Sociological Constructions of

Deviance

Sociological Constructions of

Deviance

Perspectives and Issues
in the Field

Nanette J. Davis
Portland State University

Wm. C. Brown Company Publishers
Dubuque, Iowa

PRINCIPAL THEMES IN SOCIOLOGY

Consulting Editor

Peter Manning
Michigan State University

Copyright © 1975 by Wm. C. Brown Company Publishers

Library of Congress Catalog Card Number: 74-20330

ISBN 0–697–07520–6

Second Printing, 1977

Printed in the United States of America

CONTENTS

FOREWORD

Perhaps it is inevitable that sociological typologies, taxonomies, and propositional systems will violate the reality that they intend to capture. By attempting to render coherent one segment of the social world, a theory will make obscure other of its features. Social theory will inevitably be selective and contain "blind spots" of some magnitude. The commitments of theorists to value positions not only bear on their versions of theory, but the sorts of problems chosen, their audiences, their methods, and their mode of analyzing data. All this is conventional wisdom. However, in the past decade, unexamined value positions and often inarticulated theoretical presuppositions have exercised important influences in sociology. The leap of faith by which one brings order to a domain has become, increasingly in the field of deviance, a political act. Rather than seeking to understand the exercise of power and authority, as in the nature of industrial society, and looking to sources and consequences of authority itself, deviance theorists have cast their lot with "victims." The point is not that victims do not deserve sympathy and political support. It is the almost exclusive commitment to a victim-centered theory that turns the analysis away from a historical and structured view of the political economy. But focusing on consequences, not causes of victimization, ignores the issue of how an underclass is created and how they realize or fail to realize their political destinies and choices.

The blind spots of deviance theorists, which have come to be called "labeling theory," are identified by Nanette Davis in this book, and she provides a powerful antidote to the drift into dogma which has been the apparent fate of labeling theory. It appears that for the reasons outlined in this book and elsewhere (Manning, 1973 and forthcoming), the promise of labeling theory will remain just that. The response to criticism of the perspective has not been salutory. Younger critics, with incisive logic, have identified the solipsism and conceptual poverty of the labeling perspective (Taylor, Walton, and Young, 1973; Rock, 1974), while some earlier spokesmen have become erstwhile defenders of the faith (e.g., Becker, 1972). Others have seemingly abandoned the struggle to move beyond new orthodoxy and have charted new fields of interest within sociology (e.g., Matza, Quinney, and others).

To some degree the debate between "the new sociology of deviancy" and other perspectives lacks focus; it has been long on posturing and short on results. It lacks historical grounding. Perhaps the historical grounding and sensitivity of Davis's book will bring out the forces, intellectual, social, and political, which can be said to lie "behind" the present intellectual impasse. It seems to me that uncovering the sources of the ideas, methods, and presuppositions of the sociology of deviance cannot fail to be a source of illumination.

We possess useful forerunners. In *Becoming Deviant* (1969) David Matza treated us to an allegorical tale as well as a literal accounting of the contributions of the sociology of deviance. Mills's "The Professional Ideology of Social Pathologists" (1943), Jesse Bernard's *Social Problems at Midcentury* (1957), Roscoe and Gisela Hinkle's *The Development of Modern Sociology* (1954), and John Horton's "Order and Conflict Theories . . ." (1966) can be read with Matza's book as constituting the barest sketch of the social constraints which have patterned the present concerns of the sociology of deviance. Each vacillates between a notion of history as determinate, cumulative, and evolutionary and as a socially constructed phenomenon. Paul Rock, in a paper aptly entitled "The Problem of History" (1974), identifies the problem that sociologists and historians face insofar as they continue to view history as other than a social construction, or in Collingwood's terms as a reconstruction:

> Reconstruction can be described as the mediation of the contradictions between multiple perspectives. A historian must "simultaneously" think within and about interpretive schemes that are fused, complementary and divergent at different points and in different phases and styles of research. He must reflect on and with ideas; switching back and forth between diverse frames of reference. However reflexive this process may be, history is necessarily a most complex attempt to capture reality which must treat as problematic the very schemes that make reality knowable.

I take from this the message that an understanding of historical processes involves no mere cataloging of dates, places, and "schools," but the development of a *metaperspective* on history itself. Sociologists have shown sensitivity to the problematic nature of our knowledge and belief in the reality of the present and the future, but they have treated the past gingerly, often reifying it in a fashion they would find unacceptable were they to discover such naiveté in other disciplines.

The present volume shares a shade of this ambivalence and ginger obeisance to "history." On the other hand, it avoids the trap of assuming the protective robes of a defender of the faith. This book strikes me as axial. That is, in summing analytically the development of the sociology of deviance, Davis sets out not only its flawed and meandering quality, but frankly argues for a sociology of knowledge or social constructionist view of its patterning. The book contains a vision of history and it therefore joins the above books in contributing to expanding and deepening our presently ahistorical sociology. It is, I think, fair. The book is at once *analytical* (schools of thought or perspectives are identified) and *historical* (a developmental review of ideas is woven into a view of history), and attempts to ground our present dilemmas in one of the residues of history, i.e., the emergence of sociology as a "respectable" occupation.

E. C. Hughes argued that in the past sociologists were intent upon discovering their social and political origins, their links with American society, and the structure of the social worlds in which they were expected to succeed. Now, Hughes argues, sociologists seek answers to the more ephemeral and personal questions of identity and self—who am *I*? Not surprisingly, the fragmentation of the sociology of deviance which still proceeds apace is created precisely by the crosscurrents of politicization (the "old question" of what the classes owe each other) and personalization (what the world owes me). This book, in my opinion, sets out or etches an alternative approach to deviance, for it suggests the boundaries of the past, even if its vision of the future is rather suggestive (the last chapter).

Grounded in experience, fieldwork, and careful study of the development of perspectives on the sociology of deviance, or better the *sociologies* of deviance, this book will inform and provoke students and professionals. It may do for a subfield what Friedrichs and Gouldner attempted to do for sociology proper. There is much to be learned from this book. That it is there to be learned is often unfortunately inadequate grounds for learning. For as Davis illustrates, the intellectual life is often encumbered with heavy moral, personal, and political baggage. It is only when we understand our heavy freight that we can begin to see it and not be blinded by our own visions.

Peter K. Manning
East Lansing, Michigan

REFERENCES

Becker, H. S.
1972   "Labeling Theory Reconsidered" in Paul Rock and Mary McIntosh (eds.) *Deviance and Social Control.* London: Tavistock.

Bernard, Jessie
1957   *Social Problems at Midcentury.* New York: Holt, Rinehart and Winston.

Hinkle, Roscoe and Gisela
1954   *The Development of Modern Sociology.* New York: Random House.

Horton, J.
1966   "Order and Conflict Theories of Social Problems as Competing Ideologies." *American Journal of Sociology* 71 (May): 701-713.

Manning, Peter K.
1973   "On Deviance." *Contemporary Sociology* 2 (March): 123-128.

────   "Deviance and Dogma: Some Comments on the Labeling Perspective." *British Journal of Criminology,* forthcoming.

Matza, David
1969   *Becoming Deviant.* Englewood Cliffs, N.J.: Prentice-Hall.

Mills, C. Wright
1943   "The Professional Ideology of Social Pathologists." *American Journal of Sociology* 49 (Sept.): 165-180.

Rock, Paul
1974   "The Sociology of Deviancy and Conceptions of Moral Order." *British Journal of Criminology* (April): 139-149.

────   "The Problem of History" unpublished paper, London School of Economics, March.
1974a

Taylor, Ian; P. Walton; and J. Young
1973   *The New Criminology.* London and Boston: Routledge and Kegan Paul.

PREFACE

Theory is often a formidable word in the sociological lexicon. Because it deals with abstract principles, rules, and methods, as distinguished from their social practice, theory tends to inspire a sense of awe, of apprehension about mastering what appears to be esoteric materials many levels removed from everyday social activities. Popular stereotypes provide a counter-image. Theory, as neither socially substantive nor significant, is treated as mere guesswork, unfounded opinions about human behavior that reflect only impractical or hypothetical thinking. Whether described as grand or trivial, social theory is only rarely considered in pragmatic terms, as a set of orienting ideas with profound moral, political, and practical consequences. This book examines the social sources, meanings, and implications of deviance theories—the diverse ideas, images, issues, research programs, and social policies that mark sociologists' efforts to describe, explain, and critique the changing social order.

How sociologists relate deviance to order and change often tells us as much about the thinkers as it does about their theories. By placing ideas in a social context, it becomes possible to examine their moral, political, and pragmatic meanings. In the examination of the historically grounded views of different thinkers, a critical mode is necessary for inspecting their contributions and defects. This sociology of knowledge approach, which I use to analyze various perspectives, requires both an appreciative stance, in order to understand how social influences shape ideas, and a critical stance, which evaluates these ideas from an alternative perspective. Exposing the value assumptions and political biases implicit in deviance theories demystifies the theoretical enterprise and provides a substantive critique of major ideas and research.

This book is the product of my own search for a coherent view of the relationship between persons and institutions, conducted in a context of conflicting ideas about human character and social reality. Seeking theoretical continuity, I discovered that discontinuity characterized explanations of social order and change. Reviewing these historical perspectives and issues, I found that, rather than clarifying ambiguities, deviance theories illustrate how scholarly controversies over styles of reasoning and world views produce radically different versions of social reality.

Is one picture of reality more real or authentic than another? One answer, from an extreme relativistic viewpoint, is that this depends on the perspective from which one observes events and relationships. Can any theory resolve the contradictions between alternative realities? While I have no answer to this question, I offer an alternative perspective to the ones reviewed here which qualifies this relativistic mode by addressing social theories in their relational context. But, as I argue in presenting different explanations of deviance, no theory can be all things to all persons. Theory, by definition, is a selective rendering of the world, as it categorizes reality in selective ways. Different theories, therefore, address different sets of problems, and produce different sets of facts.

My primary objection to most theoretical statements about deviance is not concerned with their selectivity, which is inevitable, but with their blind spots which obscure their social and ideological origins and their implications for managing deviants. Sociological constructions of deviance have very real social consequences for controlling human conduct, but these have been papered over or deemed irrelevant to the theory task, further confounding efforts to explain deviant phenomena.

Conventional categories impede a critical understanding of deviance in another way. By adhering to dominant definitions of deviance as abnormal, theorists fail to critique the social order that generates these stereotypes. As a result, deviance research often displays excessive concern with the problems formulated by administrators or enforcement groups. This trivializes the research product, reducing it to a rhetoric for elites that justifies their dominance over powerless groups.

However, the appreciative-critical stance also has its difficulties. While I attempt to describe the various perspectives as their theorists presented them, I also screen ideas through my own critical-conflict perspective. Thus, I could be charged with presenting only a partial portrayal, or even a distortion, of a complex rendering of deviance events. But this risk is part of the responsibility involved in articulating a fully social theory of deviance.

I wrote this book for students interested in exploring deviance beyond the shallow treatments provided in standard texts. While I have tried to simplify technical discussions of analytical modes and to summarize some of the major research illustrating these theories, the selections may not be to everyone's taste. Thus, I urge students to consult original sources; examples are included in each chapter's bibliography. The glossary furnishes a guide to terminology, which, at this stage of sociological work, is often a personal product of theorists, rather than a set of universal definitions. I strongly encourage students to not limit themselves to criticism or the construction of alternative theories, but also to do research in the critical-conflict mode suggested in the final chapter.

Intellectual debts incurred in the process of writing this book date back some years. Peter Manning, initially as dissertation advisor and, presently, as editor of this series, has been a profound influence in my coming to grips with historical and current assumptions in deviance theory. His insights into the state of the field led to my own attempts to develop new approaches to old problems. Bo Anderson, as mentor and friend, has offered extensive knowledge and a perceptive grasp of the sociological enterprise which continue to inform my scholarly work. William Form's impatience with psychological explanations of social phenomena and his insistence on a structural perspective provided a message few of his former students could dismiss. I used several of his ideas as basic building blocks for an organizational model of deviance.

This book would still be at the talking stage if it were not for the superb assistance of my student typists (and critics), Kathy Rosser and Jane Huyck, who patiently plodded through the numerous clerical duties. Also assisting were Nancy Fulton, Mary Cannon, and Andrea Thomas. Sue Shott, an able undergraduate sociologist in her own right, has been an excellent editor, mercilessly weeding out my redundancies and excess verbiage. If this book offers less than the usual tortured style of presenting theoretical ideas, I owe it to her.

Larry Reynolds, an avowed critical theorist, read my last chapter on a proposed conflict model with gusto, giving me the encouragement I needed for this new enterprise. Allen Liska read through an early draft and offered many insightful comments, and his well-informed discussions about the theory-data gap in American social theories enabled me to pinpoint several generic theoretical deficiencies which are found across sociological fields. As a longtime colleague and friend, Bernard Meltzer has never failed to provoke a series of searching questions about my theoretical and research biases. His rigorous standards of scholarship and critical advice over the years have been a primary support for my scholarly work.

To my husband, James, and children, Kathy, Sue, Liddy, Tim, Mike, and Patti, I offer my deepest gratitude for your enduring support and good humor throughout these hectic writing months.

1

INTRODUCTION

Plan of the Book

This book presents an analysis of changing sociological images of deviance. As its title implies, emphasis is on two meanings of the word—deviance as a special field of study, and deviance as a social reality constructed by sociologists. As I try to show in the chapters that follow, deviance research lacks theoretical and ideological continuity. Social perspectives have shifted over time to reflect the changing interests of sociologists in their efforts to define, describe, and explain the changing social order. The purpose of this book is to identify major themes in deviance research and to show how these have been shaped by social and ideological influences. My approach is both analytical and critical.

Problems generated by social differentiation and group conflict in industrial society, first systematically explored in the nineteenth century by Durkheim, Marx, and Weber,[1] provide the crucial issues for a sociology concerned with the nature of social order. But a persistent dilemma remained then, as now: how to account for the apparent forms of change, conceptualized by most sociologists as disorder, disintegration, or disorganization, while, at the same time, to cope with an adequate explanation of social order?

Subsequent generations of sociologists have approached this question in different ways. Styles of reflection, as W. I. Thomas has noted about his own intellectual work, are products of "diverse influences," including "trends of thought and method" and "dissent from as much as acquiescence in the models or attitudes of others."[2] The controversy over the study of social problems, social disorganization, pathology, and deviance[3] has its source in diverse modes of reasoning, and, invariably, touches upon such basic issues as the boundaries and goals of sociology, professional roles of sociologists, and public images of sociology.[4]

Shifts in deviant perspectives, then, reflect intellectual, ideological, and professional influences. As conceptual maps and theoretical rationales,

1

perspectives undergo changes in meaning and produce radically different pictures of the social world.[5]

By tracing deviant formulations over time, I arrived at six distinct conceptions, including: (1) social pathology, (2) social disorganization, (3) functionalism, (4) anomie, (5) value conflict, and (6) labeling. More recently, a political-conflict model of social control has emerged. This newer perspective attempts to shift the emphasis from the problematic moralities of assigned deviants to the larger issues of power, conflict, and ideological struggles in organizational control of human actions.[6]

The fact that sociological conceptions of deviance as a social reality have shifted over time does not imply that early and contemporary approaches lack a common tradition. Instead, the treatment of the themes social disorganization, social pathology, social control, social problems, and deviant behavior has in common a set of evaluative assumptions about the routine moral order and ways of preserving, reinforcing, attacking, reforming, or transforming it. While earlier sociologists were informed by elite groups' definitions of problems and how to correct them, recent approaches have used sociological category-making to get inside marginal groups. From this insider's perspective, they implicitly attack society and its works. This means that, whether the sociologist accepts or rejects the dominant institutions of his or her society, there is no way to avoid taking a value position on issues. The problem-defining and problem-interpreting processes are, above all, evaluations of what constitutes a social problem or a deviant act, its effects on legitimate society, and those who are defined.

The many faces of deviance reflect the sociologist's continual concern to cope with the changing impact of what Mills called the "public issues and private troubles"[7] of our time. The sociology of social problems and deviance has typically concentrated on the unconventional or problematic aspects of social life—juvenile delinquency, crime, alcoholism, prostitution, homosexuality, divorce, race relations, poverty, slums, and other social and personal "failures." Focusing on the victims of social change, rather than on the structural sources of change and social problems, has made these issues the bread and butter for sociologists of deviance.

To analyze what intellectual, political, and professional influences affected styles of sociological reasoning and choices of issues, I shall consider how theories and concepts are related to social and ideological events. This sociology of knowledge, or sociology of sociology, approach is a method for investigating the historical and social sources of ideas.[8] Changing definitions of deviance, I argue, have a social history and a political context. By illuminating the connection between the ongoing social order and the sociological constructions of this order, we may better understand how ideas are formed and transformed.

Changing constructions of deviance also reflect American sociology's persistent disengagement from critical analysis of modern institutions. European founding fathers of sociology used social problems as a vehicle for uncovering, chronicling, and explaining the social workings of modern society. Anomie, for Durkheim, and alienation, for Marx, were metaphors for a radical attack on the conventional order.[9] In their approaches, social stratification was the central mechanism of social control, contributing to unequal distribution of political and economic resources. Deviance, interpreted as social conflict, was conceived of as a normal social process that was built into ongoing social arrangements and perpetuated by powerful groups and collectivities. The power-conflict issue was largely abandoned by American sociology, which identified with the dominant laissez-faire ideology and the myth of a classless society.[10]

Yet institutionalized inequality, power and its abuses, and enduring social conflict may well be the major public (if not international) issues of our time. They deserve to be seriously addressed by a sociology willing to examine the economic and political underpinnings of institutionalized stratification.

In exploring the social and ideological bases of sociological constructions of deviance, this study will be informed by a dual consciousness: that of the sociologist examining the discipline with respect to social influences that have formed sociological perspectives, and that of the sociologist of deviance attempting to assess predominant research concerns in the field. At any given time, one or the other will prevail. The evidence for social context must necessarily be more suggestive than definitive, given the broad scope of this effort. I believe that the ambiguity of this method will be balanced by a more adequate treatment of deviance theories and research than is possible in standard, cookbook formats. In scrutinizing the variety of deviant theories and issues, my aim is not to launch a broadscale attack on previous work. Practitioners in the field are already well aware of the present state of drift,[11] and proposals for a new sociology of deviance have come from many quarters. I am offering an alternative theory of social control within this reawakened critical tradition. By constructing an organizational theory within a control perspective, I seek to redirect research efforts toward a critical sociology, a sociology that takes account of institutional order, conflict, and change.

To analyze and critique alternative approaches in deviance theory and research, the chapters are organized by theoretical schools. This provides a sequential picture of the changing social context and the different analytical modes used by sociologists to address deviance issues.

On Paradigms and Problems

This approach also places deviance studies within a larger framework of sociological thought. Changing images of social order and deviance may be elucidated by reference to paradigms. A paradigm, as defined in the philosophy of science, is a historically based, conceptual framework that guides scientific investigation.

Kuhn asserts that science proceeds from assumptions about conceptual frameworks and techniques which the working researcher accepts uncritically.[12] A comprehensive framework does one or more of the following: it indicates the basic concepts in terms of which the phenomena are to be explained; it gives some of the general relationships existing among these concepts; it provides some methodological guide to be employed in investigating the phenomena; and it indicates which research problems or questions should be investigated.

The existence of a paradigm and perceived problems gives rise to puzzles; i.e., a problem that must be solved, using the elements of the paradigm. Science, then, is essentially puzzle solving, and, for Kuhn, an inclination toward puzzle solving is the primary motivation of most researchers. When a problem does not yield to solution in terms of the prevailing paradigm, an anomaly is said to exist. Accumulation of anomalies facilitates search for a new paradigm that solves the riddle. Because paradigm shifts involve a change in world view, as well as in concepts, techniques, and research problems, they represent a discontinuity in thought, a rupture with the past in an effort to cope with persistent, unsolved issues.

The concept of paradigm, as employed by philosophers of science, is, perhaps, too rigorous when applied to the state of the art in sociological reasoning. But the process of concept and problem shift seems instructive for our purposes. Sociology emerged as an academic discipline in direct response to drastic, persistent social change. The effort to explain or explain away the transformation of persons and institutions has generated a series of paradigms, each of which addresses the order and change problem in distinctive ways.

Since a paradigm is an analytical tool, it serves as an ordering device to make explicit basic theoretical components and their interrelationships. I have identified five basic elements of the paradigm I use to present a critical review of deviance theory and research.

First, I place each theory in the larger context of social and professional conditions that have influenced or shaped thinkers. These influences range from a particular perception of social and political events held by a group of communicating scholars to professional or theoretical trends within the discipline.

Second, I show how selective perception and participation in social and professional worlds affect the perspective, or world view, of the thinker. Perspectives, as orienting frameworks, provide the conceptual mapping of social reality that serves as a basis for constructing explanations. Thus, I assume that theory is, above all, a social product that incorporates the meanings, interests, and social relations of theorists, but always in highly selective ways. In other words, only some social experiences are salient to any group of theorists. Some theories have emerged from an explicit concern with the nature and consequences of the larger social order (e.g., urbanization, lower-class deprivations). Other theories have been generated out of innovations or conflicts within the profession itself (e.g., new research techniques, repudiation of standard explanatory schemes). Theories may also be products of particular universities or sections of the country.

Locating and identifying the social sources of ideas are what a sociology of knowledge does. Analysts trace ideas to the significant social and professional meanings, articulated within a community of scholars, that contribute to a selective version of social reality while screening out alternative realities. Thus, theory and research are interrelated elements that grow out of theorists' sense of what the social world is (or is not) and how theory should address itself to particular renderings of reality.

Third, I use the concept of metaphor to focus on the dominant image of reality that characterizes any theory. The key metaphor summarizes the symbolic and cognitive style of a theoretical work and its research problems. In certain philosophy of science usages, this is often referred to as a model,[13] which is defined as a set of propositions that uses a relatively well-understood set of phenomena as an explanatory analogy for a set of phenomena that is inadequately conceptualized. For example, historically, sociology has followed in the wake of the natural sciences (physics, chemistry, and biology). To explain social processes which were only inadequately explicated in social theory (as compared with theological or philosophical explanations), early theorists, such as Durkheim, borrowed the language and imagery of biology to explain social processes. Society as an organism (in the biological sense of an integrated, functioning whole) has been a dominant motif in sociological thinking until recently.

Some of the theories I will review lack this analogous quality. The cognitive style may be highly diverse, using a medical image, an economic conception, a literary or evocative style, or a critical stance. The key metaphor distills symbolic styles without requiring further assumptions about various forms they may take in any theoretical area. Finally, a dominant metaphor sensitizes social theorists to the nature of the phenomena being studied and the appropriate research problems related to a cognitive mode.

Fourth, since sociology's claim to be a scientific (rather than philosophical) discipline requires that it produce more than speculative ideas about the world, theoretical propositions (statements of causation and relationships) must be subjected to empirical observation. Because perspectives slice the social pie differently, each theoretical mode provides a distinctive set of research themes. Ideally, research should flow from the major ideas of the theory, which have been systematized into propositional form. These provide directives for examining one set of issues, while ignoring others. A hypothesis provides an operational statement of expected relationships between given phenomena, and is checked against (selectively perceived) "facts."

Many of the theories reviewed here are severely deficient in their linkage between theory and fact. Propositions may be nonfalsifiable (incapable of being proven either true or false), or vague ideas about social causation and social processes may confound testing. Both of these conditions generate merely varied observations devoid of a consistent set of orienting ideas (eclecticism).

Another characteristic shortcoming is the prevalence of explanatory modes that feature only impressionistic ideas about the social world which resist development into propositional form or fail to inform research. Invariably, every field also has its collection of textbook truisms, propositions that have acquired authoritative status, even though they are little more than unsubstantiated assumptions.

Finally, the method of research is intimately linked to the particular perspective and conceptual apparatus that the theorist brings to the observation task. Different methods characteristically have been used for different theoretical frameworks, an observation that gives us two additional insights about the nature of a dominant paradigm.

That there is a built-in resistance to change, even when the paradigm appears to have an accumulation of unsolved theoretical problems, is the first insight. For example, in a technological society, research techniques and procedures (e.g., high-speed computers, sophisticated statistics, and bureaucratic organization of research) may change more rapidly than the ideas they are intended to support. Paradigms can be locked into fashionable orthodoxies simply because the techniques and procedures adapted to work with research designs are compellingly efficient, allowing the researcher to take theoretical shortcuts. Absorption in the research technology, often for its own sake, has been a common by-product of this situation. The theoretical enterprise thus remains in an underdeveloped state.

Secondly, a reaction to the dominant methodology (the logic of procedure) may initiate change in dominant paradigms. Dissatisfied with the research products turned out by one school, theorists may seek alternative ways of investigating the social world that are more in harmony with their own experiences and professional training. The new insights provided by these alternative methods support an altered conception of social reality.

In these chapters, I show how interrelationships between basic elements of a theory distinguish one explanatory mode from another and, also, determine the degree to which there is overlap between these analytical schemes.

The figure on pages 8-11 outlines the major paradigmatic elements of each theoretical school. These include *social and professional conditions, perspective, metaphor, themes,* and *method.* Each chapter will duplicate that portion of the figure pertaining to the particular school. Two perspectives do not qualify as paradigms. The first, social pathology, was less a puzzle-solving enterprise than an extension of social-reform ideology, and had no systematic methodology. The last, social control, is still an emerging perspective and lacks a body of research. Despite their preparadigmatic status, both are significant because the first leads into a scientific phase of work and the other moves away from traditional sociological treatments of social problems.

Summary of Chapters

The book begins with a discussion of how American sociology emerged as a discipline at the turn of the century by joining forces with a social work-social reform coalition. Deviance was conceived of as social pathology, an ethos borrowed from social Darwinism and promoted by elites and their academic and professional supporters.

Turning to the Chicago School in the 1920s, I shall discuss, in chapter three, how deviance became conceptualized as social disorganization, an approach that generated a viable body of urban studies. Freed from the constraints of philanthropic and elite control over work, the Chicago School established a tradition of firsthand investigation and appreciation of deviant life-styles in urban settings.

In chapter four, I consider how analytic deficiencies in the participant-observation case study contributed to the Functionalists' reconceptualization of deviance. The milieu sociology of the Chicago School, which

	Social Pathology	Chicago School	Functionalism
I. Social-Professional Conditions	Emergence of industrialism as dominant way of life; rise of social science to "solve" industrial problems; elite control over work; sociology as social reform; ideological style of thought	Urbanism as a way of life; a university-based discipline free from elite control; city as a social laboratory; dominance of Chicago School in American sociology; applied sociology	Economic depression and war; top sociology faculties in private schools insulated from economic and political crisis; problems pursued in relatively autonomous technical tradition rather than response to publicly salient issues; accomodation to master institutions, dominance of Eastern universities (Harvard and Columbia) in American sociology; scientific, technical style of thought
II. Perspective	Social Darwinism; social selection demands adjustment to industrial sector; problem of assimilating new immigrants; rejection of urban underclass; deviance as personal maladjustment or pathology	Ecology-Interaction; behavior a product of physical location; modified environmental determinism; duality of material and moral realms; acceptance of urban diversity, but conceived as social disorganization; deviance as "natural" or disorganized phase of urban life; change as inevitable	Structural sociology; collective determinism; social order as central concern; society held together by spontaneous processes ("voluntarism"); deviance as persistent social pattern; breakdown of moral system; e.g., defects in socialization; change as disruptive; or change as gradual evolutionary process; unanticipated consequences of purposive social action

FIGURE 1.1. Major Paradigmatic Elements of Theoretical Schools in Deviance Analysis

Anomie Theory	Value Conflict	Labeling Theory	Control Perspecive
Rise of welfare state; government financing of social science research; academics provide expertise for noneconomic social problems (e.g., racial conflict, social consequences of poverty); "professionalization" of sociology as community of specialists; tacit identification with control personnel	Professional recognition of normative pluralism; continuity of social problems approach; conflict in sociological styles of work generated focus on widespread value dissensus and norm violations; sociological response to wartime and middle-class crime; theoretical attempt to extend integrationist question to include conflict and criminality; specialization of theory in crime studies	Liberal reaction to bureaucratic state; counterintellectual tradition; humanistic orientation; identification with underdog as victim; debunking of establishment institutions and sociologies; rejection of formalistic, structural sociology; alternative professional ideologies	Developed industrial state; political economy fosters inequality of power, wealth, and authority; crisis of legitimacy: Vietnam war, student protests, urban riots, government corruption; concern with underdog alienation; disenchantment with liberal solutions to social problems; counterideological tone; radical sociologists' rejection of status quo
Variant of functionalism; theoretical focus on structural strain or malintegration of social structure; deviance as stress generated by disjuncture between goals of success and structural means for their achievement; utilitarian calculus generates deviance as response to lack of opportunity; institutionalization of self-interest (legitimization of amorality)	Normative conflict; differential social organization and association as sources of criminal and deviant behavior; law as a device of one party in conflict with another party; thus crime and punishment perpetuate cultural conflict; deviance as shared cultural tradition learned primarily in face-to-face groups; modalities of interaction stressed: priority, duration, and intensity; social psychological analysis stressed; differential identification and deviant vocabularies as crucial elements of deviant act	Secondary deviation; social control leads to deviant identity; i.e., deviance a product of negative reaction by social audiences (usually formal control agents); moral entrepreneurs create rules against the interests of underdogs; rule breaking common; social change inevitable	Critical theory, political-conflict model of social control; organizational analysis; society as struggle between conflicting groups for scarce commodities, collective activities as outcomes of organizational rivalry and coercion; deviance created by maldistribution of resources inherent in legitimate social order and maintained by exchange within and between controller groups and controlled populations

	Social Pathology	Chicago School	Functionalism
III. Metaphor	"Health-illness" referent for social order and disorder	"Web of life;" naturalism; interconnectedness of urban organizations	"Social system;" interdependence of social phenomena; deviance as essential to maintaining "system"
IV. Themes	Social Correction and amelioration: —clinical model —public opinion model —public health model	Sites and Situations: —social worlds —life cycle or career —crisis	Latent functions of deviance; boundary-maintenance and exclusion mechanisms
V. Method	Casework	Ethnography; rates and distributions	Abstract generalizations; use of secondary sources

FIGURE 1.1. Continued.

focused on sites and situations within the larger urban complex, was redefined by this later generation in terms of a systems analysis. The enhanced social prestige awarded science also contributed to large-scale studies, a methodological requirement of a systems approach. Science—as ideology and method—fostered a value-free posture, or the belief that investigators could consider functions of deviance without questioning the underlying assumptions of dominant institutions.

Chapter five takes up anomie theory, viewing it as a response to persistent problems of social control in the larger society. Juvenile delinquency, crime, poverty, and other indicators of individual departures from middle-class norms were crucial issues for anomie theorists. I stress how their use of official data (e.g., police files) reinforced both official and academic notions that deviance was concentrated among lower-class populations.

In chapter six the role of deviant motivation, said to be a product of cultural diversity and conflict by the value-conflict theorists, is explored. Rejecting the functionalist use of middle-class society as an orienting framework (with its view of deviance as disorganization and the deviant

Anomie Theory	Value Conflict	Labeling Theory	Control Persepective
Differential opportu-nity structure; varieties of official rates of deviance constitute a "normal" response by lower-class offenders to structural depriva-tion	"Criminal behavior system"—career concept emphasized systematic pattern of deviant motives and acts	"Stigma"—defining, isolating, and punish-ing the rule breaker creates and perpetuates the deviant identity	"Structural contradic-tions"—opposition and cleavage built into social structure, legiti-mating processes that foster organization generate counteracting forces
Deviance as individual adaptation; delinquent subculture; culture of poverty	Criminal behavior types; victimology	Collective rule making; social reactors; deviant careers	Political economy of control; social organi-zation of social control; responses to control by the controlled
Use of official data; statistical analysis of etiological and epidemi-ological factors	Typologies; analytical summary	Ethnography; partici-pant observation; *Verstehen* or under-standing	Methodological dilemmas and con-straints; historical model; generalizations from specific instances of changing events; *Verstehen* or understanding

as lower class), value-conflict theorists proposed a nonmoralistic approach to the study of deviant identities.

Chapter seven considers the work of the labeling theorists, a new gen-eration of dissenting scholars, who took a counterposition to functional and anomie arguments about deviant causation. Disenchanted with the status quo, and often identifying with the underdog, labeling theorists returned to the early work of the Chicago School. Deviant research gener-ated sympathetic portrayals of the urban underlife. By focusing on the varied research programs of the labeling school, I try to show how an emphasis on deviant categories, rather than on the authority structures which generated deviant types, promoted a sociology of the segmental, the exotic, and the bizarre.

In the final chapter, dealing with theories of deviance, I propose an alternative model of social control which attempts to treat devi-ance as an outcome of bureaucratic regulation. It focuses on control sys-tems rather than on the controlled. By tracing the origins of a social control perspective, I try to show how widespread, delegitimating influences in the larger society and professional reactions to traditional sociologies provide rationales and issues for research among control theorists. A preliminary attempt to delineate the formal and substantive requirements of a political-conflict approach includes some suggestive propositions and basic issues. In this departure from value-neutral approaches, I try to show how the research act joins analysis of institutional life with critical evaluation of the consequences of these social arrangements for the human condition.

NOTES

1. For representative works, see Emile Durkheim, *Suicide,* J. A. Spaulding and G. Simpson, trans. (New York: The Free Press, 1951); Karl Marx, *Selected Writings in Sociology and Social Philosophy;* and Max Weber, *The Theory of Social and Economic Organization;* A. M. Henderson and Talcott Parsons, trans. (New York: The Free Press, 1947).

2. W. I. Thomas, "Life History," Paul J. Baker, ed. *American Journal of Sociology* 79 (September 1973): 249.

3. I use the concept "deviance" as a generic term to include related sociological concerns as in social problems, pathology, disorganization, criminology, social control, anomie theory, and deviant behavior. The single definitional uniformity for all these subfields is the focus on the rule breaker as "different," thereby justifying investigation of deviant categories as isolated psychological and social phenomena. As I argue throughout the book, the spurious scientific validity of assuming "deviant" values and conduct as altogether discontinuous with more accepted ones, has placed much of deviant research in a theoretical limbo.

4. Emil Bend and Martin Vogelfanger, "A New Look at Mills' Critique," in *Mass Society in Crisis,* ed. B. Rosenberg, I. Gerver, and F. W. Howton (New York: The Macmillan Company, 1971), pp. 271-281.

5. Thomas Kuhn, *The Structure of Scientific Revolutions* (Chicago: Phoenix Publishers, 1962).

6. An overview of deviance theories, with special emphasis on contemporary approaches is found in Nanette J. Davis, "Labeling Theory in Deviance Research:

A Critique and Reconsideration," *Sociological Quarterly* 13 (Autumn 1972): 447-474.

7. C. Wright Mills, *The Sociological Imagination* (New York: Oxford Press, 1959).

8. This approach has been explicated by James E. Curtis and John W. Petras, *The Sociology of Knowledge* (New York: Praeger Publishers, 1970) and Larry T. Reynolds and Janice M. Reynolds, eds., *The Sociology of Sociology* (New York: David McKay Company, Inc., 1970). See, also, Leon Bramson, *The Political Context of Sociology* (Princeton, N.J.: Princeton Publishing Company).

9. John Horton criticizes contemporary definitions of anomie and alienation which have confused and obscured the classical meanings of these concepts in "The Dehumanization of Anomie and Alienation," *British Journal of Sociology* 15 (December 1964): 283-300.

10. For a discussion of this point, see John Pease, William H. Form, and Joan Huber Rytina, "Ideological Currents in American Stratification Literature," *The American Sociologist* 5 (May 1970): 127-138.

11. Peter K. Manning offers an insightful review of the state of deviance theory in *Contemporary Sociology* 2 (March 1973): 123-128. See, also, Richard Quinney's overview of philosophical assumptions underlying research on crime and deviance in "Crime Control in Capitalist Society: A Critical Philosophy of Legal Order," *Issues in Criminology* 8 (Spring 1973): 75-96.

12. Thomas Kuhn, *The Structure of Scientific Revolutions.* See, also, Robert

K. Merton's discussion of the uses of a paradigm for abstracting and systematizing theoretical frameworks in R. K. Merton, *Social Theory and Social Structure* (New York: The Free Press, 1957), pp. 14-16, 19-84.

13. Models, as analogues and as cognitive styles, are treated in Abraham Kaplan, *The Conduct of Inquiry* (San Francisco: Chandler Publishing Company, 1964), pp. 267, 269-272.

2

Deviance as Individual Disorganization and Amelioration

THE SOCIAL PATHOLOGISTS

> Man's history is a trail of blood. The struggle for survival has left along the road the bones of those who have fallen in the fight. It has also imprinted indelibly upon the very nature of man and upon his institutions certain qualities which make for success under some conditions of life, but make for failure under others . . .Life from birth to death is a struggle for adjustment. (John Lewis Gillin, *Social Pathology*)[1]

Social pathology has followed an erratic intellectual course. Its origins can be traced to the French Enlightment's ideal of the goodness of man. Its principles for social action can be located in efforts to join science with a welfare ideology. However, its American expression, drawn from social Darwinism principles, has explained social change and human diversity as personal failure and maladjustment. The persistence of these contradictory themes in contemporary deviance theories (however muted and metamorphasized by linguistic alterations) testifies to the endurance of the pathology conception. Structural dislocations generated by an industrial order remain largely outside the purview of deviance theories.

In equating conventional morality with health and unconventional or disapproved behavior with disease, the social pathologists divided the social order into two parts: social organization and social disorganization. The social organization sector was the moral order grounded in established norms and institutional practices. The social disorganization sector was the immoral order, conceived of as personal dislocations from the established order. Identifying, describing, and "correcting" these human failures was the pathologist's task.

14

By the nineteenth century, alliances among sociology, social work, and social reform contributed to academic sociology's dominant concern with pathology and amelioration. The early history of the alliance (to be detailed below) and the origins of the organization-disorganization classification can be traced to the rise and decline of the social science movement in America. For a résumé of major elements of this preparadigmatic framework, see figure 2.1. This chapter departs from the systematic presentation of elements, as I am attempting to trace the historical and conceptual influences on this early work.

I. Social-Professional Conditions	Emergence of industrialism as dominant way of life; rise of social science to "solve" industrial problems; elite control over work; sociology as social reform; ideological style of thought
II. Perspective	Social Darwinism; social selection demands adjustment to industrial sector; problem of assimilating new immigrants; rejection of urban underclass; deviance as personal maladjustment or pathology
III. Metaphor	"Health-illness" referent for social order and disorder
IV. Themes	Social correction and amelioration: —clinical model —public opinion model —public health model
V. Method	Casework

FIGURE 2.1.   *Social Pathology*

The Social Science Movement

By 1840, the rise of a social science movement in the United States marked the first effort to integrate European social philosophy and the application of science to social welfare.[2] Reform and science became the twin links that forged a coalition between philanthropic, charity, and reform groups and the still undifferentiated academic disciplines. This new association believed that an inclusive social science could be an effective strategy for making the transition from a theological to a secular, scientific world view. Social problems, in this analysis, were institutional defects perpetuated by outmoded customs and political interests. Building a science of society would replace magical and mythological survivals with rational explanation and social planning.

Three streams of ideas flowed into the American movement to provide the blueprint for social change. Two of these involved reform ideologies.

The third, the notion of a scientific social system, was most fully articulated by Auguste Comte.

The first of these reformist ideals was in the French tradition of the Enlightenment, and was romantic, utopian, and radical. It began with analysis of an idealized human nature, and emphasized the social evils which repressed and distorted it. By deductive logic, advocates worked out a consistent, efficient, and just social system. The other type of reformist ideology was in the British liberal tradition. Rejecting revolutionary doctrines and programs, it stressed concrete, practical forms of change. Social and economic legislation, prison reform, public health, care of the insane, and other reform programs were intended to shore up the social system.[3]

Elements of both traditions, however disparate, were incorporated into movement ideology. Utopian ideals often became part of patchwork social reforms, none of which were directed toward a systematic attack on the structural sources of social disturbances. These hodgepodge efforts led one American critic to suggest that any theory of reform would be legitimate if only because inactivity in the face of abuses is tantamount to passive support and sanction of abuses. Finding solutions, said William Elder in 1859, requires first of all a critical awareness that social change can be managed by human effort.

> We are not of those who reject a theory because some if its most remarkable points seem impracticable, or because it rudely puts us upon the defense of our most cherished opinions. But there is still stronger reason why we would not hastily reject revolutionary novelties—the feeling which we have in common with everybody else, that the system of things in which we live is not so good that it ought to be blindly defended against all change. Stubborn conservatives ought not to forget that their opposition to all proposed reforms really involves them in responsibility for all the evils which they passively maintain. The people of this generation are terribly worried with revolutions and reforms, but they would not be at peace if philanthropy, real and pretended were to desert the earth today. The world is not good enough, nor well enough . . . it must be mended, and this felt necessity will ensure every plausible reform a hearing from somebody, and those who accept it will press its claims, whether men will hear or whether they will forebear . . . We have a world to put in order, and why not receive proposals and examine the terms of all the world members who wish to make the contract?[4]

By opening the door to any and all reformers, Elder exemplified the weakness of the reformers' position. Lacking a theory of society and a

viable political support structure, the social science movement in its pre-
Civil War phase produced only a few well-intentioned, but ineffective,
reform bills. Social improvements, many advocates believed, required
knowledge of society, with amelioration guided by scientific principles
and laws. Comte's positivist treatise on society and his plan for a new type
of social organization provided academic reformers with a theoretical rationale for human betterment.

In the work of Auguste Comte, which animated many of the early
American social system-builders, the key elements of the new social science were first systematically articulated. Social science, as an ideology in
search of a theory, found Comte's large-scale conception of society to be a
good substitute for current transcendental and Christian theories of the
social order. Inherent in Comte's thought, however, was the fallacy of assuming that society was unified, coherent, and integrated. By failing to
account for the industrial order as a drastically different type of social
organization (based on heterogeneity and conflict of interests), Comte's
thought paved the way for American social science's adoption of a two-
value logic in explanations of social life. Comte's conception of social
structure, later borrowed by American theorizers, was the notion of harmonious, organic order. Departures from this order were immoral or
pathological. A brief summary of Comte's key ideas will clarify this.

Comte proposed four principles as the foundation for a theory of society
and social reform:[5] an *organismic model of society, evolution, determinism,* and *positivism.* Together, these formed the blueprint for a society
based on social order and social progress. The unexamined assumptions
and contradictions implicit in Comte's work may explain, in part, why
early American social theorists were never able to resolve the conflict
between the social welfare ideal and the proliferation of deviant forms in
industrial society.

First, Comte proposed a biological model of the social order which
held society to be a living organism subject to laws of growth, decay, and
change. The organic structure is composed of moral, intellectual, and material parts (e.g., arts, sciences, occupations, institutions) which fit together to form a unified whole. In the social organism, a harmony of
structure and function works toward a common end through action and
reaction among the parts and between parts and the environment. In the
final state of social evolution:

> Family, State, and Church are finally to be distinguished and
> harmonized, and fixed in their proper organic relations to each
> other, so as to preclude, forever their warfare or intrusion upon
> each other's provinces.[6]

For Comte, the organismic doctrine was not merely a useful analogy, but a reality. "It is the individual who is an abstraction rather than the social organism." More than the sum of individuals that comprise it, society has universal laws that transcend psychological ones. Society became the mover; human beings adjusted their needs to its demands.

Second, a theory of evolution explained social change as a natural phenomenon largely independent of human will. Organismic evolution (proceeding from theological to metaphysical to the present industrial-scientific state) is characterized by an increasing specialization of functions and a corresponding tendency toward adaptation and perfection of "organs" (i.e., institutions). Progress is built into this all-inclusive scheme of social change, and is evidenced by increasing human control over the environment. Industry and institutional life show a trend toward increasing excellence and perfection.

Aside from the metaphysical notion of progressive intellectual stages of civilization, the scheme has another basic flaw. Progress, as a generic condition of the social order, lacked specification. Progress for whom, toward what social end, and with what consequences was never stipulated. A prevailing myth in American society, the doctrine of progress, was used by social pathologists to justify the uneven struggle for existence and the maintenance of a political order that rejected interference in the "natural" order of things.[7]

Third, Comte held a deterministic view of history and the inevitability of progressive change. Stages of growth cannot be eliminated, although intelligent direction may hasten the process and lack of knowledge of the laws of change retard it. Comte stressed, as a corollary, that institutions were as perfect as their stage of social development permitted. Determinism, combined with the organic conception, undercut Comte's elaborate proposals for social reform. Unable to theoretically justify a reconstructed social order (since the order itself was preordained by scientific laws), Comte's reform schemes were reduced to ethical and theological placebos. In essence, he held that the pathologies of this largely self-regulated social system should be corrected by an altered morality. Changing personal attitudes, rather than social structures, later became a crucial theme for American social pathologists.

Fourth, positivism, or explanation of phenomena entirely by scientific laws, was proposed as a replacement for religion and metaphysics. This was more than a set of empirical procedures in the study of social regularities. Positivism was a new social regime controlled by reason, science, and moral education, the latter to be mediated through sociologists, who comprised a new priesthood of philosopher-kings. Positivism provided the

mechanism for regulating the social system by inculcating "fixed principles of social conduct." Social reform was left to public opinion which,
when it has become the great regulator of society, will eliminate conflict
and disorder by "substituting peaceable definition of duties."[8] What Comte
and later social scientists failed to recognize is that a strong state and
corporate elite can manipulate public opinion in the interests of dominant
classes.

The Comtean evolutionary doctrine, expressed as progress through
science, was assimilated into the American social science movement, providing a basic organizing principle for reformers. Armed with a theoretical
apparatus that entailed a holistic conception of society, early reform
efforts consisted of descriptions and proposals for change of the social
system. Land reform, cooperative enterprises, and profit sharing, for example, were radical efforts to change the political economy.[9] Experimental
colonies were set up to demonstrate the utility of social science theory. A
utopian belief in the regeneration of industry was the dominant theme
among colony leaders, who offered new social frontiers to conquer. In the
words of one promoter:

> We are engaged in the solution of the greatest problem that ever
> occupied the attention of man—a problem embracing every
> interest of humanity. The civilized world is convulsed with
> conflicting interests. To utilize them and elevate the race is the
> great work before us, which, when accomplished, will mark the
> most important era in the world's history. If we demonstrate the
> theory of social science in the Pacific Colony, we will do more for
> humanity than all the political systems in the world. Let us
> realize the importance of the world in which we are engaged and
> with patience, courage, and persistence we cannot fail.[10]

The flight-from-reality motif, economic failure, and internal factions all
contributed to the weakening of these movements and their eventual
disappearance from the American reform scene.

The positivistic doctrine had still other implications for some American
social system-builders. Social control through science became the guiding
principle for a revitalized social order. The industrial system itself was
seen as the primary social problem. Solutions for regulating the excesses of
this order had a strong Calvinistic tone, recommending duty, self-denial,
and abstinence. But the theoretical rationale was a conception of the social
system drawn from Comte; it exalted the primacy of society over the individual, of order over freedom, and of duty over gratification. Human rights
were eliminated in this scheme. One American follower of Comte, James
O'Connel, suggested this formula for social control:

> Reason instead of force, duties instead of "rights," knowledge
> instead of fraud; education instead of superstition; or to sum up in
> a single term, society instead of man; and the corresponding
> practice will be: abstinence, forbearance, self-denial, in the
> regulation both of property and population.[11]

By 1870, centrifugal processes began to operate in the Association of Social Science (the organizational aspect of the movement) which separated philanthropy from theoretical aspects of social science. The Conference of Charities, with its member organizations (such as the National Prison Association, National Conference of Charities and Corrections, the American Public Health Association, and the Association for the Protection of the Insane and the Prevention of Insanity), eliminated several of the applied aspects of the Association's program. Academic disciplines were left, by default, to drift in the opposite direction.

Social reform became a separate discipline, and went on to such issues as welfare, care of mental patients, abolition of alcohol (as a cure for the immigrant's ills), and feminism. The system of social reform helped to create government and private agency structures, which led quickly to the professionalization of the helping function. These professionals, the social workers, tied into the Mental Hygiene Movement with its psychological view of social problems. The social casework method, oriented toward a description of the maladjusted individual and his or her immediate problems, became the dominant style in the field. Professionalism now aimed at adjusting the individual to his or her social situation, and the change in social work from reform to amelioration was complete.[12] Social work practice became a mechanism for the maintenance of the status quo.[13]

The Association, as an inclusive social science movement, floundered because of its later specialization into subdisciplines (e.g., history, political science, economics, ethology). With official academic recognition in college curricula in the last quarter of the nineteenth century, each discipline went its own way. Sociology, alone, emerged as a general science of society from the remnants of the movement.

Utopian ideals were dampened by the efforts of sociologists to come to grips with the new social and industrial order. Slums, strikes, disease, unemployment, migratory labor, trusts, and the hosts of problems associated with new modes of making a living were not amenable to the reform plans of grand-scale system builders. Solutions for social problems became a leftover collection of social and practical principles to better the conditions of the immigrant poor.

Social science, beginning with an economic reconstruction emphasis, came to specialize in social problems, and finally merged with sociology.

By 1894, the identification of sociology with social pathology was complete. College catalogs reflect this merger, as this Vassar College description of the sociology course offering suggests:

> Sociological bearings of natural selection, heredity, environment,
> free will; physical, physiological, moral and social causes of
> abnormality, statistics of the causes of pauperism, history of the
> English poor laws, principles that should direct charity, private
> relief, charity organization, public relief, almshouses, old age
> pensions and workingmen's insurance: relief for the unemployed
> including labor colonies and the tramp problem, dependent
> children, relief of the sick, insanity; statistics of the causes of
> crime; criminal anthropology; prevention of crime; principles that
> should govern the treatment of offenders; delinquent children;
> reform of prison methods, cumulative sentence; the family
> and divorce.[14]

Philosophy of history, sociology, social problems, and social correction were all to be covered in one term!

Social problems thus had two sets of practitioners. One was the social worker, attempting to adapt the unadjusted individual to the labor market. The other was the academic social pathologist, who provided a theoretical rationale for locating the source of social problems within the individual.[15] Social Darwinism provided both ideology and theory for practitioners of this noninterventionist approach to social order.

Social Darwinism and Social Pathology

The earliest textbook use of the term, social pathology, was based on the organismic conception, and contrasted a healthy, normal society with diseased, abnormal social conditions. The conventional bias is clear in the definition of social pathology as the "study of all phenomena which are apparently inconsistent with the best interests of society, and the determination of clearly abnormal or unhealthy structures and functions."[16] Poverty, vice, crime, physical disability, and social inactivity were listed as obvious signs of social diseases. Consistent with the early idealist version of social problems, the source of individual pathology was held to be social conditions, or, as the text phrased it:

> abnormal social arrangements and functions [that] react upon
> individuals, offering opportunities for personal degeneration
> and unsocial conduct, if not actually making them necessary.[17]

Ten years later, another leading textbook abandoned the social-conditions framework and articulated a (now standard) definition of social pathology as "maladjustments in social relationships."[18] A shift from focusing on social conditions (functions and structures) to emphasizing the "antisocial" individual and his or her maladjustment had occurred. Three traditions were at work in American sociology that encouraged a psychogenic orientation to social problems. One was Comtean sociology's failure to reconcile social problems with the increased perfection of so-called higher-order industrial society. Social pathology (abnormalities of the social system) became relegated to the sidelines, away from the mainstream of social theory. The model of social organization continued to be (as in Cooley's analysis) the highly integrated, consensual society of like-minded, middle-class persons whose norms constituted the standards of society.[19] Departures from these norms were viewed as defects of the person, not faults in the structure.

Spencer's rigorous treatment of the organic conception was also popular among American social theorists, further contributing to the psychological analysis of social problems. In Spencer's scheme, the complexity of industrial society, with its "progress toward greater size, coherence, multiformity, and definiteness," required limiting "political control over personal conduct."[20] The organizing principles of industrial society, such as "voluntary cooperation" and a "decentralized regulating system for the industrial structures," carried the free-market concept into the heart of sociological theorizing. To interrupt the "mutual dependence of parts" by tinkering with the social system became anathema to American Spencerians.[21] Correcting individuals, not social systems, was the logical corollary to this natural-systems proposition.

The third, and most significant, influence on the conception of social problems was social Darwinism, a doctrine that was widely adopted by business and governing elites.[22] A highly distorted version of Charles Darwin's theory of natural selection, this popular doctrine served to justify ruthless competition and perpetuation of the status quo. In its glorification of the individual struggle for existence, social Darwinism upheld the belief that the upper classes in the present social order have survived because of their peculiar fitness in the moral order. Failure to survive implied inherent biological and social weakness and lack of fitness for the competitive struggle.

In its theoretical phase, social Darwinism accounted for the malfunctioning of social arrangements as the cost of progress. The notion that society was moving inevitably upward and onward implied that social forces must control the "backward" (those populations resistant to change). Social reform not only interfered with the normal workings of society, but also protected the least fit to the disadvantage of the fit. Writing in 1883,

Sumner raised the Darwinian question: what do social classes owe to each other? He concluded that social reforms penalized the thrifty, the energetic, and the competent by forcing them to remedy the "noisy, pushing, importunate, and incompetent."[23] Reforms could halt progress and contribute to a relapse into an earlier evolutionary stage, even into "barbarism." Natural social growth has its own, built-in timetable, said Sumner, and social architects only repeat the old errors, thus postponing any chance of real improvement. He held that the industrial system was "automatic" and "instinctive" in its operation and needed no human interference, a point emphasized in this passage:

> Society needs first of all to be freed from these meddlers [i.e., reformers]. Here we are, then, once more back at the old doctrine —*Laissez-faire*. Let us translate it into blunt English, and it will read, Mind your own business. Let every man be happy in his own way. If his sphere of action and interest impinges on that of any other man, there will have to be compromise and adjustment. Wait for the occasion. Do not attempt to generalize those interferences or to plan for them *a priori*. We have a body of laws and institutions which have grown up as occasion has occurred for adjusting rights. Let the same process go on . . . natural adjustments will . . . come about through the play of interests and the voluntary concession of the parties.[24]

With laissez-faire raised to a sociological principle, the social pathologists concentrated on identifying the pauper, the criminal, the insane, and other "degenerates" to locate where the "departures from normal human life began, and what were the malign influences that caused it."[25] The aim was to correct defects in order to equip the individual for the economic struggle, without violating the doctrines or practices of industrial elites. Guided by the doctrine of the "survival of the fittest," they defined the subject of social pathology (indeed, of sociology itself) as the study, control, and disposition of the "dependent, delinquent, and defective classes."[26]

Social Pathology and the Casework Technique

By the first decade of the twentieth century, the line between social work, social pathology, and sociology was blurred by a fusing of psychogenic explanations (called "sociological" theory), an emphasis on social problems, and the use of the casework technique. The standard text treatment of social problems combined elements of the client's case history with an eclectic interpretation of his or her "problem." Biological, medical, psychological, psychiatric, economic, and sociological approaches provided what one text called a "well-balanced" interpretation of individual ills. Sociologically, the problem individual was defined in terms of crisis, unadjustment, maladjustment, demoralization, and disorganization. Personal change (e.g., sickness, accident, loss of job or friend) created crisis situations, and was regarded as a predominantly psychiatric problem.[27]

The case study approach had two foci. One was providing a detailed description of the maladjusted person in a style designed to give student audiences the social worker's perspective. Welfare clients were typically presented as irrational, disorderly, incompetent, socially unskilled, and violence prone; traits presumed to be associated with lower-class behavior. This image was often enhanced by melodramatic flourishes. In one narrative about a disturbed family, the authors portray domestic bedlam in a style worthy of a dime novel. The following scene depicts the disintegration of a working-class family threatened by its members' persistent temper tantrums and violence:

> "So you're lifting boxes and gambling away your money are you?" he shouted, and then he added from sheer nervousness and from long habit, the most opprobrious epithet that one man can give another. Joe rose to his feet like a cat and picked up his chair by the back. The others rose with him.
>
> Obviously, if Joe was what his father called him, it was his mother who was demeaned by the epithet. Such an accusation was more than speech. It was violence. And from a husband to his son, before his wife—it was almost murder. Of course Mr. Nyack had meant nothing of the kind. He and his wife had had their daily quarrels to be sure. But he knew well enough that she had been entirely faithful to him and to his interests. His epithet to his son had been merely a manner of speaking. It had slipped out, with no reference to its meaning, because Mr. Nyack was tired and cross, and his children seemed to be smothering him with their outlandish whims. But when he saw his two daughters rising from the table against him, backed by an hysterical wife and a son ready to throw a chair at him, it entirely destroyed what self-restraint he had left after so wearing a day. He grasped his own chair aloft and threw it blindly. It hit the stove pipe, knocking it clear from the wall, and distributing the soot over the table and over the heads of the three screaming women.
>
> Joe, his feelings a blind mixture of hurt pride, chagrin, over his ill-chosen present, his realization that his mother could not be made to understand his motive, and his wild wrath over his father's unjust epithet, flew at his father and pinned him to the

floor by his throat. He began choking him so successfully that Mrs. Nyack, unable to bear more, gave a wild shriek and fell unconscious over the table. Louisa and May gave one horrified and disgusted glance at each other. Then Louisa clawed at Joe's throat, as the only available spot of attack where she could hope to weaken his grip on his father, and May, catching a pail of water from the kitchen sink, threw it impartially over all of them. By this time, the clamor had risen to such a height that the neighbors were collecting outside the door.

"Help! Help!" screamed May, ready to fly into hysterics herself, as she saw that the soot and water between them had effectually devastated the green sandals for all time.

A crowd of neighbors pushed the door open at this cry, and Joe, his ardor somewhat cooled by the water and by the presence of the newcomers, rose sulkily to his feet. His father, after some preliminary grunts and snorts, did the same. In the shamefaced silence which followed, May elbowed her way through the crowd and into the street.

"It's the last night I spend with those devils," she called back to Louisa.[28]

(From the 1925 edition of *Social Pathology* by Stuart A. Queen and Debler Martin Mann. 1940 edition by Stuart A. Queen and Jennette Row Gruener, Copyright 1940 by Thomas Y. Crowell Company, Inc., with permission of the publisher.)

The comic elements that embellish this narrative reinforced the social worker-pathologist view that clients need to be controlled for their own good.

The second focus of the case study approach was the enumeration of interpretations that could account for a maladjusted person or family. A "paste-pot eclectic psychology," to use Mills's term,[29] characterized these interpretations which focused on the absence of traits associated with the ideally adjusted person (e.g., patience, specialized knowledge, skills, optimism, love of work, moderation, will power, and other virtues of the "good life from the standpoint of the individual"[30]). The adjusted person conforms to middle-class morality and motives, and participates in the gradual progress of respectable institutions. Using the standards of the small-town, middle-class milieu, social pathologists viewed underprivileged persons as "unsocialized."[31]

The pathologists borrowed the psychogenic explanations of conduct employed by professional helpers, as well as the case study technique of social work practice. The quasi-biological term, "adaptation" (or adjustment), was linked to an entourage of such terms as "existence," "survival," and "fitness" which gained prestige from the vogue of social Darwinistic doctrine. The quasi-biological, astructural character of the adjustment concept tended to obscure specifically social content, and simple evaluations of "normalcy" (the desired state of adjustment) usually lacked definitional boundaries. When defined, the term invariably expressed the ideological preferences of the writer.

Sometimes "normal" referred to the uneventful life cycle, as in "normal life." At other times, it suggested the "forgotten man" in Sumner's analysis,[32] or, in recent parlance, "the silent majority." Normal standards may also be those held by the idealized middle-class person living out his or her small town life, unexposed to urban variety, as shown by Elliott and Merrill's discussion of one early pathologist's interpretation:

> The normal life [is] the norm [of] the healthy and uneventful
> life cycle of the average middle-class man or woman. These
> persons are never subjected to the temptations of great wealth.
> Neither do they come in contact with poverty, crime, vice, and
> other unpleasantly sordid aspects of life.[33]

For some pathologists, normality was so commonsensical a notion that it hardly needed analysis at all. It was often identified in such organismic terms as consistency, equilibrium, harmony, or stability. In some contexts, it was simply reduced to a tautology: normal is normal is normal. The following definition seems to beg the question altogether:

> While the word "normal" carries a fairly definite and, for the
> most part, accurate implication to the mind of any intelligent
> person, it is nevertheless extremely difficult to define in concrete
> terms . . . As commonly used to convey a definite idea, the word
> "normal" means that which is in harmony with the general
> make-up and organization of the object under discussion—that
> which is consistent with normal factors.[34]

Whether "normal" was defined or remained a primitive term in the evaluative calculus, it is clear that it carried clinical connotations (e.g., health, fitness, psychological stability, sound mental attitudes and habits, and personal equilibrium). "Abnormal" meant the absence of clinically established norms. In occasional analytical asides, most pathologists admitted that social change usually generated abnormality. Because a conception of emergent social structure was lacking, change became synonymous with disorganization, disorganization became equivalent to personal maladjustment, and personal maladjustment became viewed as so extensive as to include entire strata and groups. By this reasoning, social problems were reduced to a single issue, adjustment:

> All social problems grow out of *the* social problem—the problem
> of the adjustment of man to his universe, and of the social
> universe to man. The maladjustments in these relationships give
> us all our social problems.[35]

The notion of adjustment implies, on the one hand, that there is an
ordered society of competent, middle-class, success-oriented persons, and,
on the other, that there are misfits who fail to adapt to institutional requirements and goals. What reformers, social workers, and pathologists had
in mind was the immigrant, who manifested symptoms of "social breakdown," "disturbance," and "dislocation." The immigrant problem was an
early focus for the pathologist, and the concepts used to describe it became
the basis for ideal constructs of the adjusted person and models of control
of the maladjusted. How to fit the "unfit" into the conventional order was
the predominant issue. It was resolved by ameliorative strategies that excluded the urban underclass from legal and political participation.

Amelioration—Three Models of Individual Change

To correct the maladjusted, pathologists took the position that restoring
mental health and improving the social relationships of the new ethnics
was the only viable solution to social disorder. Reform panaceas had been
tried and found wanting. Dominant institutions appeared fixed and inevitable, and only gradual change without social interference could guarantee a semblance of social continuity. The immigrant must adjust to the
new environment. To accommodate the troubled and troublesome to urban,
industrial routines, three models of individual change were employed: the
clinical model, the public opinion model, and the preventive model. In all
three, reform was practical, concrete, and fragmentary. As apolitical measures, they dealt with isolated situations and their symptoms, rather than
with the economic and political context that created personal stress.

The Clinical Model

With its diagnostic and therapeutic orientation, the clinical model was
well adapted for regulating the immigrant poor. Widespread disenchantment with urban conditions by professional reformers and academics alike
reflected the strong rural bias current among American intellectuals. While
praising the virtues of smalltown milieux, pathologists attributed deprav-
ity, corruption, and poverty to the evils of the city. Ill-absorbed immigrants, with their foreign values and folkways, could not be trusted to
guide their own destinies. Widespread public suspicion of foreigners

encouraged the denial that political action could solve social problems and promoted an attack on immigrant ways of life.[36]

For governing elites, the immediate enemy was the political boss. The problems of reducing ethnic leadership influence and Americanizing the immigrant suggested the need for innovative concepts and policies. The rehabilitative approach, stressing psychological adjustment, offered one solution. In a coalition between progressive reformers (the emergent social work profession and social pathologists) the groundwork was laid for controlling the discredited urban classes. These groups were perceived as suspect moral categories requiring special precautions and extraordinary strategies of intervention.[37] Distrust of the urban population, couched in the language of personal pathology, emphasized individual therapy rather than political action or structural change.[38]

A clinical model of the poor speaks of the "patient" as diseased, ill, contagious, chronic, and in need of prophylactic measures. Intervention and cure involved programs that would restore health to the sick and remedy "natural" imperfections. Stereotypical images of the poor as uncontrollable, degraded, animalistic, and morally diseased supported a therapeutic regime designed to reshape the character of the offender. Because moral sickness was believed to be deeply rooted, systematic exploration of the patient's experiences was required. Psychological individualism became the philosophy that guided social amelioration.

By the beginning of the twentieth century, the "Americanization of the unconscious," to use Seeley's term,[39] pervaded the social-problems ethos. Commitment to the uniqueness of each individual, emotional factors in experience, unity of personality, and the necessity for dealing with the whole persons became characteristic, rhetorical goals of the people-saving agencies and their sociological allies. It also formed the basis of casework, the primary method of client management.[40]

Opposition to prevailing institutions was treated as a problem of personal maladjustment. Platt describes the invention of delinquency by the "child savers," or reformer-social-worker interests, who successfully imposed their own values and rules on a powerless minority. In doing so, they consolidated the dependent status of "problematic" youth.[41] Overall, care and cure of the poor were directed toward saving souls, rather than salvaging institutions. They adjusted the client to his or her deprivation, but did little or nothing to correct the imbalance of power.

The Public Opinion Model

For some pathologists, individual correction was too slow and inadequate to stem the tide of urban disorder. Moral education, it was proposed, would create an enlightened public opinion that would enhance social justice and restore moral and political equilibrium. Social structure was not neglected in this analysis. It was featured in the diagnosis of the problem, but eliminated in the solution. Industrialism, perceived as the source of social problems, generated new categories of ills (e.g., greed, corruption, distortion of values, and loss of moral leadership). In one analysis, this reformism was both wrong minded and simplistic because it failed to reconstruct citizen values. In an attack against urban crusaders, especially feminists, Ross lashed out at "moral pacesetters" who strike at bad personal habits, but leave untouched the "child drivers, monopoly builders, and crooked financiers."[42] Ross speaks for all social Darwinists threatened by a newly mobilized women's reform coalition:[43]

> Men rather than women are the natural foes of wrong. Men burn
> at the spectacle of injustice, women at the sight of suffering.
> "White," "decent," "fair play," "square deal," voice masculine
> conscience. Men feel instinctively that the pith of society is
> orderly struggle, competition tempered by rules of forebearance.
> The impulse of simpleminded men to put down "foul play" and
> "dirty work" is a precious safeguard of social order. But the
> impulses of simpleminded women are not so trustworthy. When
> they smother red-handed bandits with flowers they are anti-social;
> when they launch into random vice crusades they are often little
> better than pseudo-social. Now, the rise of great organizations
> for focusing the sentiments of millions of women has lately
> brought about a certain effemination of opinion. . . .[44]

While Ross recognized the hazards of random tinkering with persons and institutions, his primary concern was the threat of new control groups' substitution of their narrow class interests for the more informal controls of tradition and spontaneous group pressure. Ross remained convinced that noninterference was the democratic solution to social problems. Social order could not be based on the coercion of citizens, but only upon a "public opinion [that] guards the social peace by enforcing moral claims."[45] He believed that, in time, the normal processes of "rank, station, caste, and office" establish powerful precedents and traditions which overpower and regulate the newly initiated. There is no need for extraordinary measures of social control, since the normal social processes will work eventually.

The benefits of an educated public were often seen by pathologists as a necessary antidote to the noxious influence of increasing social controls in modern life. In their view, public opinion expressed the social imperative. It is obeyed because people trust it, dread it, and are obsessed by it.[46] The only alternative is a repressive social order which denies personal autonomy. Some writers believed that social regulation had already gone too far:

> In civilized society, laws and regulations press on the individual from all sides. Whenever one attempts to rise above the dead level of commonplace life, instantly the social screw begins to work, and down is brought upon him the tremendous weight of the socio-static press. . . Under the enormous weight of the socio-static press, under the crushing pressure of economical, political and religious regulations, there is no possibility for the individual to determine his own relations in life; there is no possibility for him to move, live, and think freely; the personal self sinks, the suggestible, subconscious, social, impersonal self rises to the surface, gets trained and cultivated, and becomes the hysterical actor in all the tragedies of historical life.[47]

The myth of a consensual public opinion that would restrain the forces of reaction, revolution, and repression was a dominant political ideal as well. A letter by Theodore Roosevelt, complimenting Edward Ross on his "constructive work" in appealing to the "general sense of right as opposed to mere class interest," indicates that elites found the concept of public opinion a useful instrument of social control. As Roosevelt concludes:

> You reject that most mischievous of socialist theses, viz.: that progress is to be secured by the strife of classes. You insist as all healthy-minded patriots should insist, that public opinion, if only sufficiently enlightened and aroused, is equal to the necessary regenerative tasks, and can yet dominate the future. Your book is wholesome and sane and I trust that its influence will be widespread.[48]

The public opinion model, an ameliorative device, rejected social reconstruction and basic reform. Betterment of the lot of the underprivileged urban populations would occur after normal increments of change resulted from education and increased assimilation of ethnics into the middle class.

The Public Health Model

The public health model of amelioration tried to arrest social disorder through prevention of social ills. It went further than either the clinical or public opinion approaches by examining institutions as the cause of social disorder. Urban organization was more than the sum of the individuals who occupied a given territory. In the city, as a political economy, were concentrated the multiple forms of industrial disorganization. Monopoly capitalism, rule by economic interest groups, law for the advantage of the few, and unresponsive corporate and government bureaucratic structures were all seen as breeding moral and physical diseases that could destroy society.

Resolution of social problems through prevention was part of the model proposed by public health.[49] Once a disease has been identified and its carriers specified, massive intervention programs are mounted. Such programs push to inoculate the population against the disease or to persuade individuals to modify their behavior in order to eliminate disease carriers. The preventive approach attempts to change only a single institution; it ignores the systematic interrelationships of institutions within the social structure. Slum clearance, antitrust laws, social insurance, public education, and individual training for migratory laborers were palliatives designed to stop the local contagion of discontent and shore up the present system.

Above all, pathologists worked to salvage society for the middle class. According to their approach, industrial conflict and widespread poverty polarized the classes, undermined democracy, and opened the door to radical change. Public and private reform would head off the encroaching specter of revolution, according to some pathologists, by extending the concept of natural rights to working and middle classes alike. Class consciousness and class antagonism were growing. Capitalism must reform itself, or face its own destruction. By expanding opportunities for the working class, by vigorous attempts to assimilate ethnics into mainstream institutions, and by more equitable distribution of wealth, the present system could be maintained. The only alternative was socialism. In an appeal to the middle class, one pathologist outlined the causes and cures of the social unrest, and concluded that basic reform was the only solution:

> The foregoing reform—and others like them—would drain the swamps and marshes of our social area so that socialism could not grow in them. But for capitalism to assume instead an uncompromising and aggressive attitude of opposition to such reforms is sheer suicidal madness. Nor is it any the less suicidal imbecility for the middle classes to drift along in smug, blind, ignorant indifference to what is happening to us all, and how it can be prevented.[50]

Pygmy solutions for giant problems, however, had little effect upon the distribution of wealth and power. As a means of shoring up the capitalistic order, fragmentary reform served only to mollify malcontents and to keep radical efforts toward institutional change in check. Impractical solutions to social problems, including both the public opinion and prevention approaches, inevitably reverted to ameliorative strategies aimed primarily at individual pathologies and their correction. Neither the political climate nor the state of sociological theory could support a viable model of the social order. Instead, social Darwinism remained the dominant ethos, explaining social variation as biological inferiority. Psychological solutions to this variation served as indoctrination techniques to adjust the "misfit" to institutional life.

Conclusion

Early American sociologists' failure to adequately conceptualize a changing social order betrays the antiurban, middle-class value preferences of these thinkers. Unchallenged values entered into the literature and were perpetuated by academics and reformers, creating an image of society as an organic model of order and health which was juxtaposed against descriptions of individual disorganization and disease.

In their preoccupation with corrective remedies for individual problems, social pathologists established a loose paradigm for coping with social problems that was grounded in obsolete images of social organization. Heterogeneity, differentiation, conflict, and change, the basic elements of the new industrial order, were viewed as problems of a society that had lost its moorings. In this early work (which set the tone for subsequent research in deviance), the pathologists' value uniformities were expressed in three ways.[51]

(1) The model of social organization that the pathologists adopted was that of a small town blown up in scale. The good society was one in which the intimacy and homogeneity of primary groups prevailed, social change occurred in a gradual and orderly fashion, and citizens were adjusted, neighborly, and helpful. Society was harmonious and continuous through time, according to this organic conception (most fully articulated in American sociology by Cooley).

(2) The concept of social disorganization utilized by pathologists often meant merely the absence of the organic society described above. Social problems were defined in terms of deviations by aggregates of individuals from the existing norms. They arise when numbers of individuals are unwilling or unable to conform to status quo standards, as a result of urbanization, immigration, and other types of social change. More and better socialization was the major ingredient for the adjustment of the individual with problems and the reduction of repercussions from social change.

(3) The value uniformities that led to typical notions of social organization and disorganization also determined the principles for selecting and

organizing textbooks and organizing the division of labor in sociology. Social problems texts, written for student audiences, characteristically had a low level of abstraction insured to perpetuate what Mills refers to as "a textbook tolerance for the commonplace."[52] Courses in deviance and social problems have been best-seller attractions. As a whole, they have little connection with larger theoretical concerns in the field. Presented as a set of isolated situations and fragmentary collections of conglomerate topics, social problems has been taught at a strictly common sense level.

The pathologist dilemma remains as pertinent now as it was then: how can the professional requirement for a theoretical framework be met within a social problems focus? The division of the field into theoretical and applied sociology suggests the extent to which the value-theory question has not yet been resolved.

The dualistic conception of the modern world persisted in the Chicago tradition, but another component, reorganization, was added to the social processes of organization and disorganization. With a more sophisticated view of the immigrant's troubles as indicators of social change, Chicago scholars abandoned the image of biological inferiority, and turned to analysis of the social processes which created such dislocations.

NOTES

1. John Lewis Gillin, *Social Pathology* (New York: The Century Co., 1933), p. 3.

2. Analysis of the social science movement in the United States is found in L. L. Bernard and Jessie Bernard, *Origins of American Sociology* (New York: Russell and Russell, Inc., 1965). See, also, A. W. Small, "Fifty Years of Sociology in the United States," *American Journal of Sociology* 21 (May 1916): 721-864.

3. Bernard and Bernard, *Origins*, p. 668.

4. Ibid., pp. 445-446.

5. For a discussion of Comte's influence in American sociology, see Howard Becker and Harry R. Barnes, *Social Thought from Lore to Science*, vol. 2 (New York: Dover Publications, Inc., 1961), chap. 15.

6. Ibid., p. 584.

7. A critical view of the doctrine of progress is offered by L. T. Hobhouse, *Social Evolution and Political Theory* (New York: Columbia University Press, 1928).

8. Becker and Barnes, *Social Thought*, p. 591.

9. A discussion of mid-nineteenth-century reform movements is found in *A Documentary History of American Industrial Society*, ed. John R. Commons (Cleveland: The A. H. Clark Company, 1910), chap. 7 and J. Bernard, *Social Problems at Midcentury* (New York: The Dryden Press, 1957), pp. 166-173.

10. Becker and Barnes, *Social Thought*, p. 367.

11. Ibid., p. 245.

12. B. Eckland, "Genetics and Sociciological Review* 32 (April 1967): 173-194.

13. For a discussion of the role of social work in control of the urban underclass, see Nanette J. Davis, "The Opaque Mandate: The Social Organization of Social Welfare," in *Social Control*, ed. P. K. Manning (The Free Press, forthcoming).

14. Bernard and Bernard, *Origins*, p. 659.

15. For a discussion of the alliance between sociology, social work, and social problems, see K. Davis, "Mental Hygiene and Class Structure," *Psychiatry* 1 (Feb-

ruary): 55-56; D. J. Kallen, D. Miller, and A. Daniels, "Sociology, Social Work, and Social Problems," *The American Sociologist* 3 (August 1968): 235-240; and D. Matza, *Becoming Deviant* (Englewood Cliffs, N.J.: Prentice-Hall, Inc., 1969), p. 18.

16. A. W. Small and George Vincent, *An Introduction to the Science of Society* (New York: American Book Co., 1894), p. 267.

17. Ibid., p. 270.

18. F. W. Blackmar and J. L. Gillin, *Outline of Sociology* (New York: Macmillan Co., 1923), p. 463.

19. Cooley tended to equate middle-class ideals and life-style with "normal" group life. Those who lacked allegiance to such ideals or patterns, he termed "abnormal." See Charles H. Cooley, *Social Organization* (New York: Charles Scribner's Sons, 1924), p. 52.

20. Herbert Spencer, "The Nature of Society," in *Theories of Society* ed. T. Parsons, E. Shils, K. Naegele, J. E. Pitts, (New York: The Free Press, 1961), p. 143.

21. Although Lester Ward adopted Spencer's evolutionary scheme, he used it as the basis for a managed society and for a lifelong polemic against Spencer and his disciples. See Israel Gerver, *Lester Frank Ward* (New York: Thomas Y. Crowell Company, 1963).

22. For an analysis of social Darwinism, see Richard Hofstadter, *Social Darwinism in American Thought* (Philadelphia: University of Pennsylvania Press, 1944).

23. William G. Sumner, *What Social Classes Owe to Each Other* (Caldwell, Idaho: The Caxton Printers, Ltd., 1952), p. 121.

24. Ibid., p. 104.

25. Samuel G. Smith, *Social Pathology* (New York: The Macmillan Co., 1923), p. 7.

26. A widespread view in American sociology stressed necessity of domination by "superior" classes who govern by intelligence and morality. This contrasted with the unsocialized "remnants," or inferior populations, whose degeneration revealed itself in various forms of suicide, insanity, crime, and vice. See, for example, F. H. Giddings, *The Elements of Sociology* (New York: The Macmillan Co., 1927), pp. 316-318.

27. S. A. Queen and D. M. Mann, *Social Pathology* (New York: Thomas Y. Crowell Company, 1925), p. 17.

28. Ibid., pp. 377-378.

29. C. W. Mills, "The Professional Ideology of Social Pathologists," *American Journal of Sociology* 49 (September 1943): 165-180.

30. H. W. Odum, *Man's Quest for Social Guidance: The Study of Social Problems* (New York: Holt Company, 1927), pp. 50-51.

31. Some social problems texts lumped all deviants—paupers, criminals, immigrants, and nonconformists, generally—with the degenerate "pseudosocial" classes. See, for example, R. M. Binder, *Major Social Problems* (New York: Prentice-Hall, Inc., 1926), p. 151.

32. Wm. M. Sumner, *Essays*, ed. M. R. Davie (New York: Thomas Y. Crowell, Co., 1963), pp. 39-41.

33. M. A. Elliott and F. E. Merrill, *Social Disorganization* (New York: Harper & Brothers, 1941), p. 17.

34. H. P. Fairchild, *Outline of Applied Sociology* (New York: The Macmillan Company, 1921), p. 16.

35. J. L. Gillin, C. G. Dittmer, and R. J. Colbert, *Social Problems* (New York: Century, 1932).

36. This struggle has been documented by Lincoln Steffens, *Shame of the Cities* (New York: Hill and Wang, 1904) and Oscar Handlin, *The Uprooted* (Grosset and Dunlap, 1951). See, also, R. H. Bremmer for a discussion of the economic and political conditions giving rise to social work *From the Depths: The Discovery of Poverty in the United States* (New York: New York University Press, 1956).

37. On this issue, see D. Matza, "Poverty and Disrepute," in *Contemporary Social Problems* ed. R. K. Merton and R. Nisbet (New York: Harcourt Brace Jovanovich, Inc.) and A. M. Platt, *The Child Savers: The Invention of Delinquency* (Chicago: The University of Chicago Press, 1969).

38. I. L. Horowitz and M. Liebowitz, "Social Deviance and Political Marginality: Toward a Redefinition of the Relation

between Sociology and Politics," *Social Problems* 15 (Winter 1968): 280-296.

39. J. R. Seeley, *The Americanization of the Unconscious* (New York: J. B. Lippincott Company, 1967).

40. C. A. Chambers, "An Historical Perspective on Political Action Vs. Individualized Treatment" in *Perspectives on Social Welfare,* ed. P. E. Weinberg (New York: The Macmillan Company, 1969), pp. 89-106.

41. Platt, *The Child Savers.*

42. E. A. Ross, *Sin and Society* (Boston: Houghton Mifflin Company, 1907), p. 97.

43. William Chafe reviews the early feminist movement, its rise and decline, in *The American Woman: Her Changing Social, Economic, and Political Roles, 1920-1970* (New York: Oxford University Press, 1972), chap. 1.

44. Ross, *Sin and Society,* pp. 94-95.

45. E. F. Borgatta and H. J. Meyer, eds., *Social Control and Foundations of Sociology: Pioneer Contributions of Edward Elsworth Ross to the Study of Society* (Boston: Beacon Hill, 1959), p. 42.

46. Ibid., p. 64.

47. B. Sidis, *The Psychology of Suggestion* (New York: 1898), pp. 311-312.

48. Ross, *Sin and Society,* chap. 11.

49. Kallen, Miller, and Daniels, "Sociology, Social Work, and Social Problems," p. 236.

50. Ross L. Finney, *Causes and Cures for the Social Unrest: An Appeal to the Middle Class* (New York: The Macmillan Company, 1922), p. 177.

51. E. Bend and M. Vogelfanger, "A New Look at Mills 'Critique,' " in B. Rosenberg, I. Gerver, and F. W. Howton, eds., *Mass Society in Crisis: Social Problems and Social Pathology* (New York: The Macmillan Company, 1971), pp. 271-281.

52. Mills, "The Professional Ideology of Social Pathologists."

3

Deviance as Social Disorganization

THE CHICAGO SCHOOL

> The process by which the authority and influence of an earlier
> culture and system of social control is undermined and eventually
> destroyed is described by [W. I.] Thomas—looking at it from
> the side of the individual—as a process of "individualization." But
> looking at it from the point of view of society and the community
> it is social disorganization. (Robert Park *et al.* "The City.")[1]

By the turn of the century, the new University of Chicago had em-
barked on the first systematic experiment in American social science.
From this point on, identifiable trends in paradigm construction by distinct schools of sociology can be discerned. By emancipating itself from a
primary social pathology-social work focus, the Chicago School established
a research program that used for theory and data what earlier writers had
discarded—the city and its diverse populations.

Rejecting both speculation and doctrine as the basis for a science of
social action, the Chicago School turned to the urban locale as a laboratory. In this setting, it studied conditions and trends of the modern metropolis as "natural" phenomena. Behaviors, as normal or abnormal, healthy or
diseased, and conventional or unconventional, were interpreted as varied
facets of the larger urban complex. A fixation on social problems and their
correction diminished. What emerged as a central concern was a pragmatic, experimental program guided by studies of the varieties of social
types. Hobos, slums, ghettos, prostitutes, immigrant communities, and delinquents, among others, were treated as natural events in a changing urban landscape. Guided by a commitment to scientific investigation, Chi-

cago scholars completed the split between academic sociology and organized welfare activity. Pre-Chicago sociology, as Albion Small describes it, was "more of a yearning than a substantial body of knowledge, a fixed point of view, or a rigorous method of research."[2] The new Chicago sociology, by creating a theoretical discipline and outlining the basic issues of contemporary sociology, cleared out certain popular nineteenth-century fallacies and errors. The religious and philanthropic temper that animated speculations about evolution, organicism, racial differences, and adjustment was replaced by deliberate attempts to investigate the meanings of the world from the subject's viewpoint.[3] Figure 3.1 summarizes the Chicago School paradigm.

I.	Social-Professional Conditions	Urbanism as a way of life; sociology as a university-based discipline free from elite control; city as a social laboratory; dominance of Chicago School in American sociology; applied sociology.
II.	Perspective	Ecology-Interaction; behavior a product of physical location; modified environmental determinism; duality of material and moral realms; acceptance of urban diversity, but conceived as social disorganization; deviance as "natural" or disorganized phase of urban life; change as inevitable.
III.	Metaphor	"Web of life"; naturalism; interconnectedness of urban organizations.
IV.	Themes	Sites and Situations: —Social worlds —Life cycle or career —Crisis
V.	Method	Ethnography; rates and distributions

FIGURE 3.1. *Chicago School Paradigm*

SOCIAL AND PROFESSIONAL CONDITIONS

Chicago and the New Sociology

Whose point of view is taken into account during the data collection process is a crucial element in studies of human behavior. Doing research, rather than talking about it, was not original with Chicago scholars. Following the lead of a line of English writers, philanthropists, and reformers (including John Howard, Charles Booth, Beatrice Webb, and others), a few nineteenth-century American sociologists carried out studies of exist-

ing social conditions and how to change them. Published work attempted
to expose social evils, to intervene and help where possible, and to advocate legislative reforms. Religious motives also drew some sociologists in
this direction for sociology had long recruited numerous restless and dissatisfied clergymen.[4] Religion and reform prompted a strong correctional
impulse, typified by Booth's description of a London lower working-class
district:

> An awful place, the worst street in the district. The inhabitants
> are mostly of lowest class and seem to lack all ideas of cleanliness
> or decency . . . the children are rarely brought up to any kind
> of work, but loaf about, and no doubt form the nucleus for future
> generations of thieves and other bad characters . . . The property
> is in very bad condition, unsanitary and overcrowded . . . A
> number of the rooms are occupied by prostitutes of the most
> pronounced order.[5]

Research of the Booth type inspired the Pittsburg Survey, a massive
effort carried out from 1909 to 1914, filling six volumes largely with the
negative features of such urban conditions as housing, sanitation, crime,
poverty, recreation, wages, industrial accidents, and public education. Information was gathered to indicate what ought to be the existing conditions and to suggest ways of improvement through welfare and political
change. The Russell Sage Foundation, using the survey technique in over
2600 special studies, focused on immoral aspects of lower-class life. The
"evil-causes-evil" theorem expressed the charity worker's bias: deviations
from middle-class propriety have no redeeming qualities. Delinquency
and crime among the poor clearly demonstrated not only the absence of
morality, but an abnormal way of life. For example, "crookin" among
working-class boys had its own traditions and rationales:

> Boys start out on "crookin" expeditions, taking anything edible
> or vendible that they can lay their hand on . . . They are quite
> nonmoral and have never learned to consider the question of
> property. Their code is the primitive code of might and they look
> upon their booty as theirs by right of conquest. Further, the
> very pressure of poverty is an incentive to stealing for various
> ends. . . When one is penniless and knows no moral code and
> sees one's elders acknowledging none, the temptation to adopt
> the tactics of the thief and the thug become almost irresistible.[6]

As long as the research problem took the conventional community's
point of view, efforts to understand and explain divergent behavior floundered in the limited categories of evil and its solution. New intellectual and

social categories were needed before sociology could establish its academic niche as an independent discipline freed from the constraints of a social reform bias.

The Chicago milieu facilitated this in two ways. One was the new University of Chicago, an innovative and richly endowed school, which fostered a spirit of creative scholarship unparalleled in American academia. The other was Chicago sociologists' research practice of making extensive observations of the urban scene from a naturalist's perspective or, as Wirth phrased it, "without offering an apology and without presenting a program."[7]

Against the background of Chicago's amazing industrial growth, digging and discovering knowledge served as the dominant rationale of university leaders for assembling a new type of faculty. Energies formerly devoted to theology and reform became channeled into education. As R.E.L. Faris notes, it was no historical accident that creative scholarship developed from this source:

> In this supporting atmosphere, then, of vigorous city and exciting new institution, the sociologists, too, were to find encouragement to dig and discover in amounts not customary in the gentler academic atmospheres where ivy sometimes grew faster than knowledge. All these secular supports may have been supplemented by the motivating optimism and selflessness prevailing in nineteenth-century Protestant theology . . . The wild enthusiasm which not long before had generated a serious intention to Christianize the entire world in a single generation became transferred in these men to more secular but similarly inspiring aims of higher education and the creation of a new science of social behavior.[8]

Ideas underwent transformation as well. While some scholars continued to pay lip service to Comte's doctrine of organicism, the dominant view of the social order held by most Chicago sociologists and their students entailed a Durkheimian conception: increased population size led to increased competition, differentiation, diversity, and impersonal relations.[9] Absence of unity, the spectacle of "a discordant medley of hundreds of thousands of individuals without any personal relations except in small selective groups," characterized the modern city.[10]

The city was a meeting place for strangers; no longer could it be conceived of as a harmonious unit. But this new historical reality presented an anomaly. On the one hand, close physical proximity connected persons and groups who shared few similarities in tastes, habits, or language. Slum dwellers and gold coast residents were geographical neighbors. On the other hand, cultural, economic, and political barriers divided classes, occupations, and groups. Social relations were typically competitive, often antagonistic. Accounting for this diversity while clinging to the notion of the community as an integral social unit was a theoretical dilemma. The Chicagoans resolved the problem in three ways.

(1) They took the social diversity of the metropolis as a starting point to formulate an ecological theory of urban organization and change.

(2) They considered observable forms of deviant behavior as transitional, or disorganized, phases of the social structure undergoing gradual or drastic reorganization. In Matza's analysis, the Chicagoans conceptualized social disorganization, but described diversity.[11]

(3) They viewed research as cumulative. This entailed a series of case studies of discrete social units or situations which were meant to show the underlying social processes of competition, differentiation, specialization, and change.

This case method proved to be a weak vehicle for conveying a general theory of social organization, a feature that appeared less significant to most sociological innovators than the research enterprise itself. Despite the reformist hangovers implicit in some of the work, the in-depth studies of groups, communities, mechanisms of communication, and processes of change begun at Chicago established a tradition of deviant studies that persist to this day. The Chicago School survives as the first American effort to systematize sociology. How Chicagoans dealt with the anomaly of deviance as an intrinsic part of the changing social order influenced later model builders, many of whom rejected or revised this earlier formulation. The fact that theory and research practice were often independent events lacking logical coherence was one condition that generated alternative formulations. Another was the overly limited scope of the theorizing itself, which left out certain crucial elements of the urban phenomena they wished to explain. Still another condition encouraging paradigm changes was historical change in the profession. Other such conditions will be further explored throughout these chapters. I turn now to the Chicago School and four interrelated elements of its paradigm: (1) the ecological-interactional perspective; (2) the "web-of-life" metaphor, (3) sites and situations as the dominant theme, and (4) ethnography and distribution rates as the chief research methods.

PERSPECTIVE

The Ecological-Interactional Perspective

In Robert Park's definition of sociology, "social control was the central fact and the central problem of society."[12] To assess this problem, investigators needed to identify those processes that specified how human collaboration worked and what conditions operated to alter or impede it. Even while the ex-newspaperman Park was directing students and encouraging colleagues to study the colorful and lively aspects of city life, he was seeking a more abstract, general approach to the study of the human community. Park found this in his own adaptation of the concepts developed by ecologists to describe the processes by which plant and animal communities develop and change.

Park derived his version of the ecological concept from three sources: Darwin's conception of plant and animal interdependencies within the natural realm, Simmel's notion of time-space properties of social relations, and Durkheim's theory of population density as determining the degree of social competition and division of labor.

The ecological framework typically started with the physical or biological facts of human existence. These provided the substratum for social organization and disorganization. In some formulations demographic criteria almost exclusively defined the community, with social problems typically conceived of as the result of physical dislocation. In the ecological model, social order and disorder follow the sequence shown in Figure 3.2.

The competition and selection processes, then, work continuously to position and displace human populations, and social problems are the result of this physical dislocation. In the words of one theorist:

> Human ecology is fundamentally interested in the effect of
> position [or location] in both time and space, upon human
> institutions and human behavior . . . These spatial relationships
> of human beings are the products of competition and selection,
> and are continuously in process of change as new factors enter to
> disturb the competitive relations or to facilitate mobility. Human
> institutions and human nature itself become accommodated to
> certain spatial relationships of human beings. As these spatial
> relationships change, the physical basis of social relations is
> altered, thereby producing social and political problems.[13]

In their theory, the human ecologists conceived of the city as a mechanism of impersonal forces that resulted in a kind of sterile production of physical forms. But this image denied the other reality: the city as a human construction, an outcome of social interaction. Since social facts, and not the physical plan of the city, were problematic, the Chicagoans had to redefine the city as a social reality. George Herbert Mead's social psychological assumptions played a crucial role in formulating an interaction-

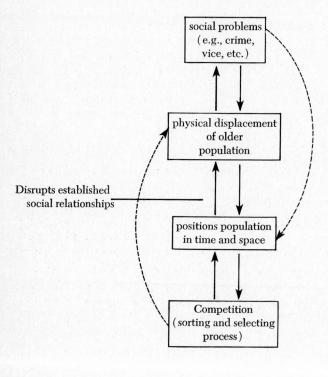

direct line of influence

------> indirect effects

FIGURE 3.2. *Ecological Model of Social Problems*

al model to supplement, if not often to replace, the ecological one.[14] This tradition stimulated a concern with the shaping and structuring of interaction by the ecology of the material world. Relating natural areas to cultural traditions generated a notion of the city as a social construct or a "state of mind." This distinctive point of view led to an outpouring of naturalistic studies. With a focus on diverse human sentiments and life-styles, deviance became not only sociologically respectable, but often the primary research emphasis. Park set the tone in his humanistic comments on the city:

> The city . . . is something more than a congeries of individual men and of social conveniences—streets, buildings, electric lights, tramways, and telephones, etc.; something more, also, than a mere constellation of institutions and administrative devices—courts, hospitals, schools, police, and civil functionaries of various sorts. The city is, rather, a state of mind, a body of customs and traditions, and of the organized attitudes and sentiments that inhere in these customs and are transmitted with this tradition. The city is not, in other words, merely a physical mechanism and an artificial construction. It is involved in the vital processes of the people who compose it; it is a product of nature, and particularly of human nature."[15]

If the community is more than an aggregate or "congeries" of individuals and social artifacts, what is it, and how did it evolve? What is the relationship between physical and social facts? How does the lack of fit between material and social realms create social problems? In proposing a general theory of social order and change, Park rejected an ideological style of thought. His questions oriented Chicago thinkers to a highly original, if still theoretically inconsistent, conception of urban society.

First, Park took a Darwinian position by asserting that competition was the active principle in ordering and regulating life. The struggle for existence regulated numbers, controlled distribution, and maintained the balance of nature. As the most elementary social process, competition determined group and institutional survival, location in the physical environment, and division of labor among groups. Analogically, the human community developed in the same way as plant and animal communities. Through symbiosis, or mutual dependence, differently positioned groups were interrelated by a biotic balance, an unending process of adjustment and readjustment.

Second, Chicagoans put moralistic predispositions aside to observe the process of institutional birth, survival, and decay. They took account of how institutions driven by competition transformed the sacred into the secular, the serious into the trivial. This implied that social change had its own internal logic, founded on market conditions and shifts in population. Thus, the newspaper underwent transition from a serious political journal catering to a restricted population to a mass commodity serving up tidbits of human interest and local trivia.[16]

Third, in the process of competitive exchange, some populations or institutions achieved a dominant position. Dominance was essentially a physical or economic fact. It ordered and stabilized the ecological patterns of the city, in this way determining the functional relation of each of the different areas of the city to all others. In effect, occupants of high land values (e.g., the central shopping district and banking area) regulated spatial arrangements. The Chicagoans preferred to think that the clustering of underprivileged populations in deteriorated areas resulted from this impersonal, unplanned process. Land values and land use were interpreted as dehumanized and depoliticized events. What the Chicagoans were sensitive to was the moral isolation of the underclass. Ecologically separated, the disreputable classes dwelt within the human community, but were not a part of it.

Fourth, while dominance tended to stabilize the community into predictable patterns of competition and interdependence, "succession," or replacement, altered these relationships by a sequence of population and land-use changes. A fascination with concepts denoting change—cycles, stages, phases, movement, mobility—enabled Chicagoans to record the alterations of urban institutions as they formed and reformed under environmental pressure.

Fifth, the moral order, or "cultural superstructure," based on communication and consensus, rested on the symbiotic base. In one sense, culture was a product of the time-space arrangements of competing groups in a scarce natural economy. In another, the cultural superstructure (traditions, norms, mores, and laws) served as an "instrument of direction and control upon the biotic substructure."[17] Social disorganization thus reflected the failure of the moral order to regulate the unrestricted ecological order. In this deregulated order, immigrants and other aliens to city life had only impersonal relations, often treating other people as part of the community "flora and fauna." A situation in which conventions and traditions of the larger society are unknown or ignored frees the alien from moral claims, turning the struggle for existence into open conflict.

Detachment from reformist circles did not free the Chicagoans from an implicit ideological position. Conventional society still provided the criteria by which investigators judged deviants as culprits and respectables as victims. In a later version, labeling theorists would reverse this sentiment to read: deviants are victims of arbitrary and irrational control by conventional social agents. Park and others in this early Chicago tradition failed to see the paradox of social control; that is, control creates and perpetuates deviant categories in the first place.

If society was everywhere a "control organization," to use Park's language, it was not conceived of as a very effective one. In fact, the social order was a tenuous, if still manageable, enterprise. Left alone, the natural order produced a kind of Hobbesian person, ruthless and self-serving. Only external constraints imposed by traditions, custom, and law made any social order possible. For the Chicagoans, the moral order could not be taken for granted. Rapid and unregulated social change broke down vital social machinery essential for stabilizing institutions and personalities. Shoring up the forces of social control appeared to be the only solution to formidable problems of regulating behavior. Yet crusader impulses were anathema to most Chicagoans. Academic freedom became identified with an antireformist posture, expressed in this statement by Park and Burgess:

> It is probably not the business of the universities to agitate
> reforms nor to attempt directly to influence public opinion in
> regard to current issues. To do this is to relax its critical attitude,
> lessen its authority in matters of fact, and jeopardize its hard-won
> academic freedom. When a university takes over the function
> of political party or a church it ceases to perform its function
> as a university.[18]

Despite the effort to incorporate interactional processes into the scheme, the ecological model of society presented a lopsided view of the social order.[19] Defining ways of life as a function of conditions of life objectified institutions, viewing them as observable, physical activities, rather than as actors' subjective role experiences. Moreover, the assumption that social institutions did not evolve, but adjusted to new conditions originating from environmental change or technological development, neglected crucial features of social life. Values and decisions of political and economic elites played no part in this analysis. Power and stratification issues may have been subsumed under the ecological rubric as competition and dominance, but these were defined as operating in impersonal, if not inscrutable, ways. Explaining the genesis of the social by reference to the natural habitat shifted the burden of adjustment from the individual to his or her institutions. When these fail to adjust, social problems arise. An oversocialized conception of humans as the product of social organization is implicit in this thinking.

Park and the Chicagoans were faced with the contradiction between social determinism and free will. In separating the physical and moral domains into a hierarchical order, the ecological theory posited that moral meanings were a product or an extension of physical placement. Environmental influences shaped persons to their settings. But the journalistic imperative dictated that description should be faithful to the individuals or groups studied. Environmental determinism eradicated free will. The naturalistic method ignored the positivistic view of the inevitability of social influences.

Ecologists never resolved this tension in their writings. Ethnographers used the image of the struggling person offered by their theory to go beyond the sketchy outline of spatial relations and their social correlates.[20] In the cultural version of ecological analysis, social placement came to provide the contributing condition for social disorganization and deviant conduct. Within these situational constraints, persons had a limited freedom of action. Deviance was an option, not a necessity; but it was an option that depended on external pressures of selection and seclusion of individuals. Once isolated milieux were identified, the interactional tradition led them out of ecology as such. Proceeding in a largely atheoretical fashion, the Chicagoans documented conformity and deviance as natural patterns of urban life. The ecological model served only as a backdrop for the more vibrant urban scenarios they preferred to describe.

METAPHOR

The Web of Life

Ecological theorists, like the organicists before them, borrowed their language and imagery from biology, this time from naturalistic studies of plant and animal life. Darwin's popularity in earlier academic circles had elevated the idea of "struggle for existence" to the status of a natural law. In siding with industrialists and elites, social scientists not only justified the exploitation of workers and the environment, but also rationalized a noninterventionist stance toward the political order.

In adopting a biological analogy for social life, human ecologists took the struggle for existence as a constant. Preferring to think of themselves as detached scientists, the Chicago writers strongly rejected any overt ideological position that would align them with either the capitalistic order or its reformers. But, as I will show later, an implicit identification with dominant institutions affected both theory and method.

In a fairly sophisticated treatment of the biological enterprise, ecologists focused on how competition promoted both stability and change, unity and variety, through mutual adjustment of populations and their environments. The "web-of-life" metaphor distilled in a brief phrase the notion of a complex system of interdependencies that transcended isolated individuals.

The biological metaphor had a compelling simplicity. It suggested that competition was essentially a benign process. Through selection, populations and institutions developed a symbiotic interdependence, with change and adjustment tending toward a state of equilibrium. Social intervention disturbed the natural order of growth, decay, and death that characterized all natural communities. Social order existed at the material level, even if not at the cultural level. In Park's words:

> The unity of the social group may be compared to that of the plant communities. In these communities, the relation between the individual species which compose them seems at first wholly fortuitous and external. Cooperation and community, so far as it exists, consists merely in the fact that within a given geographical area, certain species come together merely because each happens to provide by its presence an environment in which the life of the other is easier, more secure, than if they lived in isolation. . . .[21]

What Chicagoans had to reconcile was the fact of cultural diversity with a conception of symbiotic order. What kind of order, they questioned, existed in inner-city districts where over 90 percent of the households were headed by foreign-born or Negro residents?[22] The biological metaphor made the city a comprehensible unit, even if socially inexplicable. It took physical formation as a framework within which community organization supposedly tended toward equilibrium and adjustment. Community integration, in these terms, resulted from universal participation in the market or in the sharing of city services. For the Chicagoans, a naive fascination with the wonders of urban technocracy (which they identified with civilization) led them to endow physical arrangements with a sociological mystique. Burgess, for one, believed that public utilities provided the main connecting mechanisms linking consumers into a common universe. He wrote:

> The existence of civilized man [depends on] water supply, sewage disposal, gas, electricity. These utilities represent, and in a sense symbolize, the great co-operative mechanism of impersonal services which underlies the essential solidarity of human life in the urban environment, a solidarity that rests upon the communal use of public utilities and the division of labor, rather than upon any vital cultural unity.[23]

A Durkheimian conception of solidarity blinded investigators to more ruthless forms of economic and political conflict perpetuated by dominant institutions. The web notion was based on a monolithic conception of culture, and phenomena that did not fit into this scheme (e.g., politics, delin-

quents, gangsters, slum dwellers) were interpreted as social disorganization or social problems. The web image portrayed the city as a network
of interacting institutions, but dismissed deviant forms as peripheral, transitory, or unstable.

The biotic metaphor, moreover, was not consistent. The tendency to
move from "as if" statements to reality statements often befuddled the
ecologist's enterprise. What began as comparisons between phenomena
evolved into the rule that all behavior was adaptive, regardless of social
origin or function. In theory, deviance needed no extraordinary accounting; it was part and parcel of the urban milieu. Slums, the ghetto, immigrants, hobos, and taxi dancers demonstrated the various modes of urban
organization. Adaptation as a social process carried no moral baggage; it
was strictly an impersonal process by which competing populations located
themselves in an environment and coped with geographical barriers, population movements, and physical distances.

While the biotic metaphor abjured the old organic notion of normal-
abnormal social types, it prevented a conception of deviance as a permanent feature of urban life. Adjustment meant fitting into a new social order,
and assimilation was a natural and inevitable process experienced by all
social "species." With time, all maladjusted groups or institutions would be
accommodated to the competitive conditions of industrial life. Observers
could count on increasing stability and status for underprivileged populations. Cressey makes this point in describing immigrant movements in
Chicago:

> Immigrant stocks follow a regular sequence of settlement in
> successive areas of increasing stability and status. An immigrant
> group on its arrival settles in a compact colony in a low-rent
> industrial center of the city. These congested areas of first
> settlement are characterized by the perpetuation of the group, as
> it improves its economic and social standing, moves outward to
> some more desirable residential district, creating an area of
> second settlement. [Here] the group is not so closely concentrated
> physically, there is less cultural solidarity, and more American
> standards of living are adopted. The last stage in this series
> of movements is one of gradual dispersion through cosmopolitan
> residential districts marking the disintegration of the group
> and the absorption of the individuals into the general American
> population.[24]

The Chicagoans not only perceived change as inevitable, but implied
that it tended toward a desirable end: social integration. The melting pot,
in time, would eradicate urban pockets of deviance. Even the slum, the low-

est point of urban disorganization, would rise from its submerged status and be absorbed into the urban order.[25] Like urban renewal advocates some generations later, the Chicagoans believed that, once dominant institutions entered the deviant scene, social reorganization would proceed. They could not foresee the social turmoil of the sixties and seventies that was induced by master institutions: wide-scale student protest and urban riots, a crisis of legitimacy in the national government, and an international oil problem that threatened the industrial order at its roots.

The Chicagoans were right in one respect: deviance does alter in form and function. Delinquency may be only a stage in a boy's career rather than a lifetime pursuit. Their predictions, however, were incorrect. Deviance is not eliminated in industrial societies. With their static conception of culture and social stratification, ecologists placed deviance on the theoretical fringe. It was a phenomenon on its way to becoming something else (usually a stable, socially approved form of social organization). An ideological fixation on stability and social control, despite evidence to the contrary, led Chicagoans to stress external constraints on conduct, while negating the reactions of the constrained. This one-sided view has severe limitations for a theory of deviance, as Taylor, Walton, and Young emphasize:

> There is no sense of men struggling against social arrangements
> as such; no sense of a social structure ridden by inequalities
> and contradictions, and no sense of men acting to change the
> range of options.[26]

Political struggle had no place in the scheme. The ideology defined appropriate and deviant behavior in territorial terms. Persons competed for social space, and, in doing so, were dislocated from traditional supports; but once they were assimilated into the middle class and socialized into a consumer society, competition would take less drastic forms.

In the meantime, scholars could remain detached from social problems and focus on such technical concerns as training graduate students, collecting data on exotic populations, and analyzing the statistical incidence of deviance. An assumption that features of American life were self-regulating discouraged theorists from critically examining fundamental postulates of the political economy. One consequence of this has been the persistent tendency to trace social disorganization to morally objectionable behavior. I would argue that criminality, deviance, and social problems are more than territorial problems limited to local residents. They are intimately connected with the master institutions and the contradictory systems of social relations and rewards that these institutions generate.[27]

In the final analysis, the ecological model, though promising a holistic conception of the community, delivered only a fragmented image of the urban order. The theory failed to resolve the split between physical and moral realms or the dualistic notion of social organization. In its physical aspects, urban transportation and commodity exchange tied all participants into a common world. But in its moral concerns, the human community consisted of a series of isolated, geographical regions divided by culture, language, class, and caste. Organizationally, this produced politically opposing social worlds. Segregation of individuals into relatively limited areas of interaction and communication separated respectables from deviants, with each world unreconciled to the other.

In assessing the problems of community and political action, the Chicagoans blamed the mix of urban cultures for initiating conflict, and crystallizing differences into a bifurcated political structure. The culture-conflict argument turned social differences into liabilities, and transformed political conflicts into unintelligible contests. Yearning after a cooperative and symbiotic balance between the species, ecologists often found a war between species. Rather than a tightly woven web, the community net appeared, to many observers, to be splintered by an array of disintegrating elements. Crime, poverty, vice, culture conflicts, and even mobility were lumped together as violations of the conventional order.

Other social influences were at work to subdue this pessimistic image. The Chicagoans were pragmatic by philosophical preference and personal experience. Many were deeply involved in current affairs as government and agency consultants or as social activists and reformers.[28] Although theory dictated that they separate personal values from intellectual work, the Chicagoans wanted the city to work, but not in the old reformers' way. They felt a curious blend of amazement that such a complex structure could exist in the first place, admiration for the technical order that seemed to hold it together, and possibly, a secret relish for the urban underlife.

An overwhelming commitment to social organization, at whatever phase of development, also restrained the Chicagoans from writing off deviant phenomena as pathological. Instead, adherence to naturalism, in the journalistic tradition, encouraged investigators to enter the world of the deviant. "From the outside, deviants, like racial minorities, tend to look alike," Matza notes,[29] but, from the inside, deviant phenomena manifested variety not only in traditions and norms, but also in complex modes of organization. Matza comments on the felicitous link between appreciation of deviance and the subjective view which subverted the correctional conception of pathology:

The view of this phenomena yielded by this perspective is interior, in contrast to the external view yielded by a more objective perspective. The deviant phenomenon is seen from the inside. Consequently, many of the categories having their origin in evaluations made from the outside become difficult to maintain since they achieve little prominence in the interpretation and definitions of deviant subjects. Such was the fate of the central theoretic ideas forwarded by the Chicagoans. The subversion and eventual decline of the conceptions of pathology and disorganization resulted partly from the dedicated entry into deviant worlds by the Chicagoans themselves.[30]

By entering deviant worlds, investigators discovered that what was stable about these worlds was not the persons or groups composing them. Instead stability resided in the continuity of an area or the perpetuation of certain social conditions. Sites and situations, rather than groups, played the overwhelming role in structuring the city naturally. Despite its inability to tie the disparate strands of the urban structure together, the Chicago School managed to suspend conventional morality and comprehend diversity. The conception of peculiar worlds with their own logic and integrity occupied a fundamental place in its study of social life.

THEMES

Sites and Situations

Theoretically, the community web embraced all forms of human interaction—conventional and deviant alike. Pragmatically, what ecologists attempted to explain was how new social forms displaced traditional lifestyles and disrupted social arrangements. The naturalist's stress on sites and situations involved three themes that dominated ethnographic studies: social worlds, life cycle, and crisis. These themes expressed the ecological perspective as an analytical tool for studying institutional and social processes. On balance, though, the research often dispensed with general, abstract explanations, and described only particular events. As Shils observed, the "tendency towards the repetition of disconnected investigation"[31] was a chronic shortcoming of this school.

Social Worlds

The term "social worlds" describes the attempt to portray life as it was experienced by similarly located participants. A sociological rule held that interactions and meanings came from the actor's position. Ecological settings were equated with situated conduct to yield typical deviant forms. Thus, slums gave rise to distinctive codes of action; the ghetto had its own internalized rules and roles; the taxi dance hall fostered the "sex game," a mutual exploitation of buyer and seller. The conception of social worlds as autonomous and integral social units tended to enhance the idea of city life as fragmented, a babel of cultures and traditions. The notion was that social worlds came into being through ecological processes, but were maintained through social isolation.

Since social worlds were separated both physically and morally, each world developed its unique "scheme of life," its norms, codes, and rationales. Schemes emerged from repetitive interaction and standardized relations between participants. Viewing the taxi dance hall as a social organization, Paul G. Cressey describes how codes reflected the particular types of relationships:

> The taxi-dancer dominates the social world, because of the peculiar organization of the taxi-dance hall. The patrons are, for the most part, transient and casual in their attendance. The girls, on the other hand, have a definite and rather permanent economic relationship to the establishment. In their contacts with one another and with the patrons they set the mode, provide a certain scheme of life, and set the immediate standards of conduct for both taxi-dancers and patrons. External standards of conduct may be maintained by the management, but the most direct control remains with the group of girls who dominate the life of the establishment and who have evolved certain codes and techniques of control.[32]

Conflict and exploitation facilitated code making. For taxi dancers, learning to substitute utilitarian relationships for romantic ones was achieved after repeated failures. For the Chicagoans, the city was an ever treacherous, if fascinating, assemblage of social types.

How did the various social worlds—slum district, hobohemia, bohemia, ghetto, vice quarters, immigrant colonies—come into being? The Chicagoans offered two explanations. The first was voluntary segregation, a naturally occurring phenomenon. Population clustering in certain areas might be based on occupational grouping, kinship or religious ties, common language, or a community of ideas and interests. The assumption was that neither political pressure nor deliberate design operated toward the founding of most locally separated communities. Population drift, defined as a sifting and resifting process, distributed groups among separate cultural areas. Once groups were assigned a place by fortuitous and arbitrary choices, isolation acted to maintain community integrity and continuity. Geographical clusters of immigrants, hobos, or prostitutes manifested such self-selecting processes.

Alternatively, some writers attributed the isolation of social worlds to compulsory segregation, an outcome of competition and dominance. This was theoretically more tenable, but less well documented in the research. In the competitive struggle, socially advantaged groups pushed despised or minority populations into restricted areas. "Accommodate or die" meant that subjected populations had to develop a modus operandi or face extinction as an identifiable group. Distribution and grouping, rather than a natural sorting process, caused social distance through conflict relationships.

Under forced segregation, deviant worlds functioned as a mode of adjustment, a response to conflict, and (from an administrative standpoint) an instrument of control. In the ghettoized history of the Jews, documented by Louis Wirth, the fact that benign self-selection processes did not operate for most minorities or deviants becomes obvious.[33]

Lacking a power conception of intergroup relations, the Chicagoans referred to the sequence of compulsory and voluntary segregation as *overlap*. They needed a neutral term for what they imagined were natural, politically unrestricted selection processes. Overlapping suggested the impingement of one world on another. Solidarity within worlds was the result of conflict between worlds.

Aside from the limited treatment provided by the overlap conception, research rarely explored the mode of interconnectedness between worlds. A narrow focus on special worlds led to detailed description and classification, much of it theoretically unproductive. For example, Cressey never mentions the purpose served by his listing of thirteen different types of public dance halls.[34] The comparative issue is dropped, never to appear again. In the naturalist's tradition, description for its own sake often superseded theoretical rationales for data analysis.

While the Chicagoans failed to discern links between social worlds, typically perceiving them as tenuous or nonexistent, they excelled in describing cohesion and persistence within social worlds. The message was that social structures persist despite population movement, generational changes, and succession. Outsiders, or those with a correctional perspective, saw deviant worlds as disordered, lawless communities, while insiders perceived them as highly organized groups that endured over time because of local loyalties and traditions. Gang life takes on a different meaning from this perspective, as shown by William F. Whyte's study of Italian streetcorner boys. Whyte explains that Cornerville participants

conceive society as a closely knit hierarchical organization in
which people's positions and obligations to one another are
defined and recognized.[35]

For Whyte, Cornerville's problems really boil down to a disjuncture
between the slum organization and the conventional society. Not a lack of
organization, but a *different* kind of organization characterized the Italian
district. Penalizing the immigrant because he or she fails to express fully
Americanized traits ignores the restricted opportunities available to foreign, working-class persons. The rackets, local political structure, and
symbolic attachment to Italy serve as indigeneous mechanisms of adjustment, a point later made by functionalists. Although most Chicagoans
displayed ignorance of stratification issues as a factor in poverty, Whyte
recognized that reform depended on a change in formal authority. The
caretaker ethic was as obsolete in Cornerville as it is in contemporary
ghetto management. Whyte's prescription sounds much like an anthropologist's advice to colonial administrators:

> Respect the native culture and deal with the society through
> its leaders. That is certainly a minimum requirement for dealing
> effectively with Cornerville, but is it a sufficient requirement?
> Can any program be effective if all the top positions of formal
> authority are held by people who are aliens to Cornerville? What
> is the net effect upon the individual when he has to subordinate
> himself to people that he recognizes are different from his own?[36]

In the labeling version of this statement, Howard S. Becker raised the
power issue as central to the ways in which dominant groups define and
treat deviants.[37]

The Life Cycle

The utility of the ecological perspective in the break with pathology
notions of deviance was especially evident in the natural history approach.
The idea was appealingly simple. Social forms followed the same growth
and decline processes as natural ones. The life cycle constituted observed
modifications in content and function (e.g., stages, cycles, or shifts). New
situations were the primary source of change. Failure to adapt to new
institutional demands generated nonadaptive behavior, i.e., social disorganization.

Ogburn held that social problems were generated by the gap between a
runaway technology and sluggish, ill-adapted institutions,[38] but most Chicagoans took the more complicated view that technological and social
change produced transformation in the forms of deviation that exist in a

society. Deviancies are born, they flourish, and they die. What freezes them into semipermanent form may be their ability to nucleate sentiments and demands that remain unexpressed in legitimate forms. For example, taxi dancing, as a deviant occupation, provided fictional romances for mobile, unmarried males (often foreign-born). This occupation's persistence in the urban milieu depended on the availability of this type of clientele. Marriage and Americanization enabled the foreign-born to express sexual needs in more conventional ways, sharply reducing clientele ranks, and the occupation phased out under competition from legitimate forms of sexual expression.

Inexplicable behaviors became normalized by using the life cycle approach. The "evil-causes-evil" theory of deviance, which identified "bad" behavior with immorality, underwent revision. The Chicagoans' use of personal documents reflected their view of the process of becoming deviant as an outcome of a series of social experiences and self-definitions. The Chicago studies revamped simpleminded, biological assumptions of deviance causation by showing the significance of the group in deviant behavior. Delinquency research nicely illustrates how the Chicagoans conceived of the movement into deviance as a normally occurring event.

Shaw and his associates used the life history approach to document four stages of the criminal career: play group or gang, initial delinquency, confirmed delinquency, and professional criminal.[39] In stage one, peer group formation characterized both deteriorated areas and middle-class residential districts. Play groups were universal, spontaneous in origin, and served as the media through which values, attitudes, and interests were acquired. What differentiated these groups were variations in culture, moral standards, and social activities. Disorganized areas produced gangs with codes oriented toward law-breaking behavior. The boy's contact with the gang brought him into direct association with criminal modes of behavior.

For Shaw and McKay, the origin of deviance inhered in the neighborhood tradition, not in the person. Delinquency was a product of social placement, "preserved and transmitted [by] the unsupervised play group and the more highly organized delinquent and criminal gangs."[40]

Stage two marked the entrance into delinquent behavior. Starting with petty thievery and truancy, the boy learned specialized techniques to avoid detection. The lack of neighborhood checks encouraged the risky enterprise. Peer approval and thrills were won by committing illicit acts without getting caught.

Repeated success in mini-delinquent acts led to definitions of delinquency as a game with its own rules and practices. By stage three, planning "jobs" became a more systematic affair with the behavior system beginning to revolve around the deviant behavior. Prison typically confirmed the deviant identity; the boy perceived himself as an outcast from conventional society. Turning to the delinquent gang, often his only source of social support, he was further isolated from conventional values. At the final stage, professional crime became a way of life. Conformity to criminal codes and ideals constituted the primary mode of organizing the personality and social relationships.

In classifying stages of behavior, researchers often gave the impression that deviant careers were inevitable, given certain social conditions and experiences. Thrasher rejected this explanation, and offered an alternative one: gang life was a contributing factor to a criminal career. He stated:

> The gang is [not] a "cause" of crime. It would be more accurate to say that the gang is an important contributing factor, facilitating the commission of crime and greatly extending its spread and range. The organization of the gang and the protection which it affords, especially in combination with a ring or a syndicate, make it a superior instrument for the execution of criminal enterprises.[41]

Significantly, criminal types are made, not born. As moral outsiders, denied interaction with the conventional world, criminals flourished in segregated settings. For the Chicagoans, crime was a tenable occupation that was nourished by the control device of isolating offenders. Thus, social exclusion perpetuated a variety of deviant types, a point that became a central tenet of modern labeling theory.

All phases of the social career were deemed equally significant: organization, disorganization, and reorganization were natural processes of growth and change. The Chicagoans found in urban settings the truncated history of many institutions, usually relatively short-lived forms that failed to survive in a competitive milieu. When Samuel Kuchelow described the behavior sequence of a dying church, he had in mind the intimate link between an institution and its setting. Change the setting—Catholic Poles, Jews, and Bohemians replaced established, Protestant groups—and the character of the institution must change as well.[42] Monroe Park Church began as a mission; it ended as a community center. For the Chicagoans imbued with an ironic appreciation of change, secularism was the ubiquitous force that first dislocated, then destroyed traditional institutions. But what moralists saw as defects requiring reform, the Chicago School regarded as transitory and preparatory for a new order of life.

In the Chicago studies, deviance became a central societal concern implicit in the convulsions of a changing social structure. Attempts to identify the processes that aid in its production led to the reduction of multifaceted phenomena to neat causal episodes that have a beginning, middle, and end. As discontinuous and cyclical events in social life, deviance represented a break in the conventional order that gave rise to new ways of life. In turn, new social forms waxed or waned as they continuously adapted to situations. In documenting institutional or personal careers, research focused on crisis as the prime mover of social change. How institutions or groups confronted, coped with, or resolved crisis determined their ability to survive.

Crisis

Chicago scholars took an opposing tack to both earlier and later studies of social organization. The assumption of an ideal social order with integrated, if not immutable, institutional forms implies that variation from its norms signifies deviance. But, in conceiving of institutional continuity and identity as a problematic enterprise, the Chicagoans examined the sources and consequences of contingencies that threatened or strengthened the social unit. Such contingencies produced a crisis, which exposed the structure of a social situation. Since a crisis was a break with routine, requiring alternative behavior, the career line was formed, in part, by the series of responses to crisis situations.

In some cases, crisis was depicted simply as the presence of optional courses of action: the unemployed streetcorner leader can withdraw from the gang or become dependent on former followers. In either event, unemployment altered his social identity and relationships.

In other instances, crisis represented any outside interference with a group's isolation that forced organizational modifications. The internal system, external forces model was further elaborated by functionalists to explain deviance. W. I. Thomas and F. Znaniecki envisioned crisis as the collision between social worlds. They noted that this occurs

> whenever external tendencies not harmonizing with the organized
> activities are introduced into the system, when the workmen in
> the factory start a strike or the soldiers of the army corps a
> mutiny. Then the isolation disappears; the system enters, through
> the individuals . . .into relation with the whole complexity of
> social life. And this lack of real isolation which characterizes a
> system of organized activity only at moments of crisis, is a
> permanent feature of all [groups] . . .[43]

Under conditions of crisis, the group's vulnerability to external pressures threatened its very integrity, often leading to a collapse of the institution.

This process was not merely a matter of impersonal forces, a favorite notion of some writers. Thomas and Znaniecki took account of the role of dominant institutions (political and social authorities) in deliberately quashing the immigrant's traditional institutions. An idea implicit in the work of the Chicagoans, but never fully developed, was the notion that social disorganization could be willfully induced as well as naturally developed.

In most of the research, crisis was invariably, if somewhat vaguely, related to social disorganization, a process set in motion by external conditions. But the reader is often left baffled by the apparent tautology: external conditions———➤social disorganization———➤crisis———➤social disorganization, where the index is the same as that used for personal disorganization. Social disorganization was a psychological problem. This is apparent in Cavan and Ranck's studies of families coping with depression.[44] In this sequence, depression created unemployment or loss of income, altering family status and roles, demoralizing members, and contributing to maladjusted behavior (excessive worrying, debts, nervous breakdown, suicidal thoughts, and evasion of responsibility). Reorganization seems to imply the restoration of group life to a predepression level of operation or the absence of crisis-induced behaviors. In tending to equate disorganization with mental strain, role change, or dependency, this work is reminiscent of the pathologists.

Most Chicagoan accounts of disorganization differed from earlier reports in their conception of crisis as shaping alternative institutional outcomes: one direction leading to reintegration, the other contributing to disintegration. They were less certain about what factors constituted these opposing tendencies. Organized versus disorganized, integrated versus disintegrated, and adaptable versus unadaptable were concepts that were intuitively arrived at. The terms could not explain why one group or institution was unified while another was disordered. Lacking a clear specification of conceptual categories, the Chicagoans often lapsed into a simplistic formula: social change produced social disorganization. The formula persisted in later renditions of deviance accounting. Social disorganization was almost invariably attributed to the transition from preindustrial or folk society to urban, industrial civilization. The study of social problems as disorganized behavior patterns became the description of consequences of social change.[45] For subsequent generations of textbook writers, deviance has represented the social products of modernization: secularization, individualization, heterogeneity, and social diversity.

Methods for Studying the Urban Scene

A dominant perspective typically has a preferred, if not primary, re-search style, and the Chicago School's method was ethnography, the continuous observation and monitoring of events as they unfold in their natural settings. Sampling opinions, survey data, and the study of con-trived situations in a laboratory setting had little appeal. The ethnographic method tied in well with a professional commitment to intimate and de-tailed inspection of urban life. A collection of intensive descriptions of spe-cific sections or social circles, the ethnographic approach provided a series of portraits that exemplified the diversity and pluralism of the metropolis. This method, however, had certain inherent defects.

The case studies focusing on encapsulation of areas and groupings typically took a microscopic point of view. Social bonds, under such inten-sive scrutiny, often appeared to be based on a series of disconnected, tightly bound social units, each isolated from the other, an urban web fragmented by discrete events and activities. While reliance on ethnogra-phy and the insider's perspective freed the Chicagoans from a rural, Protes-tant bias, it confirmed the earlier notion that social change led to a dis-jointed social order.

Moreover, the case study technique often lapsed into a kind of histori-cism that denied the existence of a general science of society.[46] Were case materials drawn from normal, typical, or extreme populations? Did they attempt to test any of the ecological hypotheses regarding segregation and urban interdependence? Finally, did the research achieve an integrative description of urban social organization? These are methodological ques-tions that were ignored by Chicagoans.

Despite the demonstration of specific modes of adaptation and life-styles of ethnics, social classes, and outcasts, the case studies were non-cumulative, bereft of systematic analytic summary. Deviant phenomena, perhaps, have never been described more completely. Undoubtedly, these close-up portrayals of urban life picked up more detail than necessary for pattern analysis. The result was a blurred picture of the urban framework. By stressing ethnographic minutiae, the Chicago School undermined efforts to build a generalizing science. However, by dramatizing the ubiquity of illicit worlds in modern life, the studies dispelled earlier notions about deviance as extraordinary behavior. Functionalists took the next theoretical step in constructing deviance, considering it to be an integral, permanent feature of industrial organizations, essential for maintaining social order.

The Chicagoans also used the demographic method to measure the concentration or dispersion of deviant types. Mapping rates and distributions of suicide, venereal disease, alcoholism, mental illness, crime, vice, and other indicators of social disorganization supported the assumption that behavior had an ecological base. Distribution data contributed to the formulation of a general sociological rule: deviant types are concentrated among the poor, foreign-born, black, or other minority populations. Mapmaking and numerical tabulations appeared, to most social scientists, to be objective and irrefutable social facts. For example, data revealed that schizophrenia came predominantly from hobo, rooming house, and slum areas and especially from populations that are a numerical minority.[47] This supposedly demonstrated the relationship between deteriorated areas and deteriorated mentality and behavior. It seemed obvious that a breakdown in communication and social control (which occurred primarily in heterogeneous, transitional urban areas) caused deviance.

Chicagoans, like later social analysts, mistook the official count (data taken from police files, mental hospital records, census data, and so on) for the whole picture. The greater visibility of lower class offenders, combined with the lack of institutional safeguards to protect their privacy and civil rights, exposed this population to agency detection and control. Subtle forms of data collecting (e.g., victim-reported crime or personal documents) were not included in these demographic methods.

In summary, the Chicago studies had a divided methodology that led in different directions. Ethnography promoted the idea of deviance as a natural, if transitory, phase of social organization. Rate analysis, using official records, contributed to public and scientific stereotypes of deviants as categorical outcasts, morally distinct from middle-class groups. The theoretical struggle between these alternative methods and concepts is still unresolved. Functionalists later repeated the demographic fallacy, but added a new, affirmative dimension: deviant phenomena survive because they meet persistent social needs.

Conclusion

The Chicago School noticed and recorded the diversity of urban life. In so doing, they transformed the older definition of deviance as individual pathology to a conception of deviance as a natural, transitional phenomenon. Starting with an ecological perspective, they took account of the ways in which new, often aberrational, social forms replaced conventional social organizations. Entering deviant worlds, and taking the subjective viewpoint, produced a sociological portfolio of unique urban groupings and happenings. The Chicagoans were not successful, however, in tying these disparate pictures together.

What the Chicagoans failed to recognize was the persistence of deviance in modern life. The social organization, disorganization, and reorganization schemes assumed that deviance was a temporary phase of maladjustment that would either pass away or alter under conditions of natural environmental changes. The question of how authority systems and the normative social order generated deviant forms was outside their purview. This question would be considered by later formulators of deviance theory.

The Chicago legacy of appreciation of differences was carried into subsequent deviance formulations, but with different results. Functionalists rejected the insider's view to generalize about the endurance of certain patterns—deviant or conventional—that survive in modern society. Labeling theorists reversed the functionalist priority to identify with the deviant enterprise. Lifting the burden of deviance causation off the "victims," they placed it squarely on the "victimizers," members of conventional society who react to, define, and stigmatize deviant conduct. Value-conflict theorists took an intermediate position. Under Sutherland, the Chicago School's conception of disorganization was transmuted to differential social organization.[48] This approach made deviant behavior socially explicable, no longer a "product" of impersonal forces of systemic needs. The level of explanation, however, remained limited to individuals and their definitions of the situation.

None of the later approaches adequately specified the role of social change in modifying the forms deviance takes. Nor did they offer a sociological theory of political economy. In the functionalists' work, to which I now turn, the longing for a moral and social consensus all but eliminated a critical theory of social stratification. Structures of power, authority, and interest were obscured by the image of society as a social system, an assemblage of interdependent parts forming a complex, unitary whole.

NOTES

1. R. E. Park, E. W. Burgess, and R. D. McKenzie, *The City* (Chicago: The University of Chicago Press, 1925), p. 106.

2. Albion W. Small, "Fifty Years of Sociology in the United States: 1865-1915,"*American Journal of Sociology* 21 (May 1916): 721-864.

3. For an overview of the Chicago School, see, for example: T. V. Smith and Leonard D. White, *Chicago: An Experiment in Social Science Research* (Originally published by the University of Chicago: 1929), (New York: Greenwood Press, 1968); Robert E. L. Faris, *Chicago Sociology: 1920-1932* (San Francisco: Chandler Publishing Company, 1967); Ralph E. Turner, ed., *Robert E. Park: Selected Papers* (Chicago: The

University of Chicago Press, 1967); and James F. Short, Jr., ed., *The Social Fabric of the Metropolis* (Chicago: The University of Chicago Press, 1971).

4. Faris, *Chicago Sociology: 1920-1932*, p. 7.

5. Charles Booth, *Life and Labour of the People of London*, vol. I, 1892, pp. 10-11; and Pauline V. Young, *Scientific Social Surveys and Research* (Englewood Cliffs, N.J.: Prentice-Hall, 1939), p. 13.

6. *West Side Studies* (New York: Russell Sage Foundations, 1914), pp. 142-143.

7. Louis Wirth, *The Ghetto* (Chicago: The University of Chicago Press, 1928).

8. Faris, *Chicago Sociology: 1920-1932*, pp. 26-27.

9. For an elaboration of this view, see Louis Wirth, "Urbanism as a Way of Life," *American Journal of Sociology* 40 (July 1938): 46-63.

10. Cecil C. North, "The City as a Community: An Introduction to a Research Project," in *The Urban Community*, ed. E. W. Burgess (Chicago: University of Chicago Press, 1926), pp. 233-237.

11. David Matza, *Becoming Deviant* (Englewood Cliffs, N.J.: Prentice-Hall, 1969), p. 48.

12. Turner, ed., *Robert E. Park: Selected Papers*, p. xi. Park provided the major impetus both for the naturalistic study of social life as well as for the type of social problems emphasized. See, Short, ed., *The Social Fabric of the Metropolis*, p. xxix.

13. Roderick D. McKenzie, "The Ecological Approach to the Study of the Human Community," *The American Journal of Sociology* 30 (November 1924).

14. A discussion of this tradition is found in Bernard N. Meltzer, "Mead's Social Psychology," in *Symbolic Interactions*, 2nd ed., ed. Jerome G. Manis and Bernard N. Melzer (Boston: Allyn and Bacon, Inc., 1972).

15. Robert E. Park, *Human Communities* (New York: The Free Press, 1952), p. 227.

16. Helen MacGill Hughes, *News and the Human Interest Story* (Chicago: University of Chicago Press, 1940).

17. Park, *Human Communities*, p. 158.

18. Robert E. Park and Ernest W. Burgess, *Introduction to the Science of Sociology*, 3rd ed. (Chicago: University of Chicago Press, 1969), p. 833.

19. A critical evaluation of the ecological model is found in Walter L. Wallace, ed., *Sociological Theory* (Chicago: Aldine Publishing Company, 1969), pp. 17-18.

20. For examples of this work, see Everett C. Hughes, *The Growth of an Institution: The Chicago Real Estate Board* series 2, monograph 1 (Chicago: The Society for Social Research of the University of Chicago, 1931); W. I. Thomas, "The Immigrant Community," in J. F. Short, Jr., ed., *The Social Fabric of the Metropolis*, pp. 120-130; Louis Wirth, *The Ghetto*; Nels Anderson, *The Hobo: The Sociology of the Homeless Man* (Chicago: University of Chicago Press, 1923); Harvey W. Zorbaugh, *Gold Coast and Slum* (Chicago: University of Chicago Press, 1929); and Paul G. Cressey, *The Taxi-Dance Hall: A Sociological Study of Commercialized Recreation and City Life* (Chicago: University of Chicago Press, 1932).

21. Park and Burgess, *Introduction to the Science of Sociology*, pp. 200-201.

22. S. P. Breckinridge and L. D. White, "Urban Growth and Problems of Social Control," in *Chicago: An Experiment in Social Science Research*, ed. Smith and White (New York: Greenwood Press, 1968), p. 204.

23. Ernest W. Burgess, "Urban Areas," in *Chicago: An Experiment in Social Science Research*, ed. Smith and White, pp. 123-124.

24. Paul Frederick Cressey, "Population Succession in Chicago: 1898-1930," *American Journal of Sociology* 44 (July 1938): 61.

25. Zorbaugh, *Gold Coast and Slum*, p. 7.

26. Ian Taylor, Paul Walton, and Jock Young, *The New Criminology: For a Social Theory of Deviance* (London: Routledge & Kegan Paul, 1973), p. 114.

27. Ibid, p. 120.

28. This was pointed out by Bernard N. Meltzer, a former Chicago student (in conversation).

29. Matza, *Becoming Deviant*, p. 28.

30. Ibid., p. 25.

31. Edward Shils, *The Present State of American Sociology* (Glencoe, Ill.: The Free Press, 1948), pp. 54-55.

32. Paul G. Cressey, "Population Succession in Chicago: 1898-1930," p. 38.

33. Wirth, "Urbanism as a Way of Life."

34. Cressey, "Population Succession in Chicago: 1898-1930," pp. 20-23.

35. William F. Whyte, *Street Corner Society: The Social Structure of an Italian Slum* (Chicago: University of Chicago Press, 1943), p. 268.

36. Ibid., p. 275.

37. Howard S. Becker, *Outsiders: Studies in the Sociology of Deviance* (New York: The Free Press, 1963).

38. William F. Ogburn, *Social Change* (New York: The Viking Press, 1922).

39. Clifford R. Shaw, *The Natural History of a Delinquent Career* (Chicago: University of Chicago Press, 1931); idem, *The Jack-Roller: A Delinquent Boy's Own Story* (Chicago: University of Chicago Press, 1930).

40. Clifford R. Shaw and Henry D. McKay, "Male Juvenile Delinquency as Group Behavior," in *The Social Fabric of the Metropolis,* ed. Short (Chicago: University of Chicago Press, 1971), p. 260.

41. Frederic M. Thrasher, *The Gang* (Chicago: University of Chicago Press, 1927), pp. 381-382.

42. Samuel C. Kincheloe, "The Behavior Sequence of a Dying Church," in *The Social Fabric of the Metropolis,* ed. Short, pp. 167-189.

43. William I. Thomas and Florian Znaniecki, *The Polish Peasant in Europe and America,* vol. I (New York: Alfred A. Knopf, 1927), p. 11.

44. Ruth Shonle Cavan and Katerine H. Ranck, *The Family and the Depression: A Study of One Hundred Chicago Families* (Chicago: University of Chicago Press, 1938).

45. A conception of change as the causal factor in social problems is evident across sociological generations of textbook writers. See, for example, Robert E. L. Faris, *Social Disorganization* (New York: The Ronald Press Company, 1948) and Russell R. Dynes, Alfred C. Clarke, Simon Dinitz, and Ewao Ishino, *Social Problems: Dissensus and Deviation in an Industrial Society* (New York: Oxford University Press, 1964). In some texts, social problems are identified as products of urban society with its derivations of mass culture and alienation, as in *Social Problems: Persistent Challenges,* ed. Edward C. McDonagh and Jon E. Simpson (New York: Holt, Rinehart and Winston, Inc., 1965).

46. For a discussion of methodological problems of using case materials in a generalizing science, see Gideon Sjoberg and Roger Nett, *A Methodology for Social Research* (New York: Harper & Row, 1968), 257-264.

47. Robert E. L. Faris, "Demography of Urban Psychotics with Special Reference to Schizophrenia," *American Sociological Review* 3 (Spring 1938): 203.

48. Edwin H. Sutherland and Donald Cressey, *Principles of Criminology,* 7th ed. (Philadelphia: Lippincott, 1966).

4

Deviance from a Distance

THE FUNCTIONALIST APPROACH

> It may be said that the definition of the deviant as a criminal overwhelmingly emphasizes the negative side. It constitutes a kind of extrusion from the social group, with little concern for his return. He is used rather in a sense as a "scapegoat" on whom to project sentiments in such a context as to strengthen the institutionalized values. What happens to *him* becomes secondary. (Talcott Parsons, *The Social System*)[1]

Introduction

In the last chapter, I identified the Chicago School's primary focus on deviant worlds. By delineating the shape and texture of urban life, the Chicagoans initiated a tradition of firsthand investigation of alternative lifestyles that remains unparalleled in American sociology. In their view, deviance was more than an intrinsic part of the social order; it often constituted the crucial events of a rapidly changing milieu.

Functionalists reversed this scheme. Taking social order as a fact of life, these normative theorists proceed to ask how and by what means the stability of society persists. Rather than examining integrated social units, they proposed a highly abstract theory that posited the interdependence of social phenomena. In their model of society, shared values and norms hold the multiple worlds of modern life together.

In a surprising twist of logic, functionalists conceive of deviance as making a fundamental contribution to this order. They note that, without deviance, no one would know the boundaries of "normality." Nor can any society long endure without safety valves to drain off the excess energy generated by the pressures of conforming to institutional routines. Through deviant outbursts, conflict may be contained. When channeled into nonlegitimate forms, hostilities are less likely to erupt as a serious threat to the social unit.

The effects of unity and diversity on the social order could not be examined by intimate observation or participation in discrete social groups. Studying deviance from a distance provides a global perspective. With a holistic view, deviance is interpreted as an analytical property of a social system which is as essential to society as conformity. While deviance is inherently problematic, it also performs an appropriate functional role: keeping the mainstream society intact.

The functionalist paradigm offers the most formidable sociological effort to date to construct a full-scale explanation of the mechanisms that account for social continuity. However, its many philosophical and theoretical loopholes have come under repeated criticism.[2] Functionalists emphasize stability rather than change, and structure rather than process. Talcott Parsons' articulation of the concept of integration (the ways in which a society is bonded) helped to make stability an overarching concern in American sociology until recently. As a model for what society should be, rather than what it is, functional theory provides an unorthodox, incomplete solution to the problem of maintaining a well-ordered social system. Deviance is salvaged as an integral element in the social equation. What is typically missing in the scheme is a recognition that tendencies within the normative order generate deviance, and that there are negative consequences of this order for politically powerless groups locked out of the system.

The remainder of this chapter further describes the functional paradigm by considering the structural-functional perspective and how social and professional conditions contributed to its theory formulation. I will also examine the "social system" as the dominant metaphor, major functionalist themes (latent functions of deviance, deviance as boundary maintaining, and mechanisms for containing deviance), and methods of analysis (abstract generalizations of social relations drawn largely from secondary sources). Figure 4.1 presents the highlights of these five dimensions.

SOCIAL AND PROFESSIONAL CONDITIONS

Olympians on the Mountaintop

When Talcott Parsons published his first theoretical synthesis, *The Structure of Social Action*,[3] in 1937, Western industrial states were in the worst depression they had ever experienced, and were on the brink of World

I.	Social-Professional Conditions	Economic depression and war; top sociology faculties in private schools insulated from economic and political crisis; problems pursued in relatively autonomous technical tradition rather than response to publicly salient issues; accomodation to master institutions; dominance of Eastern universities (Harvard & Columbia) in American sociology; scientific-technical style of thought
II.	Perspective	Structural sociology; collective determinism; social order as central concern; society held together by spontaneous processes ("voluntarism"); deviance as persistent social pattern; breakdown of moral system, e.g., defects in socialization; change as disruptive; or change as gradual evolutionary process; unanticipated consequences of purposive social action
III.	Metaphor	"Social system"; interdependence of social phenomena; deviance as essential to maintaining "system"
IV.	Themes	Latent functions of deviance; boundary-maintenance and exclusion mechanisms
V.	Method	Abstract generalizations; use of secondary sources

FIGURE 4.1.   *Functionalism Paradigm*

War II. To many intellectuals, industrial, and particularly capitalistic, societies appeared doomed. Free enterprise had failed; the democratic state was not equipped to cope with the internal strains and conflicts that generated radical political movements, both on the right and the left.

Avoiding the near-hysterical response of many thinkers, Parsons dispassionately looked at the nature of modern industrial society, and, with a blend of intellectual tools taken mainly from nineteenth-century sociologists and twentieth-century anthropologists, fashioned a formal theory of social order. He explored the possibilities of science for generating potentially useful knowledge and applying it to the solution of critical human problems.[4]

In their effort to come to grips with the problem of rationality in modern society and the role of science in safeguarding Western values, Parsons and his disciples moved away from the world of concrete social action and analyzed social patterns many levels removed from the participating actors. The esoteric writing often associated with the functionalist school reflects the professional preference for detachment. Aloof from specific social problems, functionalists seemed to be saying that the crisis of the social system could be seen only from above. If analysts were at the same level as participants, they might be caught up in immediate controversies and parochial interests, thereby contaminating their scientific objectivity.

Parson's view of society as a total system separated theorists not only from crisis society, but also from the ideological extremes of accepting the traditional map of social order and rejecting the counter-map offered by revolutionary theorists.

Detached objectivity required an appropriate social milieu to create and foster scholarly sentiments. Harvard University, as a training ground for America's elite, provided isolation from immediate problems and a tradition of intellectual excellence. The risk-taking enterprise of building a new theory and launching a discipleship free from the politics of social reform was facilitated in this sheltered environment. Harvard afforded what Gouldner calls an "institutional incubator" for this new theory. He writes:

> Well-endowed, recruiting most of its undergraduates from an
> elite who had relatively little difficulty in paying the tuition,
> surrounded and permeated by an aura of money and Family,
> having regular intercourse with men of power and influence,
> Harvard is part of the American Establishment and a training and
> recruiting ground for its elite. It is a relatively protected milieu,
> better able than most to maintain the continuity of technical
> academic interests, more successfully resist the politicalization of
> graduate students of sociology, and more easily control the press
> and mute the clamor of current social tensions.[5]

In its social-political significance, though, functional theory has a built-in class bias. It tends to promote system values over alternative moralities, and favors social stability over social change.

By upholding the middle-class concepts of "freedom" and "democracy" (to be established through social regulation of personal interests), functionalists intend to resolve the tensions of industrial strife. Seemingly value-neutral, these new technicians of social order opt for doctrines that depict American society as a bureaucratic, conformist organization. Their tacit acceptance of elite definitions of social order is related to the belief that tightly imposed social rules within a model of "engineered consent" are a necessary antidote for social disorganization.

A conservative rendering of the social structure is an inevitable by-product of this rule-oriented predisposition. Although value commitments are veiled in the language of technical theory, functionalists use the official, dominant ideology as the chief frame of reference for evaluating social system needs and individual behavior. C. Wright Mills comments on the irony of functionalist value-free pretensions. Striving to be disconnected from the struggle, they end up as apologists for the status quo. Mills says:

The ideological significance of this great theory—in its dominant trend—resolves to be justifications of stable forms of social rule. Opportunities before it to acquire even more direct political significance if conservatives should find themselves in need of an even more detailed justification of their rule.[6]

The problems of rationality and order, as these are experienced by threatened urban middle classes, are the twin axes of Parsonian functionalist theory. An image of the wholeness of society is communicated, for unity and diversity are incorporated under the overarching rubric of common morality. Social deviance, when examined in this way, turns out to be a social good, still another mechanism for preserving cherished values and beliefs. From the top of the mountain, these modern Olympians survey the social landscape, revealing patterns that are invisible to those at lower reaches. While such patterns present an overly general and abstract picture (often bearing little relevance to concrete human experience), functional theory, as a topographic model of the ideal society, proposes a set of guidelines for survival of existing social arrangements.

PERSPECTIVE

The Calculus of Consensus

The structural-functional approach has premised two assumptions about the nature of any group or society.[7] One states that all social groups or collectivities have a system of culturally structured, shared symbols that is accepted by most participants. This provides the primary social meanings, or normative orientation, that imposes order by forcing participants to interact within the conventions of the symbolic system. Because social actors share a common pool of cognitive meanings and expectations, interaction can proceed smoothly. The pattern of interactions constitutes a structure of stable organization of roles that contributes to the persistence or functioning of the social group. In brief, society is possible because actors organize goals and behaviors around shared moral standards.

The theory further presumes that social structures, as relatively definite and enduring social relations, operate interdependently to form a coordinated whole. For functionalists, the well-ordered society is a well-integrated society. Not only do actors willingly fit into their appropriate niche in the division of labor but, bound together by common interests and sentiments, they perform those necessary tasks that keep society going.

But is social order or consensus really as simple as these initial assumptions would suggest? Contrary to the accusations of many detractors of functional theory, Parsons and company recognize the hazards of taking the collective conscience for granted. Reacting against the Spencerian doctrine of the "economic man," Parsons posed a conception of the person as a voluntary actor, one who evaluates the situation and behaves in terms that are meaningful to him or her. Profit is only one consideration in the calculus. Institutional rules, common standards of decency, beliefs in the "good society," and occupational interests are other elements that figure in the design. Moreover, much behavior is irrational. It lacks a cognitive orientation, but satisfies biological or psychological needs. This means that structure is indeterminate. The common culture provides the blueprint, but concrete behavior approximates the design; it does not duplicate it.

Consensus, then, is a problem. The issue is the implementation of social agreement that fosters personal freedom without conflicting with socially necessary regulation of wants. Theorists resolved this by postulating a relationship between goals and needs that defined the various organizational frameworks as necessary and automatic developments which met these social requirements.[8]

This strategy proved fatal to attempts to explain deviant behavior. Classic functional theory ignores both how deviance may be generated from lack of identification with an organization, as well as the consequences for the system when actors fail to internalize institutional norms.

Theorists never adequately resolved the freedom-constraint problem. In proposing social prerequisites for an enduring order, functionalists replaced voluntarism with collective determinism. The normative solution to social order bypassed unconventional ideologies and practices that lead to tension and change, and adopted a conventional rendering of dominant moral codes. This becomes apparent when the consensus argument is examined.

Functionalists argue that individuals make autonomous social commitments, yet successful functioning of the system demands that these commitments conform to institutional requirements. How does this arrangement happen? How do persons willingly comply, and receive just enough gratification to continue to be motivated to perform those tasks necessary for group survival?

Parsons offered four solutions to the problem of social order: socialization, profit, persuasion, and coercion. Each solution considers how society regulates deviance by shaping, motivating, tracking, encouraging, or coercing persons to conform.

Socialization acts as the elemental social constraint because it is the process by which individuals internalize rules. For example, the child learns that it is rewarded for inhibiting aggression and expressing socially approved behavior. Significantly, once a person establishes a social relationship based on mutual expectations and gratifications, it is not problematical.[9] If, however, external conditions upset the equilibrium of interaction, there are tendencies to deviance.[10] The impact of these influences requires that socialization be an ongoing process. Learning at one stage of the life cycle may make persons unfit for roles at later points of the personal career. This means that psychological mechanisms are an inadequate means of assuring social stability. Curbing deviance requires more than the reciprocal processes in ordinary social relationships.

The second line of defense for the social order is profit, which is not limited to money. As one element of the social exchange, money gains its value by its potential uses, not by any intrinsic worth. To calculate profit, actors sum the benefits of a transaction over costs, evaluations which include material or social factors. Considerations of profit can motivate persons to stay on approved social tracks.

The system survives by rewarding good role performers. Elites carry the crucial burden here. Entrepreneurial groups, as "bearers of the conception of social order," formulate social goals, making certain the rewards are commensurate with expectations.[11] If this fails, institutional keepers have to find supplementary or alternative means of motivating the discontent.

Persuasion is an additional instrument elites use to develop consensus. This maximizes the individual's identification with a given social order by influencing his or her definition of the situation. Education, an integral part of the persuasion system, uses science and rational techniques to shape behavior by appealing to the actor's "reality principle" and emotional maturity.

Persuasion, though, entails some risk. It easily becomes propaganda, if it attempts to define situations in a one-sided manner. When revolutionary or disruptive, such propaganda undermines the institutional system.

But Parsons hedged on this one. He recognized that private and public agencies employ propaganda when they deliberately attempt to reinforce or strengthen attachment to basic institutional values. Yet his concern for preserving institutions by defusing tension and conflict led him to abandon his value-neutral posture. Social policy, it turns out, should take a definite direction. Parsons stressed that propaganda serves as

> "reinforcement"; of strengthening attachment to the basic
> institutional patterns and cultural traditions of the society and
> deliberately and systematically counteracting the very important
> and existing deviant tendencies. Few would question that this is
> the direction that propaganda should take in relation to the
> internal situation since, in this great crisis, it is fundamentally

preservation of continuity with the great traditions and institutional patterns of Western society that is at stake.[12]

While functionalists believe that socialization, incentive systems, and persuasion induce most people to conform to dominant social rules, they also recognize that deviance is part and parcel of a competitive social order. Taking Durkheim's view, deviance is normal, as it defines the boundaries of right conduct.[13] By marking the outer edges of group life, deviant forms give the inner structure its special character. In this way, people in the nondeviant group develop an orderly sense of their own cultural identity.

Holding social order as a constant, theorists considered the ways in which deviance performed vital functions in the society, in effect contributing to the continuity of that order. By demonstrating the strains within the system, deviance provokes countermeasures to tighten institutional loopholes or innovate sluggish institutions. As long as deviance and social control are locked together in a mutual process, functionalists accord deviance a basic role in the social system.

However, carried too far, deviance may disrupt the ongoing order. Sometimes, more forceful mechanisms are needed to interrupt the vicious circle of deviancy that can shatter the social structure. The vicious circle turns in two directions: alienation or overconformity. Both can take active or passive forms, as Figure 4.2 shows.[14]

	Alienation			*Overconformity*	
	Active Form	*Passive Form*		*Active Form*	*Passive Form*
Rejection	Aggressiveness	Withdrawal	Seductability	Dominance	Submission
Compulsive Avoidance of Responsibility	Incorrigibility	Evasion	Compulsive Responsibility	Compulsive Enforcement	Perfectionism

FIGURE 4.2.   *Alternative Forms of Deviant Behavior*

Deviance is many faceted from a systemic point of view. On the one hand, persons may have only a limited commitment to a system of relations. Alienation, whether expressed as aggressive attack on the system or withdrawal from an untenable situation, reflects explicit forms of rejection.

Alienation may also work more subtly, as in uncontrollable outbursts, acting out behaviors (e.g., illness), or avoiding social obligations. The latter forms take longer to corrode the system, but their effects may be deleterious in the long run by undermining or destroying social relationships.

On the other hand, persons may overcommit themselves to a system of relations at the loss of personal integrity or ability to make situational adjustments to new demands. Overconformity may involve dubious or exploitative transactions between authority and subordinates that corrupt the authority system. It may also take the form of an inflexible response to events: following rules to the letter, obsessive concern with detail, or inability to adapt to new social conditions. The paradox of social order is that it may require members to have just enough detachment from ongoing relations to permit moral evaluations, to accommodate to new rules, and to modify outmoded practices.

While the model does not exclude institutional gatekeepers from engaging in any particular behavioral extremes, functionalists tend to be more concerned with common-garden-variety deviance. Studies feature proletariat crime, rather than white-collar offenses and lower-class rule-evasion rather than corporate and government fraud.

"Deviant binges," in James Old's analysis, must be contained.[15] If socialization fails, if the individual lacks emotional ties with others, if there is no respect for the regulatory norms, or if the individual cannot be manipulated by material or social rewards, then the social structure is threatened. Bringing the deviant into line requires stronger measures. When all else fails, coercion solves the problem of order.

For functionalists, the power of the state to restrain deviance is the trump card in society's hand. Used as a last resort against recalcitrants, it denies freedom or inflicts injury. The role of enforcement is to reintegrate the social group by mobilizing collective sentiments against moral outsiders. What happens to the deviant is of minor concern.[16]

But there are some hazards in this form of control. First, the uncertainty of sanctions may actually encourage more deviance. If persons find they can violate norms and get away with it, the threat of coercion has little impact on their offending behavior.

Second, the existence of ambivalence in the larger society about the need for sanctions, appropriate types of sanctions, and mitigating influences (such as age, sex, and race) may lead controllers to adopt a law-and-order mentality. Overreaction further isolates the deviant and prevents reintegration with the society.

Third, punishment may actually be irrelevant to the deviant although highly pertinent to reinstitutionalizing conventional values. In this sense, criminals may be needed to strengthen the collective conscience when it becomes flabby or inert.

Fourth, the possibility of corruption of enforcers inheres in the close connection between criminals and officials. Enforcement tactics, imposed on a recalcitrant population, may depend for their success on granting concessions to criminals. While this may prove functional from the enforcer's point of view, it is highly dysfunctional from society's standpoint.

Functionalists realize that coercive measures may breed social disorder (a crucial consideration later emphasized by labeling theorists). But, in their essential belief that social balance can be achieved only by containing deviance, they played down the inherent tendencies of power and control to assume irrational and undemocratic forms. As an act of faith, they sided with the sentiments of the urban middle class and governing elites who stand to lose the most from a disruptive social order.[17] From the functionalist perspective, the social order appears beneficent. Because American society fosters such ideals as individualism, free enterprise, open opportunity, compromise politics, and mitigation of overt conflict through co-optation of opponents, it seemed to be adaptive with minimum state interference. Functionalists never denied that power and its abuses were endemic to the structure. What they stressed, though, were the fair rules of the game, the middle-class talent for arbitrating differences. As long as power is dispersed and social managers limit power by recourse to "consent," a harmonious society is possible.[18]

The normative solution to social order provides no answers to the crucial question of structural sources and consequences of deviance, and ignores the role of conventional norms in generating deviance. Positing coercive control as one mechanism society uses to keep deviants in their place, functionalists failed to see how such measures can undermine standard values and institutions.

Unresolved social tensions are swept under the rug. While Hobbes and later conflict theorists were primarily interested in transforming a society characterized by civil war into one characterized by civil peace, normative theorists were concerned with identifying social integration in social systems in which the problem of order has been solved. The system metaphor that permeates this work presents an image of society that is congruent with the notion that benign transactions hold the disparate social parts together. Once the assumption of interdependence is made, system theorists go on to other matters: locating maintenance strategies and focusing on modes of control.

In the final analysis, the basis of social order is the compulsion to conform. The system is greater than the social atoms that constitute it. Human freedom and choice become sacrificed to system needs. The calculus of consensus, theoretically derived from social differences, is actually constructed from shared values among influential groups. By metamorphasizing the moral codes of social managers into prerequisites for social maintenance, functionalists inadvertently modeled society after the well-organized bureaucratic state. Deviance, if well-controlled, helps to lubricate the system and keep it functioning in high gear.

METAPHOR

Society as System

A dominant metaphor not only sensitizes social theorists to the nature of a problem, but also defines concepts and organizes major themes. For functionalists, an updated image of society as a system provided a unified view of society modeled after biology, classical mechanics, and the new science of cybernetics. The system concept has been the center of some of the most crucial sociological issues, such as the bases of the social order, the nature of social causation, and the place of change in sociological analysis.

In brief, the system construct posits the interrelationship and interdependence of parts to form a functioning whole (the organic concept), the stability of the internal environment (the equilibrium concept), and the maintenance of boundaries (social patterns that maintain their integrity over time). In the next section, I shall consider some representative work that demonstrates the functionalists' use of the system concept to describe deviant behavior. The implications and limitations of the concepts of integration, equilibrium, and boundary maintenance for a theory of deviance will be examined below.

Integration

Interdependence, or integration, is a beguiling idea. It suggests that in any given social system, all social structures are interrelated. It is not individual actors that are interdependent, though, but aspects of their behavior (e.g., roles, values, interests, motivations).

By definition, order and integration are equivalent processes. A system (e.g., society) or a subsystem (e.g., the family) can be said to be integrated if roles are mutually complementary, with actors performing in terms of norms that are grounded in common values. The basic referent for such interaction is the collectivity, or larger society.

On the societal level, integration is realized when groups are hierarchically ordered in a division of labor that produces socially useful outcomes. Stratification is a functional imperative for the maintenance of social order.

The integration notion contains four fallacies which seriously detract from its utility as an adequate explanation of deviant processes.[19] In the first place, it focuses on the problem of maintaining a system in which the participants have already internalized norms prohibiting the use of force and fraud, rather than on the emergence of relevant norms. Fixated on the issue of order, functionalists tend to regard deviations from ideal patterns as problems requiring resocialization or social control. This is linked to their dominant theoretical orientation. By locating norms in a hypothetical cultural system which determines concrete social action, they failed to take account of the gap between ideal and real behavior.

Ideally, political minorities have the same incentives and opportunities for success as middle-class groups. But the systematic bias built into dominant-subordinate relations prevents most lower-income groups from entering the system in the first place. Proletariat crime, as Bell recognized, may be an alternative route for realizing the dominant social values.[20] Emergent norms among deprived groups reflect what Rodman called the "value stretch," the effort to adapt to social exigencies by developing situational norms. Highly valued ghetto roles, such as bootlegging, prostitution, pimping, and racketeering, reflect social heterogeneity and occupational diversity in a situation of structured scarcity.[21]

In a word, saying and doing are independent events. An individual's value assertions and his or her actual performance of the social act are rarely equivalent. Even assuming that law-abiding persons internalize dominant norms, there are situations, contingencies and value conflicts, resulting from multiple group memberships that may alter actual behavior.[22]

In the second place, the notion of integration tends to confuse the problem of establishing a well-ordered system with the problem of increasing the level of integration in the system in which order already prevails. By equating order with integration, functionalists betray their ideological preference for the well-run society in which rewards tend to be concentrated in the have classes and the have-nots have no choice but to accept their lot.

According to Davis and Moore, the stratification system gets society's important jobs done by offering high inducements for certain occupations and low incentives for less valued work.[23] In industrial societies, doctors, lawyers, and other professionals require years of specialized training for developing the high levels of competence required for these roles. Monetary rewards and social esteem are said to motivate the able to undergo extensive investment in a functionally requisite role.

This argument justifies the inequalities of the social order; it does not explain the widespread alienation and withdrawal from the differential reward structure by millions of have-nots. A society can be ordered by force but it cannot be integrated so easily. Threatening a general strike in 1974, British coal miners and basic-industry workers demonstrated their rejection of a scarcity ideology that fosters heavy sacrifices for low rankers while maintaining rewards for the affluent.

The normative solution to order does not allow for the possibility that the creation of socially integrated systems, which are based on common values, may involve certain attitudes and behavior different from those required to establish socially ordered systems, which are based on the internal division of labor. For example, prisons are well ordered, but not highly integrated. Actually, these are two different dimensions that vary the state of the system, as the following figure shows.

Highly ordered	Highly integrated (e.g., monastery, Mennonite Community)
Highly ordered	Poorly integrated (e.g., prisons, concentration camp)
Poorly ordered	Highly integrated (e.g., hippie commune)
Poorly ordered	Poorly integrated (e.g., urban ghetto school)

FIGURE 4.3. *Differentials in Order and Integration in Concrete Social Systems*

Increasing the level of order may actually undermine integration as Gouldner shows in his study of management-worker relations in a gypsum factory.[24] When a new management group assumed control, they intervened to bring behavior in line with rules by tightening up "indulgency patterns" (systematic worker borrowing or use of tools and equipment). Underdogs retaliated with wildcat strikes. By violating the informal expectations of workers, management broke down the social bonds between ranks. This suggests that effective integration may depend upon a highly flexible order. Norms may serve as guidelines for action, but, in practice, may be widely evaded.

Effecting a transition from a poorly integrated structure to a highly integrated one may require a dictatorial mandate. Revolutionary governments that demand almost total conformity may wipe out their opposition by murder, banishment, or brainwashing. Clashing value systems often safeguard rights for political minorities, a point made by functionalists themselves in support of democratic values.

In the third place, the integration notion seriously underestimates the degree of conflict that may be generated by shared values, which certainly are no guarantee of civil peace. The functionalists' claim that American society is largely oriented toward success norms, ignores the might-have-beens, the social casualties who lose out in the competitive struggle. Without "cooling-out" mechanisms, as Goffman shows,[25] losers would be unwilling to abide by the rules. Conflict is inevitable in any scarcity system in which the ideology emphasizes structural openness and the realities demonstrate structural closure. Chinoy's study of industrial workers shows the extent to which underdogs have abandoned the American Dream.[26] High rates of suicide and mental illness among low rankers and increasing evidence of industrial sabotage[27] also suggest reconsideration of the integration assumption.

Finally, the integration conception neglects the role of norms based on self-interest in the creation and maintenance of social systems. Contrary to the functionalist argument, a viable social organization depends on participants' expectations of gain in relation to perceived investments. This suggests two considerations. One is that social participants have different definitions of interests dependent on time, place, circumstances, and other situational contingencies. This is apparent in such instances as the decreased tolerance level for misbehavior in nuclear families, which may act as the primary factor leading to mental hospital admission.[28] The family interests in keeping the breadwinner (or other socially productive persons) within the system may decline with a change in the gratifications he or she is able to provide when socially defined as an outsider.

The second consideration is that interests are not necessarily linked to a specific organizational base, but may represent a composite derived from investments in a variety of systems. For example, a value commitment to a job may be a complex matter, as Becker points out, in which the social actor takes account of non-job-related matters.[29] Collegial relationships, location in a specific community, children's school and friends, spouse's preference, recreational opportunities, and alternative work opportunities are all part of the investment-gains calculus. Norms and interests are more complicated and variable matters than functionalists seem to grasp.

Equilibrium

Closely related to the idea of integration is the assumption that a system maintains equilibrium. This means that stability characterizes the system in exchanges with environing systems because of built-in mechanisms that balance any "tilting" tendencies the system may have. Parsons, the systems builder par excellence, goes so far as to say that a system *must* exhibit a "tendency to self-maintenance," using an analogy he draws from the model of classical mechanics. Balanced between inertia and action and reaction, social systems are said to display continuity even as the parts undergo mutual adjustment and change. Parsons found this balance of stability and flexibility in the American two-party system, and asserts that

> at any given time, a relative equilibrating balance in a pluralistic
> society is maintained so that conflicts and divisive tendencies
> are controlled and more or less fully resolved.[30]

In Parsons' view, since power in the system is merely the capacity to get things done in the collective interest, power politics obviously provide the arrangements and strategies that lead to stability, integration, and other system-maintaining functions.

But is this the case? Does consensus politics really embrace the diversity of interests that is reflected in class divisions? Can it reconcile individual and collective utilities, especially the utility of the more powerful and still account for that of the less powerful? The equilibrium model leads functionalists to paint a Panglossian picture of society as coherent, orderly, and the best of all possible worlds.

Evidence suggests an alternative rendering of the majority political scene. "Manipulated consensus," using Edelman's term,[31] is the primary strategy elites use to maintain rule. Historically, powerless groups have been systematically excluded from this political game. The poor, American Indians, Chicanos, blacks, youth, and women, as politically deprived groups, have had little input and few benefits under this system. By restricting the number of players that get into the game, elites can better control the outcome.

A similar point has been made by Buckley, who argues that, in Parsons' model, deviance and strains of various types are treated as residual. The model includes primarily "those determinate relations making up an institutionalized dominant structure of conformity to role expectations."[32] If the fixed point of reference were shifted from the institutionalized structure to the alternative structure of strains and deviance, the question would change, and the answers would lead to a different set of crucial problems: power, stratification, conflict, ideology, and vested interests.

Equilibrium notions really predict little about how the system will change, what types of changes (internal or external) are likely, and whether the outcomes will be continuous or discontinuous with the past. It seems apparent that the functionalists cannot handle conflict and change, given their preoccupation with stability models.

Again, what are the limits of change beyond which a system could be said to be disintegrated? This is a matter of the observer's perspective. For white segregationists, the 1973 election of a black mayor in Detroit may represent the dissolution of the political order. For liberals, and some radicals, it indicates that the system can be responsive to minority demands.

The action-reaction principle, which posits that change in one part of the system contributes to changes in related parts, suggests what Sorokin calls "homemade versions" of physico-mathematical laws. Applied to societies, the principle is "meaningless, imitative verbiage."[33] Without reference to time, place, direction, and type or extent of change, such mechanistic laws provide no guides for examining observable action.

We could easily propose the reverse: change in one unit of the system has few or no consequences for change in related units. For example, despite psychiatry's altered emphasis on the therapeutic milieu for restoring patients' health, custodial treatment is the pervasive pattern in American state-supported mental institutions, with one notable exception. The rich get therapy; the poor are placed in custody.[34]

Boundary Maintenance

A system is supposed to maintain its integrity (its relative autonomy) despite interaction with its environment or other subsystems. Exchange between systems defines the outer limits of behavior by reinforcing internal bonds in a subsystem. However, in modern society, systems often merge together, lose their identity, and have low functional autonomy. Parsons recognized the police-criminal coalition as an inherent strain in enforcement. My own observation of the abortion movement in Michigan suggests that antisystem reformers became prosystem, abortion-service administrators after legalization. Collectivities change, and the line between systems becomes blurred as social roles are transformed.

The notion of functional autonomy may be a myth rather than social reality. The overlapping of social groups in American society tends to erase boundary lines between systems. C. Wright Mills showed this by delineating the ruling class as an "interlocking directorate," in which elites form out of combinations drawn from the political, economic, military, and professional spheres.[35]

The functionalists want it both ways. They hold that power is widely dispersed among the electorate, while, at the same time, they cling to the idea that the political system is autonomous, and can serve as arbitrator for the collective will, uncontaminated by conflicts and mutually contradictory demands.

Functional autonomy, like interdependence and equilibrium, is a matter of degree for any observed system. The medical system, for example, probably has a relatively high degree of functional autonomy. Control over licensing, self-regulation of practice, high professional skills combined with secrecy, and dominance over (but not ultimate responsibility for) the hospital setting as workplace function to afford the medical occupation a wide latitude of control over work. Patients, by contrast, may have little or no choice of practitioners (especially with the increased trend toward closed practices), hospital settings, modes of treatment, or costs. Lacking a counterorganization to offset the medical institution, patients often face a take-it-or-leave-it treatment system.[36]

The system analogy tends to shape the problems of the real world into ones that fit the model. Because the underside of society is left out, the world appears to conform to neat images of order, stability, and continuity. Whatever does not fit can be examined for its latent function (the unintended and unrecognized consequences of persistent social practices). In this way, even the "seamier" aspects of social life may be considered in terms of their contribution to institutional maintenance.

The systems approach resolves deviance into a balance act. As deviance rears its head, social control automatically enters to put it down. When deviance is too blatant to be ignored, its function for the institutional order is explained. In this way, respectables are assured that all things conduce to the general good. As I shall elucidate in the next section, functionalists approach deviance both appreciatively, as it is implicit in social organization, and distantly, as it is not the central focus of their concern.

THEMES

Making the World One: Functionalists Look at Deviance

Undergirding the conceptual superstructure that functionalists have raised is a single, overarching conviction that the world is whole and that all elements support unity. Presuming that investigators must stand outside the melee in order to detect structural patterns, functionalists examine how deviance contributes to the grand design. They employ three themes to account for the persistence of deviance. Two of these, latent functions and boundary maintenance, take a positive view of deviance. The third theme, illegitimacy and exclusion, describes deviance in terms of how society contains or seals off deviance from the institutional order. The empirical work, however, is drawn primarily from secondary sources, and illustrates, rather than tests, functionalist propositions.

Latency

Kingsley Davis takes up the universal social problem of regulating sexual behavior, in which pressures for nonconformity often outweigh tendencies to conformity.[37] While he holds that "sex norms are like other norms in that they help get the business of society accomplished,"[38] the sex drive is probably impossible to regulate in terms of ideal norms; tendencies to deviance encourage the drive to be expressed in nonlegitimate ways. How does society manage to channel sex in the interests of institutional stability and simultaneously provide an escape valve for those persons with pent-up sexual energy? This question was answered by revealing the latent functions of illegitimate behavior which contribute to the integrity of marriage and the family system. Female prostitution manifests these functions.

Two mechanisms are built into the illegitimate structure of prostitution to regulate it in the interests of dominant norms. First, prostitution is defined as evil, since it serves no socially recognized goals. Because it divorces intercourse from reproduction and sentimental social relationships, prostitution is condemned as a vice. The woman who willingly trades sex for money loses social esteem because promiscuity is linked to emotional indifference and lack of a stable relationship. Thus, society regulates the behavior by outlawing the act and the seller.

Second, prostitution provides males with a sexual outlet that has limited liability. Unlike courtship, friendship, or marriage, prostitution requires no obligation other than a fee, and involves no emotional interference with other roles. In this way, the contraband act presents no threat to institutionalized relations.

Not only is this deviant behavior contained within safe limits, but, paradoxically, it is intimately bound up with the structure of the family. Prostitution protects the traditional family system by restricting sexual irregularity among respectable wives and mothers. No other institution can meet the needs of unattached males as well as prostitution, according to Davis.

> Enabling a small number of women to take care of the needs of a large number of men, it is the most convenient sexual outlet for armies and for the legions of strangers, perverts, and physically repulsive in our midst. It performs a role which apparently no other institution fully performs.[39]

At one stroke, Davis demonstrates the systemic connection between legitimacy and deviance. Unlawful behavior, condemned by conventional society and its enforcers, actually shores up respectable institutions. Furthermore, the consequences are not all negative for the prostitute. Even for the working-class girl turned hustler, conditions of life are greatly improved. In no other lower status occupation can she earn so much. Everyone seems to gain, as long as the existing system of dominant relations is taken for granted.

Reversing commonsense explanations of deviance, functionalists seek to uncover unintended functions that keep a complex, mobile society on track. They assume that, if a social pattern persists, it must perform positive functions that are not adequately fulfilled by other existing structures. The latent functions they reveal are not obvious to the participants, and must be teased out by sociologists probing the interdependence of social life.

Merton masterfully makes this point in his analysis of the urban political machine.[40] Examining reformers' accounts of boss politics as corrupt, Merton placed the machine in the context of American political arrangements. As a generic type of social organization, the machine has emerged to meet the needs of the deprived and disenfranchised. It does this by organizing, centralizing, and maintaining, in good working condition, the scattered fragments of power. Boss rule was an antidote to the official system in which no one had legitimate authority to act. If the system did move, it typically neglected diverse subgroups whose distinctive needs were left unsatisfied. "The lawlessness of the extraofficial democracy was merely the counterpoise of the legalism of the official democracy," Merton observes.[41] He lists the following functions performed by the political machine.

1) The Machine humanized and personalized assistance to the needy (e.g., foodbaskets and jobs, legal and extralegal advice, helping the bright boy to a political scholarship, serving as intermediary between the law and the offender, consoling the bereaved). A whole range of crisis services, unavailable from legitimate agencies, were provided by local politicos.

2) Not only was aid furnished, but the manner in which it was provided was significant. Without legal or bureaucratic entanglements or invasion of "client" privacy, the unprofessional techniques of the precinct captain got the job done with no questions asked. For social marginals, the distant, impersonal, and professional style of the welfare worker had little appeal.

3) The feudal-type political apparatus put together by the Boss minimized economic inefficiency while maximizing political privileges for both underdogs and topdogs. Business corporations gained by regulated competition, organized by an economic czar, that was free from political scrutiny and control. In effect, the Boss held the balance of power in the urban political structure. Holding the strings of diverse government bureaus and agencies, he rationalized the relations between public and private business. As a political ambassador for the privilege-seeking business community, the Boss negotiated the alien world of government, thereby perpetuating his rule and welding a link between conventionals and marginals.

In discussing how the machine performed an integral role in the urban economy, Merton offers neither apologies nor reforms for the illegal structure. Even the machine appears to fit into the grand design. By seeking consequences of social practices and reasoning back to the institutional sources of such practices, Merton took the underworld of politicos, crime, and the rackets as basic to the ongoing order. Despite the apparently antipodal interests of legitimate and illegitimate groups, he found, on closer examination, that the two organizations were complementary. The underworld supported the overworld by bringing together the loose strands of power that characterized urban politics. Function unites apparent structural disparities. The world is made one, after all.

In contrast with the deft touch that Davis and Merton display in disassembling social parts and reconstituting a whole, Gans presents a clumsy attempt to show the positive functions of poverty.[42] Structural poverty is a very difficult phenomenon to justify, even for conservative analysts (although Banfield comes close to doing just that in his analysis of *The Unheavenly City*[43]). Even among social pathologists, poverty was an embarrassing evil to be eliminated with industrial growth or corrected as immigrants assimilated into the all-embracing mainstream.

Gans does not set out to defend poverty. Trying to imitate Merton's classic analysis of the machine, Gans exposes poverty as a major prop for holding the present system together. He raises a typical functionalist question: does poverty have positive functions that explain its persistence? His answer reveals a prevailing contradiction in functional theory. Asserting that social science was objective and value free, functionalists failed to see that, by identifying positive functions with benefits for the ongoing system, they take their stand with the elite.

Using system adaptation as the reference point, Gans lists fifteen latent functions that poverty serves, including keeping wages down, making certain dirty work is done, providing a large labor pool, and maintaining markets for spoiled or defective commodities rejected by the affluent. Poverty also offers the nonpoor vicarious participation in the poor's alleged uninhibited sexual indulgence, promotes mobility for the middle class by eliminating the lower class from competition, and creates employment for professionals and other custodians of order. The list goes on. The capstone of the analysis is that the role of the poor has the significant political function of reducing conflict, thereby promoting stability. Gans writes:

> The poor have played an important role in shaping the American
> political process; because they vote and participate less than
> other groups, the political system has often been free to ignore
> them. This has not only made American politics more centrist . . .
> but it has also added to the stability of the political process . . .
> If the 15% of the population below the federal "poverty line"
> participated fully in the political process, they would almost
> certainly demand better jobs and higher incomes . . . [requiring]
> income distribution and would thus generate further political
> conflict between the haves and the have-nots.[44]

Gans identifies the basic latent functions for the beneficiaries of the system. In doing so, he lays bare the ideological skeleton hidden in the functionalist closet. The system turns out to be the dominant institutions, activated by just enough deviance to make it workable for the affluents and governing elites. Gans tries to extricate himself by showing how the same practices that reinforce the economic and political institutions are dysfunctional for those pushed into the basement of the system, but this feeble effort to present both sides only exacerbates his theoretical predicament.

If, as he claims, the stratification system is untenable for the poor, and change requires social costs the affluent refuse to consider, the only possible alternatives are radical reorganization of the system by underdogs or maintenance of the status quo by topdogs. As his single reference point has been the functions for the dominant system, he can hardly reverse himself and discuss how the system would operate if the poor were used for the focal point. The only conclusion his argument allows is that, given system needs, inequality and disenfranchisement are inevitable costs of social stability. Gans makes this point explicitly:

> Consequently, a functional analysis must conclude that poverty
> persists not only because it satisfies a number of functions but
> also because many of the functional alternatives to poverty would
> be quite dysfunctional for the more affluent members of
> society.[45]

Unintentionally, Gans supplies grist for the mill of social caretakers who shape policy to technical accounting schemes. Social change is dismissed as simply too expensive to work.

Preserving Moral Boundaries

Fascinated with the issue of constancy and stability in social systems, functionalists tend to concentrate on social mechanisms that pull community members together, giving them a sense of we-feeling, of collective identity. Some writers focused on taboos or rituals (such as funeral rites or court proceedings) as socially universal means of fostering solidarity and shared moral values.[46]

To demonstrate the role of deviance in defining morality, Kai Erikson examines a historical case: the Puritan pattern of isolating and treating offenders.[47] In this insightful attempt to extend functionalist analysis to historical materials, Erikson considers how the values and attitudes of Puritan settlers in seventeenth-century Massachusetts led to institutionalized ways of coping with deviant behavior. In the process, settlers also carved out the boundaries of socially approved conduct. Morality is known by its opposites, evil and immorality. Deviance supplies an important service to society "by patrolling the outer edges of group space and by providing a contrast which gives the rest of the community some sense of their own territorial identity."[48]

Erikson proceeds to explicate his thesis by proceeding on three fronts. The first deals with the relations between the moral order of a community and behavior that is defined as violating moral limits. Different social orders generate different types of deviance. A society that extolls property and material success will have a greater volume of theft than those that do not. Since Puritans emphasized religious orthodoxy as interpreted by clerical leaders, deviations tended to take the form of violations against the theocratic code. Crime was an offense, first, against God, and, second, against the community of believers.

The shapes of the devil came in two forms: heresy and witchcraft. Among Puritans, the tolerated margin for religious error was very narrow. If a community of saints was to maintain its moral landmarks, sinners had to be named, punished, and purged from the community. The boundaries of conformity reflected the values that represented the core of Puritan consciousness. Deviation and conformity, while on opposite sides of the law, stem from the same cultural vocabulary. Erikson states:

> If deviation and conformity are so alike, it is not surprising that
> deviant behavior should appear in a community at exactly

those points where it is most feared. Men who fear witches soon
find themselves surrounded by them; men who become jealous of
private property soon encounter eager thieves. And if it is not
always easy to know whether fear creates the deviance or deviance the fear, the affinity of the two has been a continuous source
of wonder in human affairs.[49]

Another theme considers how the volume of deviance tends to be
linked to the organization of social control. Communities define deviance
to encompass a range of behavior roughly equivalent to the capacity of its
control apparatus. Taking offense records over a thirty-year period, Erikson notes that the number of persons charged with crime tended to change
very little from one point in time to the next. The conviction rate, though,
fluctuated appreciably, leading Erikson to conclude that "crime waves"
almost doubled the number of offenses, even though the size of the deviant
population remained relatively constant.

Erikson surmises that communities tend to have a fixed pool of deviants which varies little despite changes in criminal definitions and enforcement practices. Crime waves, rather than adding to the deviant pool,
displace one deviant population with another. The "Quaker invasion" in
the Puritan settlement may have induced a higher degree of conformity
among citizens. Alternatively, it may have led enforcers to develop "quotas" to keep the deviant population stabilized. In either event, the result
was the same: the offender rate remained constant.

Moreover, disparities between offender rates and conviction rates reflect changes in social definitions of moral boundaries. What is most highly
threatening will be most severely sanctioned. Social control acts to make
visible the often blurred margins of moral behavior. By altering conviction
rates, account is taken of new threats to the social order. Control is adaptive in that new offenses replace earlier ones; new ranks of offenders move
into the vacuum left by former ones.

The third theme deals with the way a society handles its deviant members by channeling certain populations into deviant careers. Deployment
patterns, however arrived at, are society's means of stabilizing the volume
of deviance appearing in community life. Puritans saw deviance as a special property of a class of people who were frozen into deviant attitudes.
The doctrine of predestination interfaced with a rigid stratification order
to lock people into nearly permanent deviant roles. Reintegration (passage
from immoral to moral status) was thus precluded for most deviants.
Branding, mutilating, or banishing offenders stabilized deviance by creating a pariah class. For Erikson, this pattern reflects the Puritan belief in
the irreversibility of human nature, an image that lingers on in modern
assessments of convicted offenders as a permanently defective class.

Erikson's adaptation of functional theory takes the equilibrium notion to its ultimate conclusion. Deviance is more than a balancing mechanism for society; it is necessary for social order. Criminal codes are used by a well-integrated, stable consensus to unite all segments of society.

The value-consensus idea has long pervaded theories of criminality. In this view, the legal process regulates, harmonizes, and reconciles conflicting desires or competing classes in order to enhance the welfare of the larger social order. One exponent of this position holds that the collective conscience and criminal law are mutually supportive:

> The state of criminal law continues to be—as it should—a decisive reflection of the social consciousness of a society. What kind of conduct an organized community considers, at a given time, sufficiently condemnable to impose official sanctions, impairing the life, liberty, or property of the offender is a barometer of the moral and social thinking of a community.[50]

However, crucial components of social life are missing in this analysis making it unsuitable for an adequate explanation of deviance. Later formulators have attacked the many shortcomings of this approach. I shall emphasize three limitations.

First, illustrating the social equilibrium conception by reference to seventeenth-century Puritan data is to compare the proverbial "apples and oranges." A theocratic, highly authoritarian state in a preindustrial stage has few similarities with twentieth-century urban society. Even assuming that consensus is shaped by social definitions and treatment of deviance, it is unrealistic to assert that a monolithic morality exists anywhere but in a preliterate, religious, or totalitarian community. Erikson depended on court and other official records to make his case. One wonders if even the Puritan community was as cohesive as Erikson suggests. In Puritan America, deviants had few opportunities to air grievances. A one-sided data-collection process could contribute to the erroneous notion that rank-and-file citizens were highly integrated into the moral order.

Second, the notion that order is preserved by stabilizing the volume of deviance is based on the assumption that social control is inherently inelastic, an argument that cannot be supported by evidence from contemporary control systems. This position conveniently ignores expansion and contraction tendencies of the control apparatus itself. Referrals to mental hospitals, jails, or other confinement settings probably approximate the total number of slots available in such institutions. However, this neglects the role of enforcement agencies in generating statistics to reflect occupational interests and prerequisites. When enforcers systematically manipulate the offense rate, taxpayers and legislators may loosen the purse strings to expand existing facilities, experiment with different modes of institutional treatment, or redefine widespread norm violations (e.g., the redefinition of alcohol abuse as a sickness rather than a crime). The role of "moral entrepreneurs" in initiating, shaping, or blocking legislation (thus modifying control strategies) is also ignored. Antidrug laws, aimed primarily at lower-status users, suggest the impact of such entrepreneurs in federal agencies, which are the primary beneficiaries of these unenforceable laws.[51] A more adequate characterization of modern enforcement practices would include their elastic quality, evident in changes in the degree and types of control.

Third, the functionalist idea that law reflects the values and needs of society completely neglects the symbolic function of criminal law in a diverse society. Joseph Gusfield argues that the persistence of certain widely violated laws justifies, for the public, the dominance of certain social ideals and norms.[52] The American Temperance Movement, which enacted the Prohibition Amendment, attempted to enhance and glorify the social status of smalltown, Protestant middle-class groups. While the law was unenforceable, it did serve to demean and degrade the urban, working-class, Catholic immigrant groups. Pressure to legislate private morality probably reflects a lack of moral agreement rather than the reverse.

Overall, the functionalists fail to present a convincing argument for the function of deviance in shoring up moral boundaries. In the first place, they overlook the thousands of criminal statutes that are inconsistent and anachronistic, a casuality of changing social norms, new technology, scientific knowledge, and, occasionally, community hysteria.[53] Laws are often hastily enacted products of emotional reaction or indignation by selected social groups to difficult situations. As Robert Park once said, "We are always passing laws in America. We might as well get up and dance. The laws are largely to relieve emotion, and the legislatures are quite aware of that fact."[54]

The systems approach to deviance proposes a final solution to offensive behavior: the use of containment mechanisms to guarantee social peace by forcibly restricting the influence deviants have on the normative order.

Containing Deviance—Illegitimacy and Exclusion

Containment mechanisms operate to keep the system stabilized. As independent factors, they limit the impact of deviance on the social body. Social definitions of an act as illegitimate deny participants the opportunity to press claims for social esteem or influence. What functionalists are saying is that since deviance persists, it obviously must be making a contribution to the social order. Unrestrained, however, it could destroy that order, and societies therefore develop mechanisms that keep offenders morally isolated from respectable others.

This depicts the normative order as an internal system with external strains (e.g., deviance and conflict) kept within bounds to avoid changing the smoothly operating internal order. Parsons argues that the illness-therapy situation is a typical example of society's efforts to contain deviance by "automatic control mechanisms."[55]

Because illness is institutionally defined as deviant behavior, the sick role is an illegitimate role. Regarded as pathological, the sick individual loses his or her claim to influence others or to receive the standard benefits of interaction. Treated as a patient, the person becomes a social dependent whose well-being has been transferred from his or her own hands to that of the physician.

Most people do not remain in the sick role, despite its secondary gains, because automatic steering controls usually deter them. Society excludes the sick by isolating them in segregated institutions (hospitals, psychiatric wards, nursing homes, etc.). Sick people do not compose a group or a movement, but only a statistical class. This means that they have no impact on the social system, and cannot organize to legitimate their role.

Moreover, they are encouraged by therapists to abandon the sick role for a more "mature" adjustment. Isolated from others and deprived of alternative channels of support, the patient conforms to the physician's expectations. Failure to conform may result in social rejection, in which the patient is treated as a malingerer by the hospital staff, and, thereby, loses the few advantages the role provides. In the doctor-patient relationship, Parsons says, "the propaganda of reinforcement would be simply an extension of many of the automatic but latent functions of existing institutional patterns."[56] The sick role not only isolates and insulates the deviant, but also exposes the person to reintegrative forces.

Illness relates to three systemic elements. It provides an alternative deviant outlet for expressing individual frustrations and strains. It also supports an elaborate professional system of health workers, and demonstrates the ability of the social system to regulate defectors in the interests of perpetuating order.

Let us consider one other case of the Parsonian containment notion: race relations as a source of potential social conflict. Parsons describes and analyzes this potentially explosive state of affairs. Whites internalize the universal norms of equality, yet they behave in terms of local patterns of "white supremacy." Role conflict and social strain result, but Parsons believes that separating conflict groups by segregation of contexts makes it possible to avoid overt struggle. Of course, conflict could lead to social change by undermining the value bases of the established order. This hardly seems to be a viable approach, since

> this possibility is potentially so dangerous to the stability of a given institutional system that it may be presumed that one of the major functions of the mechanisms of social control is to forestall the establishment of a claim to legitimacy [for acts] which are alienative relative to the major institutionalized patterns of the social system.[57]

Institutional racism provides a balancing mechanism for curbing social conflict. By keeping minorities in their place, it reinforces social inequality and preserves the political status quo.

The moral evaluation is clear. Under the banner of a value-free sociology, functionalists tend to follow the conventional lead by tracking down deviance as a problem to be controlled, and thus avoid analyzing the established power structure's creation of deviance. Their analysis implies that the powerful are morally superior, and should not be held responsible for causing deviance within the society.[58]

Neither illness on the individual level nor racism on the social level are analyzed as problematic to the victims. The viewpoint of the powerless is not mentioned. By implicitly holding the general public's stereotyped notion that the powerless are more deviant than the powerful, functionalists can wash their hands of controlled populations. The ideological undercurrent of this thinking sensitizes theorists to those deviant acts and social problems that present difficulties to social caretakers. Nonelitist solutions to the problem of order are not proposed. Critical commentary and suggestions for change are left to ideologists, journalists, reformers, and other nonsociologists whose occupational prerequisites would not be violated by negative evaluation of power arrangements.

Classic functionalism fails to deal with deviance as an internal property of the system. Deviance is viewed as external system disturbances, to be systematically put down if it threatens the ongoing order. This failure to account for structural sources of deviance in the normative order is linked to a preferred methodological style of selective observation without falsification and insight without precise procedures.

The Methodological Fallacy

Avoiding direct confrontation with deviant subjects, functionalists considered the meanings of deviant phenomena for the larger system. Their view is holistic and abstract, and typically lacks grounding in concrete social organizations.

For the most part, functionalists' work depends largely on the ability of the observer to consider functions performed by partial structures, correlations, integrations, and so on. Theorists translated the anthropological method of analyzing total societies to a complex urban milieu, often omitting direct observation of structures and functions, and adopted an "as if" approach. Social phenomena are viewed as if they are unfolding toward the achievement of definite ends. The historical process can be interpreted as possessing objective goal-directedness, a philosophical position that leads to assumptions of transpersonal finality.[59]

A methodological fallacy is built into this reasoning. By asserting that all social arrangements positively contribute to the order and integration of the system, theorists need neither scientific tools nor rigorous logic to support their case. The canons of science require that propositions be stated in such a way that they may be falsified by intersubjective observations. Intuitive hunches about the social world, often stated in universalistic terms, are not enough. The scientist is also obligated to study negative cases to ascertain if a given proposition can be supported or must be modified by the evidence. Data collection that depends primarily on the scholar's insights or use of secondary sources is susceptible to highly selective perception guided by personal experiences or occupational interests. Since the system cannot be studied *en toto* (except, perhaps, as an abstract mathematical model), research focuses on subsystems that are assumed to be related. No clear evidence exists, however, as to how these are related, the conditions of linkage, and the factors that contribute to the lack of connectedness between certain parts.

Undoubtedly, the logic of multiple causation further complicates the problem of isolating indispensable functions from those that are neutral or have a negative impact on the system. The notion of interdependence of parts becomes a slogan that masks social complexity and lack of fit between elements.

Moreover, the use of secondary sources encourages investigators to construct a picture of the structure that ignores the meanings of that structure to participants. Functionalists do not discuss the extent to which social practices serve or subvert particular groups' needs and goals, who they are functional for, and the circumstances under which their functions have impact.

System goals are conceived of as unitary processes, but generalizations about goals in an abstract, *post hoc* fashion ignore the process by which specific organizational goals are created, struggled over, and negotiated.

Unitary processes hardly characterize the administration of justice, for example. Police discretion, selective application of the criminal law, and wide latitude in interpreting criminal law in action suggest that much law enforcement is detrimental to the goals of criminal law and the administration of justice.

Investigating deviant phenomena in one time and place produces an erroneous view of the degree to which social control works to harmonize social relations. While the persecution of witches in colonial America may have removed troublesome persons from respectable ranks, vigorous enforcement may have also disrupted family relations, undermined trust between neighbors, critically reduced the labor force, and violated expectations held by rulers and ruled. A one-dimensional view of the social enterprise blinds theorists to the consequences of control, such as the creation and maintenance of deviance and widespread rule evasion among the controllers themselves.

Despite functionalists' dedication to scientific "purity," the methods they employ are relatively primitive and tend to reinforce metaphysical assumptions. Finality and purpose, as built into the system, are notions that are closer to a medievalist interpretation of society than to empirical propositions about actual operations of social structure. Postulating a grand design, functionalists produce only limited data. The scheme is too top-heavy to be penetrated in depth by investigators. There is too much that must be taken on faith and too little questioning of basic assumptions. Seen from a distance, deviance remains an underexplored terrain.

Conclusion

Functionalists abandoned earlier views of deviance as pathological or disorganizing to propose an alternative proposition: deviance is not only integral to the social system, but necessary for its existence. The argument hinges on several assumptions. First, deviance is a persistent social fact in all societies; therefore, it satisfies basic social needs or goals. Second, since all parts of the social system are interrelated, deviance is thus an elemental force that contributes to the functioning of this unitary system. Third, deviance provides a balancing mechanism that stabilizes the ongoing social order and defines the boundaries of good and evil. Without deviance, normality could not be specified.

Functions are presumed to be either manifest or latent. The distinction stresses the difference between intended and unintended consequences of a social or cultural unit. As nonparticipants in the social struggle, functional sociologists overlook the contradictions and conflicts built into any system of relations.

Their methodological preference helps to create and reinforce this holistic vision of society. The grand design is built out of materials drawn primarily from intuition or the logic of multiple causation. Neither approach encourages cautious statements about the contributions of parts to wholes, nor the type and extent of integration of a particular social system.

By constructing configurations of ideal social patterns to fit a systems model, functionalists fail to generate either a methodology for investigating the stresses and strains in a system or a body of valid data that demonstrates how social practices may shore up or alter a social structure. Presuming that social actors internalize values which motivate conformity, functionalists overlook a crucial point: conventional norms may also generate conditions for widespread rule violation.

In an effort to curb the theoretical excesses of unreconstructed functionalism, anomie theorists attempted to retain its holistic perspective while avoiding self-justifying and self-defeating images of collective determinism. "Middle-range" theory, more modest in its efforts to account for deviant phenomena, replaced grand theory.

In the next chapter, I shall consider how anomie theorists took the first step toward accounting for internal contradictions and lack of consensus. Their assumption of discontinuity fostered a wide range of studies of lower-class crime and delinquency, but anomie theory itself accords little recognition to the interaction between deviants and society or to middle-class violations.

NOTES

1. Talcott Parsons, *The Social System* (Glencoe, Ill.: The Free Press, 1951), p. 312.

2. Herman Turk and Richard L. Simpson have edited a series of papers that provide an appreciative and critical view of selected aspects of functional theory in *Institutions and Social Exchange: The Sociologies of Talcott Parsons and George C. Homans* (Indianapolis: The Bobbs-Merrill Company, Inc., 1971). The most detailed, critical examination of Parsons' theory is in Alvin W. Gouldner, *The Coming Crisis of Western Sociology* (New York: Basic Books, Inc., 1970).

3. Talcott Parsons, *The Structure of Social Action* (New York: McGraw-Hill, 1937). Talcott Parsons, by far, has been the dominant figure in functional theory, if not in American sociology. His work bridges four decades, and includes books and essays analyzing economic, political, sociological, and psychological theories. This chapter takes up *selected* issues in functional theory. No attempt is made to cover Parsons' comprehensive, if not global, approach to sociological theory building.

4. Parsons provides an intellectual autobiography in "On Building Social System Theory: A Personal History," *Daedalus* (Fall 1970): 881. See, also, a bibliography of his works (1928-1952) in Talcott Parsons, *Essays in Sociological Theory* (Glencoe, Ill.: The Free Press, 3rd Printing, 1963), pp. 440-445.

5. Gouldner, *The Coming Crisis of Western Sociology*, p. 174.

6. C. Wright Mills, *The Sociological Imagination* (New York: Oxford University Press, 1959), p. 49. See, also, N. V. Novikov's critique of Parsonian theory "Modern American Capitalism and Par-

sons' Theory of Social Action," in *The Sociology of Sociology,* ed. Larry T. Reynolds and Janice M. Reynolds (New York: David McKay, Inc., 1970), pp. 256-273.

7. Representative works in the structural-functional paradigm include T. Parsons, *The Social System;* Robert Merton, *Social Theory and Social Structure* (New York: The Free Press, 1957); Marion Levy, *The Structure of Society* (Princeton, N.J.: Princeton University Press, 1952); and Kingsley Davis, *Human Society* (New York: The Macmillan Co., 1949).

8. S. N. Eisenstadt, "Societal Goals, Systemic Needs, Social Interaction, and Individual Behavior: Some Tentative Explanations," in *Institutions and Social Exchange: The Sociologies of Talcott Parsons and George C. Homans,* ed. Turk and Simpson, pp. 36-55.

9. Parsons, *The Social System,* p. 205.

10. Ibid., p. 206.

11. Eisenstadt, *Institutions and Social Exchange: The Sociologies of Talcott Parsons and George C. Homans,* p. 45.

12. Parsons, *Essays in Sociological Theory,* p. 172.

13. Emile Durkheim, *The Rules of Sociological Method,* trans. S. Solovay and J. Mueller, ed. George E. G. Catlin (Glencoe, Ill.: The Free Press, 1950), pp. 65-75.

14. Parsons, *The Social System,* pp. 323-324.

15. James Olds, "Analysis of Deviance," in *Lab Bulletin* 3, Laboratory of Social Relations, Harvard University (May 1951): 1-9.

16. Parsons, *The Social System,* p. 310.

17. Robin M. Williams, Jr., *American Society* (New York: Alfred A. Knopf, 1960), p. 44.

18. Ibid., p. 280.

19. This analysis largely draws on Desmond P. Ellis, "The Hobbesian Problem of Order: A Critical Appraisal of the Normative Solution," *The American Sociological Review* 36 (August 1971): 692-703.

20. Daniel Bell, "Crime as an American Way of Life," in *End of Ideology* (New York: The Free Press of Glencoe, Inc., rev. ed., 1962), chap. 3.

21. Hyman Rodman, "The Lower-Class Value Stretch," *Social Forces* XLII

(December 1963): 205-215. Ulf Hannerz describes ghetto roles in *Soulside: Inquiries into Ghetto Culture and Community* (New York: Columbia University Press, 1969).

22. For further discussion, see I. Deutscher, "Looking Backwards: Case Studies on the Progress of Methodology in Sociological Research," *American Sociologist* 4 (February 1969): 35-41 and H. Ehrlich, "Attitudes, Behavior, and the Intervening Variables," *American Sociologist* 4 (February 1969): 29-34.

23. Kingsley Davis and W. E. Moore, "Some Principles of Stratification," *The American Sociological Review* 5 (May 1945): 242-249. Melvin M. Tumin critically responds to this paper in "Some Principles of Stratification: A Critical Analysis," *The American Sociological Review* 18 (August 1953): 383-387.

24. Alvin Gouldner, *Wildcat Strike* (New York: Harper & Row, paperback edition, 1965).

25. Erving Goffman, "On Cooling the Mark Out: Some Aspects of Adaptation to Failure," in *Human Behavior and Social Processes,* ed. Arnold M. Rose (Boston: Houghton Mifflin Company, 1962), pp. 482-505.

26. Ely Chinoy, *Automobile Workers and the American Dream* (New York: Random House, 1955).

27. So-called "meaningless" behavior may indicate alternative responses to unresolvable frustrations and conflicts of work. This is suggested in Laurie Taylor and Paul Walton, "Industrial Sabotage: Motives and Meanings," in *Images of Deviance,* ed. Stanley Cohen (Baltimore: Penguin Books, 1971), pp. 219-245.

28. M. Hammer, "Influence of Small Social Networks as Factors in Mental Hospital Admission," *Human Organization* 22 (Winter 1963-1964): 243-251.

29. Howard S. Becker, "Notes on the Concept of Commitment," *American Journal of Sociology* 64 (July 1960): 32-40.

30. Parsons, *The Social System,* p. 482.

31. Jacob M. Edelman, *The Symbolic Uses of Politics* (Urbana: University of Illinois Press, 1964).

32. Walter Buckley, *Sociology and Modern Systems Theory* (Englewood Cliffs, N. J.: Prentice-Hall, 1967), p. 29.

33. Pitirim A. Sorokin, *Sociological Theories of Today* (New York: Harper & Row, 1966), p. 54.

34. The organization of mental hospitals is discussed in Albert Deutsch, *The Mentally Ill in America* (New York: Columbia University Press, 1949).

35. C. Wright Mills, *The Power Elite* (New York: Oxford University Press, 1959).

36. An excellent analysis of the medical organization and health care system is found in Eliot Friedson, *Professional Dominance: The Social Structure of Medical Care* (New York: Atherton Press, 1970).

37. Kingsley Davis, "Prostitution," in *Contemporary Social Problems*, 3rd ed., ed. Robert K. Merton and Robert Nisbet (New York: Harcourt Brace Jovanovich, Inc., 1971).

38. Ibid., p. 341.

39. Davis, "Prostitution," p. 351.

40. Merton, *Social Theory and Social Structure*, pp. 71-82.

41. Ibid., p. 73.

42. Herbert J. Gans, "The Positive Functions of Poverty," *American Journal of Sociology* 78 (September 1972): 275-289.

43. Edward C. Banfield, *The Unheavenly City: The Nature of Our Urban Cities* (Boston: Little, Brown and Company, 1970).

44. Gans, "The Positive Functions of Poverty," p. 283.

45. Ibid., p. 287.

46. Jesse R. Pitts, "Social Structure and the Motivation of Deviant and Conforming Behavior," in *Theories of Society*, ed. T. Parsons, E. Shils, K. D. Naegele, and J. R. Pitts (New York: The Free Press, 1961), p. 871.

47. Kai T. Erikson, *Wayward Puritans: A Study in the Sociology of Deviance* (New York: John C. Wiley & Sons, Inc., 1966).

48. Ibid., p. 46.

49. Erikson, *Wayward Puritans: A Study in the Sociology of Deviance*, p. 22.

50. Wolfgang Friedmann, *Law in a Changing Society* (Berkeley: University of California Press, 1959), p. 165.

51. Howard S. Becker, *Outsiders: Studies in the Sociology of Deviance* (New York: Free Press, 1963), chaps. 7 and 8.

52. Joseph R. Gusfield, *Symbolic Crusade: Status Politics and the American Temperance Movement* (Urbana: University of Illinois Press, 1966).

53. Stuart L. Hills, *Crime, Power and Morality* (Scranton, Pa.: Chandler Publishing Company, 1971), chap. 1.

54. Edwin H. Sutherland and Donald R. Cressey, *Principles of Criminology*, 8th ed. (Philadelphia: Lippincott, 1970), p. 10.

55. Parsons, *The Social System*, p. 10.

56. Ibid., p. 313.

57. Parsons, *The Social System*, pp. 282-283.

58. Alex Thio, "Class Bias in the Sociology of Deviance," *American Sociologist* 8 (February 1973): 1-12.

59. Methodological issues in functional theory are discussed in Nicholas S. Timasheff, *Sociological Theory*, 3rd ed. (New York: Random House, 1967), chap. 17 and Arthur L. Stinchcombe, *Constructing Social Theories* (New York: Harcourt, Brace and World, Inc., 1968), pp. 80-93.

5

Uncovering Deviant Behavior through Official Data

ANOMIE THEORY

> Our primary aim is to discover how some *social structures exert a definite pressure upon certain persons in the society to engage in non-conforming rather than conforming conduct.* If we can locate groups peculiarly subject to such pressures, we should expect to find fairly high rates of deviant behavior in these groups. Our perspective is sociological . . . We look at variations in the *rates* of deviant behavior, not at its incidence. (Robert Merton, *Social Theory and Social Structure*)[1]

Introduction

Functional theory labored to make American society whole. Committed to the present society, theorists overlooked its dilemmas, contradictions, tensions, and malintegrative propensities. By grafting a systems conception to the analysis of institutional life, functionalists imposed an image of order and unity on industrial society that violated the realities of class, conflict, and change.

Anomie theorists did not totally abandon this holistic image. Instead, they drastically modified the functionalist scheme by assuming that contradictions are implicit in a stratified order in which the culture dictates success goals for all citizens, while institutional access to these goals is limited to the upper strata. Despite the American dream of "making it," lower-class strata are excluded from the competitive game. These underdogs retaliate by choosing deviant alternatives over legitimate ones.

Anomie theorists emphasized that neither biological nor psychological variations account for the choice of deviance. It is the faulty social structure that is the culprit in this case. Egalitarian beliefs, fostered in an open-class society, are said to have the contradictory effect of encouraging unlawful or nonconformist behavior. Deviance is not merely problematic for the society, requiring intensified social control; it also signifies the deep alienation of many Americans from the dominant values and approved life-styles.

Anomie theory represents American sociology's first genuine theoretical break with a general theory of society, developing instead a special theory of deviance. The Chicago School and functionalist theories were sociologies of society, not limited to the study of deviance. Robert Merton, a student of Parsons and the chief formulator of anomie theory, attempted to salvage functionalism by scaling down its claim to be a master conceptual scheme. He proposed theories of the "middle range" that would encompass only restricted fields of experience. Such theories, modeled after the natural sciences, could be tested and refined by highly sophisticated methods using statistics, high-speed computers, mathematical models, and so on.[2]

With the impetus of multiple-theory development, deviance became a special topic, reinforcing the earlier social problems trend of separating studies of offenders and their acts from theoretical sociology. As an occupational specialty, the field became identified with studies of the peculiarities of lower-class life, including alleged high rates of criminality, delinquency, suicide, drug use, and alcoholism.

Uncovering deviance required neither an excursion into the urban underlife nor exposure to lower-class informants. Violators were known and counted by their official recorders (police, jailers, psychiatrists, and social workers). Slum boys lost the unique qualities described by Shaw and associates in the Chicago era. Data drawn from police files utilized objective measurements to correlate clusters of variables that identified "anomie," or normlessness, as instability among working-class boys.[3]

The theory and research, to be described in this chapter, moved little beyond Merton's initial, provocative effort to relate certain properties of the social structure to personal adaptations and life-styles. Despite the reams of literature devoted to explicating, testing, reformulating, restating, and regurgitating Merton's notions of the gap between cultural goals and structural means and consequent deviant behavior, the anomie formulation remains a stunted theoretical product. I will argue that the failure of these abortive efforts to develop a viable theory of deviance is due to the social-professional conditions of sociology itself. As established professionals, government and business consultants, and tacit representatives of the control apparatus, sociologists found that uncovering deviance brought its own official rewards. Critiquing the social order that generated offenders was deemed unnecessary for the technical-professional task. As "experts" in domestic social problems, researchers often tended to become methodological ritualists, losing sight of the theoretical question of stratification and the possibility of equalizing social resources. Figure 5.1 abstracts the major elements of the anomie paradigm to be covered in the chapter.

I. Social-Professional Conditions	Rise of welfare state; government financing of social science research; academics provide expertise for noneconomic social problems (e.g., racial conflict, social consequences of poverty); "professionalization" of sociology as community of specialists; tacit identification with control personnel
II. Perspective	Variant of functionalism; theoretical focus on structural strain or malintegration of social structure; deviance as stress generated by disjuncture between goals of success and structural means for their achievement; utilitarian calculus generates deviance as response to lack of opportunity; institutionalization of self-interest (legitimization of amorality)
III. Metaphor	"Differential opportunity structure"; varieties of official rates of deviance constitute a "normal" response by lower-class offenders to structural deprivation
IV. Themes	Deviance as individual adaptation; delinquent subculture; culture of poverty
V. Method	Use of official data; statistical analysis of etiological and epidemiological factors

FIGURE 5.1. *Anomie Theory Paradigm*

SOCIAL AND PROFESSIONAL CONDITIONS

The Technical Model of Work—Welfare Statism and Professional Sociology

Social welfare has been around a long time, emerging at approximately the same time as the industrial state. From the English Poor Laws in the sixteenth century to the modern era, private and public ameliorative efforts have attempted to mitigate, if inadequately, the hardships imposed on deprived populations left stranded by the dislocations of a market economy.[4]

"Welfare statism," though, is a newer concept more appropriately related to those social policies of capitalistic states designed to regulate the poor in the interests of controlling civil disorder.[5] The welfare system is politically fragmented, conforms to market demands, and acts as the instrument of discriminatory social institutions. It operates to preserve unequal distribution, justifying this by claiming to fulfill functional necessities of public order.[6]

Sociologists have hardly played an indifferent role in the welfare institution. On the contrary, the trend toward professionalism (a shift from discipline to occupation) stimulated sociological efforts to apply notions of social change to the reconstruction of slums and social control of delinquency.[7]

The professional role that fostered this involvement is not unique to sociology. This professional trend is irresistible in a highly bureaucratic society, in which occupational claims to professionalism are means of gaining the prerogatives of independence of judgment, esoteric knowledge, and relative immunity from outside criticism. These prerogatives became part of the working definition of the sociologist's role.

With the expansion of federal funding for social science research, sociologists moved into the professionalization of reform.[8] As part of the state apparatus, professional intervention tried to transform the political and social life of poor and minority communities in the interests of organized professionals and government administrators. The fate of the poor came to be shaped by professional reform, which was presumed to have a special ability to anticipate and correct social problems.

As early as 1940, as Janowitz notes, a new breed of sociologist had emerged. He or she was an applied survey research specialist, whose generalized techniques could be adapted by a wide variety of clients.[9] The model was that of the operations research engineer. Client-oriented and cost-conscious, this new social engineer was rarely critical or theoretical, and often became the vassal, rather than the lord, of welfare baronies. With few exceptions,[10] sociologists' participation in the proliferation of public commissions and national studies during the 1960s produced little material of lasting scholarly worth. Janowitz sums up this effort:

> One is often struck . . . by the absence of the kind of integrated
> sociological perspective which characterized the early
> commissions [pre-1945]. Perhaps the generous funding which
> brought with it increased bureaucratization deterred the kind
> of intellectual leadership which could produce a more
> unified approach.[11]

The engineering model, coupled with professional claims to autonomy, offered individual entrepreneurs the flexibility to move readily from classroom to research shop to consulting office. The situation, however, had defects as well as merits. Partially freed from dependence on university budgeting and the constraints of professional control, sociologists became willing servants of defense, government, and business contractors. For example, "Project Camelot," underwritten by the United States Army in 1965, involved sociologists in military intelligence studies to control leftist insurgency activities. Leaving aside the dubious social advantages gained from such studies, the project itself was deemed a disaster. It did, however, arouse academic critics, who began to take serious second looks at the claims of a purportedly value-free social science that could be bought and sold as a market commodity.[12]

Merton, however, who is a meticulous social critic and rigorous thinker, never intended that sociologists should abandon the intellectual enterprise and replace it with full-time, bureaucratic commitment to practical or policy issues. Merton warned against intellectuals assuming the role of technical specialists who attend only to their own limited tasks, abdicating social responsibility to favor administrators.[13] He did concede that, in a continuously anomic situation, the specialist is obliged to try to cope with social disorganization by advising the powerful and agitating public opinion.

This mandate, together with the natural science doctrine of value-free sociology,[14] appeared to exempt the organizational researcher in poverty, parole, or delinquency programs from moral evaluation of crucial public issues. The milieu and the mentality of postwar products of sociology graduate schools have a direct bearing on the tendency to subordinate scientific or humanistic concerns to institutional needs. C. Wright Mills characterizes this milieu in the following manner:

> Their positions change—from the academic to the bureaucratic;
> their publics change—from movements of reformers to circles of
> decision makers; and their problems change—from those of their
> own choice to those of their new clients. The scholars
> themselves tend to become less intellectually insurgent and more
> administratively practical. Generally accepting the *status quo*,
> they tend to formulate problems out of the troubles and
> issues that administrators believe they face.[15]

The professional-technical model, adopted by postwar sociologists, offered a rationale for social intervention and participation in policy decisions. Deviance research became an official product, manipulated by contracting parties to control troublesome social behavior. Neither research questions nor political solutions were determined by the social scientist. Not only is the research product trivialized by such constraints, but, even more damaging, the exploration of alternative assumptions and problems is virtually excluded because of adherence to traditional morality and politics.

As specialists in deviant behavior among the deprived, anomie theorists uncovered certain persistent troubles in stratified society. They designed problems, however, to maximize the merits of middle-class conformity and minimize the innovative character of lower-class nonconformity, testifying to their dominant political allegiances (despite their claims to be value free). Using official data furnished by institutional caretakers simplified the technical task and reinforced theoretical assumptions that deviance was concentrated among lower-class populations.

PERSPECTIVE

Fission and Fusion in American Society

"Fission" is a splitting of a structure into discrete parts; "fusion" refers to a blending of units into a whole. Merton uses both images to convey his notion of American society as culturally whole and structurally divided. He thus breaks away from the classical functional paradigm (which views deviance as a source of integration and consensus), and studies the institutional strains and contradictions reflected in deviance. Social structures are not seen as unifying and reinforcing, for they generate circumstances in which infringement of social codes constitutes a "normal (that is to say, an expectable) response."[16] Using evidence of widespread deviance among lower-class populations, Merton reasons that pressures toward deviation vary within different social structures. While he recognizes the many shapes and patterns of deviance in different social structures, he assumes that social contradictions tend to accumulate in the lower strata. It is in underclass groups that the universal belief in the American dream is most violated by institutional closure, Merton stresses:

> It is only when a system of cultural values extols, virtually
> above all else, certain *common* success-goals for the *population at
> large* while the social structure rigorously restricts or completely
> closes access to approved modes of reaching those goals *for a
> considerable part of the same population,* that deviant behavior
> ensues on a large scale.[17]

Merton borrows his initial conception of anomie from Durkheim. According to Durkheim, anomie is a general condition of industrial society, a state of institutional normlessness. The anomic society is one in which confusion in moral codes leads to contradictory or highly egoistic behavior. Merton's formulation of anomie is broader in orientation and more specific in application than Durkheim's. Arguing that deviance is a consequence of disjuncture between cultural goals and institutional access to goals, Merton focuses primarily on the lack of integration between economic values and opportunities for jobs and education. In his scheme, "culture" is transmuted into the ideology of the marketplace. "Structure" consists of the legitimate channels for tracking high achievers into upwardly mobile status positions.

Assuming the priority of the economic order, Merton traces deviance to the clash between idealized goals and class-restricted means. He does not claim that everyone internalizes the desire to win (such a state of affairs would undermine the competitive order he supports), but he does assert that, given the internalization of achievement norms and the structural blockages impeding legitimate solutions, individuals are likely to choose illegitimate solutions.

Essentially, Merton has taken up the issue of the great deception, perpetuated by official ideology that "everyone can make it if he tries." But he never examines this myth as a possible rhetorical device that has political utility for keeping the "masses" in their place. Nor does he indicate the conditions under which certain groups or individuals are likely to believe or discredit the success credo. Merton simply assumes that the success doctrine is a cultural imperative that cuts across class strata, groups, and interests. Culture remains whole, while structure is fragmented into the haves and have-nots.

It is, perhaps, a matter of historical interest that Merton should fix upon one dominant norm, monetary gain, as the crucial independent variable that causes alienation and lawbreaking among the economically disadvantaged. Taking the Horatio Alger myth as a serious sociological proposition, he undercuts his own assumptions about the diversity and pluralism of American life and mores. While Merton vehemently denies that the utilitarian doctrine of "Economic Man" is a viable explanation of human motives, it is precisely this model that is implicit in his scheme of the nearly universal, competitive yearning for success (met with inevitable failure for most) which drives the frustrated into deviant acts.

Anomie appears to take on the character of a social disease. Trapped in no-win, low-esteem jobs, manual workers are infected with the contagion of success goals, but lack the institutional therapy of education and job opportunity that restores health. The only surcease of such individual deprivation is temporary and illegitimate (e.g., crime, mental disorder, withdrawal through drugs or alcohol, rebellion, and so on). On the societal level individual deviant choices generate a vicious circle. An increase in individual deviance undermines legitimate norms for others, leading to a spiraling of deviance until it is counteracted by social control. Merton reasons that:

> A mounting frequency of deviant but "successful" behavior tends to lessen and, as an extreme potentiality, to eliminate the legitimacy of the institutional norms for others in the system . . . As anomie spreads and is intensified, this, in turn, creates a more acutely anomic situation for still others and initially less vulnerable individuals in the social system . . . with cumulatively disruptive consequences for the normative structure, unless counteracting mechanisms of control are called into play.[18]

In a typically anomic society, Merton says, anything is permissible. Conspicuous consumption dominates public morality; self-interest justifies opportunism and greed. Restricting opportunity eventually nourishes deviance because it undermines the fair rules of the game. Because social rewards bear little resemblance to social worth, deviant choices are considered no more immoral than legitimate ones, as evidenced by the popular myths about nineteenth-century American entrepreneurs, the "robber barons," that are now second and third generation elites. Merton seems to be saying that anomie invokes a kind of Gresham's law by depreciating the moral currency; bad morality drives out the good.

Despite Merton's revisionist critique of functionalism (including his denial that all parts are necessarily integrated or functional), he retains the universalistic culture perspective while introducing a relativistic notion of structure. Society as system controls social disorganization in the interests of the legitimate order, and society as cleavage between classes and groups requires social intervention to modify economic and social inequalities in access to the good life.

In social policy matters, Merton appears to take a social Keynesian point of view: prime the social pump of equal opportunity for the able, regardless of their class position, and the system will be strengthened and endure. Unlike the economist Keynes (who made millions of dollars from the declining stock market in the 1930s), Merton sees little social utility in the disorganizing influences of modern life. Like most functionalists, he envisions society as whole, and is dismayed when he discovers how shattered it is by personal alienation and lawbreaking. Since he depends almost exclusively on official institutional records to make his case, he is left in a precarious theoretical position.

The competitive order must be preserved for the meritorious (those who make it legally) to protect them from the criminals, delinquents, sluggards, mentally deranged, and revolutionaries, who, after all, are clustered in the lower class. However, unless rules are flexible enough to allow the incorporation of aspiring working-class boys, who constitute the greatest threat to the system, anomie will increase beyond society's tolerance level.

Merton does not blame the lower class for widespread deviance. Such behavior merely represents an adjustive response to structurally induced strain. Essentially, the fault lies in the structure. Nonetheless, changing the economic, political, and legal institutions to accommodate all the high achievers would alter the rules of the game and undercut the position of "merit" (which is identified with middle-class mores and manners) as the chief criterion for participation.

Perhaps the inconsistencies in Merton's argument account for his lack of specific social solutions to the problem of anomie.[19] The polarities in Merton's thinking include mixed images and contradictory statements, as I show in the following contrast set.

(1a) Culture as a uniform set of values, beliefs, and goals.	(1b) Structure as splintered into classes, interests, and conflicting groups.
(2a) Images of unity and order promoted by a more efficient control apparatus.	(2b) Images of normative and institutional breakdown generated mainly by lower-class dissenters.
(3a) Deviant adaptations imply evaluations of options and alternative rewards.	(3b) Deviant adaptation implies simple utilitarian motives and reactions to strain.
(4a) Deviance as functional; innovates and regenerates the legitimate structure.	(4b) Deviance as dysfunctional; undermines and destroys legitimate structure.
(5a) Collective determinism.	(5b) Individual opportunism.
(6a) Protected meritocracy within the competitive system.	(6b) Social action to open up opportunities within deprived communities.
(7a) Preserve moral and legal order.	(7b) Change social policy to alter moral and legal order.
(8a) Moral regeneration.	(8b) Technical manipulation of system.

FIGURE 5.2.   *Polarities in Merton*

Critics have attacked Merton's anomie formulation on several grounds,[20] including the simplicity of his monolithic culture concept, the fixation on lower-class violations, *ad hoc* reasoning from rates and proportions, and the indeterminacy of the theory. Other weaknesses of anomie theory are the confusion between structural and personal aspects of anomie, neglect of anomie among the successful, a conceptual blurring of distinct and separate conditions that equates anomie with a variety of social and personal ills, and the overgeneralization of anomie to embrace generic conditions of urban life and social change. There are other substantive and ideological charges as well.

Merton's formulation, which accounts primarily for present rate patterns, says nothing about different historical patterns of deviance or the social changes in definitions and enforcement patterns that alter the distribution of deviant behavior. This is a serious omission for a theory of deviance. Merton's lack of situational specificity is related to his view of culture as an entity that "defines, regulates, and controls." He reifies culture as a behaving unit, confusing associational value order with individual hierarchies of values. Lemert takes strong exception to this version of culture:

> The empirically more tenable alternative is that only human beings define, regulate, and control behavior of other human beings. Beyond this it is dubious that clear and exclusive referents can be found either for a "cultural system," or a "cultural hierarchy of values." This is not to deny the existence of hierarchies of values, but merely to insist that only individuals have hierarchies of values ... To claim otherwise forces the animistic admission that cultures *feel* for and against things, or that they feel more strongly about some things than others.[21]

The cultural determinism argument further emphasizes that, in a well-integrated culture, conformity is a taken-for-granted occurrence. Malintegration, on the other hand, induces deviance and disruption. Culture, however, is actually nothing more than a set of rules that take their meaning only in the context of a particular act in progress. No values or rules constitute ends all of the time or means all of the time. Goals (e.g., making money) may become means in a different context (e.g., gaining power, status, love, etc.).[22] Ends and means are not predetermined by cultural mandate, as Merton insists, but take their meanings from the situation.

Despite serious theoretical flaws (most of which were uncorrected by later formulations), anomie theory has generated a proliferation of research applications in deviance and institutional studies.[23] On the whole, this research features such conventional deviance topics as crime, delinquency, suicide, mental disorders, alcoholism, and drug addiction. The rationale for such studies is built into the theory. Deviance rates demonstrate anomic social conditions, and, since rates are defined and administered primarily by institutional caretakers, the sources of data and analysis may be obtained from legitimate control practitioners. Neither rates nor control practices were deemed problematical by this school.

"Differential opportunity structure," a neutral term, became the dominant metaphor that replaced the vocabulary of stratification or political ideology. The overwhelming concern with structurally induced deprivation encouraged preoccupation with the issues of economic determinism, the link between poverty and crime, and deviant motivations.

METAPHOR

Differential Opportunity Structure

Anomie theorists bypassed consideration of political and economic inequalities in institutional life to identify the differential opportunty structure as the source of deviance. Because merits and rewards are out of joint for lower-class persons, the deprived worker often sees little connection between the ideology of achievement and the legitimate means for realizing ideal goals. Alienation and withdrawal from the legitimate structure offer escapes from an unfair or mystifying situation. In this sense, deviance is the normal response of lower-class offenders to institutional blockages.

The opportunity-structure concept contains three interrelated assumptions. Behavior is viewed as economically motivated, a direct link between poverty and crime is posited, and deviant motivation is explained as an outcome of deprivation. These notions underlie much of anomie research. In the next section, I will consider the extent to which this imagery detracts from the theoretical effort to construct a sociology of deviance.

Economic Causation

American sociologists have wrestled with two competing theories of stratification which I call the unitary-ranking system versus the multiple-ranking system. The initial ideas originated from Karl Marx and Max Weber, both of whom attempted to explain the sources of social inequality in industrial society.[24]

For Marx the basis of the social order was the economic relationship, which reflected the mode of economic organization in any given society. The two-class (or, at most, three-class) system was divided by wealth, which was determined by location in the economic order. The entire social system was maintained and controlled at the top by systematically excluding those in low ranks from any share in the power and reward structure. Observing early industrialization in England, Marx saw no sign of a "circulating elite" or a movement of have-nots into the circle of affluent decision makers. The economic order, a basically unstable system because it rested on force, determined the direction of political affairs and ideological realities for social participants.

Rejecting this conception of a monolithic economic order, Weber proposed that other aspects of society, especially ideology, be considered as prime movers of social action. The economic location of classes, while providing crucial constraints for behavior (without determining it), was not the only source of social order and change. Indeed, in many historical instances, ideology influenced the direction of social organization, as in the expression of Protestant concepts (e.g., personal salvation, good works, and deferred gratification) in capitalistic enterprises. Moreover, Weber demonstrated that multiple-interest groups operate in any concrete social situation. Unlike crude coercion theories, Weber's multiple-ranking conception emphasized the give-and-take between conflict groups, and stressed the loopholes in the structure that permit opposition groups to form and alter social arrangements.[25]

By posing this contrast analysis, I wish to show how anomie theorists were snared by the official statistics bait and fell into the trap of an economic causation theory. In brief, the anomie argument implies that economics determine ideology. Like Marx, theorists hold that it is not necessarily the structural position of the participant that determines his or her ideas, but, rather, the ideology of the dominant class. Success aspirations, however unrealistic for the disadvantaged, are promulgated by this dominant class to justify their own economic advantages.

But, unlike Marx, Merton and others did leave loopholes for the "oppressed." Deviance is the alternative to the class struggle, a substitute behavior for the disenfranchised, but one that is unlikely to alter the system of social exclusion. As I will show later, in Merton's typology of individual adaptations, his deviants are puppets, caught in a system they neither create nor understand. Since the ideology is unified, and is a false one for those at the bottom, the disenfranchised can only act out their desperation in illegitimate ways. As a rule, no counter ideology or political opposition is generated by these outsiders. Their adaptations remain isolated, individualized reactions, disconnected from the political scene.

Merton regrets that the class structure is "not fully open at each level to men of good capacity."[26] However, he never questions whether the standards that separate the deserving from the undeserving are themselves unethical and discriminatory. Social classes are inevitable and functional, according to his argument. Social exclusion of the less-than-gifted becomes justified as necessary for the preservation of the system for "men of good capacity."

Deviance theory, when transformed into economic determinism is a theory of lawlessness among the disadvantaged. It says nothing about norm violations among the powerful or conformity among the disinherited.

The Poverty-Crime Linkage

Merton and his followers essentially agree that the class system is good, but question the open-class ideology that promises without delivering. They tend to concentrate on the low-ranking, true believers who continue to attempt (but must, inevitably, fail) to achieve the American dream. It is an open-and-shut case. If the able low ranker is denied access to the legitimate ladder of success, he or she simply erects his or her own ladder, advancing in the world of rackets and politics. Educational and occupational closure create stress, leading to deviant behavior. Merton writes:

> Despite our persisting open-class ideology, advance toward the
> success-goal is relatively rare and notably difficult for those
> armed with little formal education and few economic resources.
> The dominant pressure leads toward the gradual attentuation of
> legitimate, but by and large ineffectual, strivings and the
> increasing use of illegitimate, but more or less effective,
> expedients.[27]

The triad of poverty, limited opportunity, and the assignment of cultural goals is the source of the high correlation between poverty and crime found in American society.

Merton erroneously assumes that crime statistics are valid (a point I will take up in a later section). Since the poor tend to be greatly overrepresented in the crime records, *ipso facto,* this group must experience the greatest pressure toward anomie. However, because institutional caretakers tend to concentrate on controlling the underclass, there are few elites who are publically prosecuted or jailed. In a provocative statement made by Daniel Bell, an alternative explanation for the source of criminality is suggested. Bell holds that crime is shaped by dominant institutions and by "characteristics of the American economy, American ethnic groups, and American politics."[28]

To erect a theory of deviant behavior on the specious evidence of rates of institutional inmates is damaging enough. To further assert that the poor have the type of personal and political resources to negotiate and succeed in the illicit order defies sound sociological reasoning. Theorists fail to consider the possibility that powerlessness and deprivation, rather than stimulating acute pressure to engage in criminal behavior, may encourage low rankers to substitute alternative values and private codes of conduct.[29] Whether private or collective solutions to deprivation, these alternative codes probably express open disenchantment with the prevailing ideology. Dissociation from achievement norms among the poor may be the rule, rather than the exception, as Merton claims.

Deviant Motivations

If Merton had remained faithful to the original Durkheimian rendition of anomie, he would have considered the more general issue of breakdown in the controlling and regulatory functions of institutional life.[30] This concern would have drawn attention to the absence of moral guidelines that are clear and consensually accepted. Under conditions of uncertainty and ambiguity, weakened institutional commitments trigger deviant solutions. If anomie is viewed in this way, different interpretations follow.[31]

First, the motivation to engage in deviance would be analyzed as more homogeneously spread throughout the population. Investigators would seek the "hidden figures" of crime among business executives and professionals as well as among economically disadvantaged persons. Second, the assumption of widespread norm violation would lead researchers to study conventional social organizations, stable working-class neighborhoods, and suburban areas, rather than delinquent gangs. Third, if theorists were to assume that there is little normative consensus in American society (no widespread and accepted means to obtain valid ends), then contradictions in the system of values would logically be the crucial issue, not differentiation in the social structure. But none of these considerations are recognized in the anomie paradigm.

For Merton modified, almost beyond recognition, Durkheim's conception of anomie because it did not fit the official facts. The idea of cultural underemphasis on means as a widespread phenomenon in American society was abandoned as anomie came to be associated with the status problems of the lower strata. By transforming the conception of anomie to fit the official distribution of deviance, Merton shifted from a structural theory of deviance to a social psychological explanation of wrongdoing.

Differential access to legitimate opportunity becomes a matter of relative deprivation, an individual's assessment of his or her chances to succeed in terms of aspirations, experiences, and perceived opportunities. Deviant motivation, I would argue, is not a simple outcome of differential location in the social structure, but rather it involves a complex process that includes identification with a reference group in which some members achieve upward mobility, a desire to succeed coupled with failure in legitimate settings, a perception of alternative opportunities that are deviant, and access to participation in the deviant enterprise. This is very different from saying, as Merton does, that social structures exert pressures on individuals that drive them into deviant solutions.

Anomie theory never resolved the contradictions in the notion of a deterministic structure that allowed individual values and choice. The differential opportunity scheme merely explicates one possible source of deviant motivation (a success ideology in a virtually closed class structure). But even here, Merton and others failed. It is one thing to assert that deprivation leads to deviance, and still another to demonstrate this by using a one-sided data-collection process. Relying on official statistics, investigators neglected to take account of the actor's definition of the situation.

The anomie formulation underwent three transformations as an explanation of deviant behavior, changing its focus from individual adaptations to delinquent subcultures to the "culture of poverty." While the scope of the theory widened to embrace a broader conception of structural sources, the emphasis on the lower class as inherently pathological and disorganized remained.

THEMES

Deviant Solutions as Modes of Individual Adaptation

Merton emphasizes that, in a situation of disequilibrium between cultural goals and institutional norms "those located in places in the social structure which are particularly exposed to such stresses are more likely than others to exhibit deviant behavior."[32] Classifying modes of individual adaptations link social actions to social structure. Most deviant behavior is neither socially uniform nor psychologically aberrant, and the form it takes is determined by the individual's structural location. Merton's scheme classifies behavior according to the acceptance or rejection of cultural goals and institutional means.

Conformity. Like many functionalists, Merton assumes that most persons conform most of the time. Thus, compliance and institutional loyalty are nonproblematic. Internalized rules create a recognized set of expectations for behavior that perpetuates social stability and continuity. Individual adaptations that reject either ends or means, or both, are, by definition, deviant.

Modes of Adaptation	Cultural Goals	Institutionalized Means
I Conformity	+	+
II Innovation	+	−
III Ritualism	−	+
IV Retreatism	−	−
V Rebellion	±	±

+ = Acceptance; − = rejection; ± = rejection of prevailing values and substitution of new values.

FIGURE 5.3.   *A Typology of Modes of Individual Adaptation*[33]

Innovation. The acceptance of pecuniary goals with the rejection of legitimate means (e.g., education, job training) implies the use of expedient or illegitimate channels to achievement. Although Merton later amended his almost exclusive focus on lower-class law violations, research continued to emphasize the correlation between lower-class status and criminal behavior.[34]

Ritualism. By scaling down the lofty, impossible goals of success while compulsively abiding by institutional norms, the ritualist plays it safe. He or she will become a bureaucratic virtuoso. Such avoidance of high ambitions clearly represents a departure from the cultural model of active striving to move up in the social hierarchy. Lower-middle-class respectables, caught up in lower-echelon, organizational routines, are most likely to respond with ritualistic performances. Merton suggests that this is a probable standard adjustment of white-collar workers.[35] Anomie researchers, however, did not follow up on this deviant type, preferring the conventional pursuit of proletariat misdeeds.

Retreatism. While innovators provide the possibility of regenerating the system, the frustrated who reject both cultural goals and institutional means adopt escape mechanisms such as "defeatism, quietism, and retreatism." Repudiating the legitimate order, retreaters take a private rather than collective solution to failure. Psychotics, pariahs, vagrants, chronic drunkards, drug addicts, and other social isolates express a mode of withdrawal that is largely disconnected from traditional and new cultural codes.

Rebellion. Not all deviant acts represent conventional law-violating behavior. Merton also accounted for rebels who may be political activists or radical agents of social change. When persons withdraw allegiance from the existing structure and transfer support to new groups with counter-ideologies, they may be engaging in the process of institution making rather than simple rule breaking. Merton has admitted that rebellion may even be functional for the basic goals of a group:

> In the history of every society, one supposes, some of its culture heroes eventually come to be regarded as heroic in part because they are held to have had the courage and the vision to challenge the beliefs and routines of their society. The rebel, revolutionary, non-conformist, heretic or renegade of an earlier day is often the culture hero of today. Moreover, the accumulations of dysfunctions in a social system is often the prelude to concerted social change that may bring the system closer to the values that enjoy the respect of members of the society.[36]

Conventional texts on deviant behavior seldom treat the radical nonconformists and social movements as sources of new ideologies and reinstitutionalization. Since conformity is not at issue, innovation and retreatism have received the greatest amount of research attention.

However, Merton's classification of deviant types represents an all-encompassing scheme that can account for a range of deviant behaviors. Essentially, it is an ideal type, similar to Parsons's conception of deviance as inclusive of both alienation and overconformity. In fact, these two schemes overlap in significant ways. Both typologies relate deviance to structural sources; both emphasize psychological aspects of adjustment to inadequate or poor socialization; both grant the positive contribution of innovation to shoring up the social structure; and both schemes identify social control as the major mechanism for checking the spread of deviance through the conventional structure.[37]

Merton makes claims, however, about the direct relationship of a fragmented structure to a psychological counterpart of anomie that are not included in Parsons's scheme. These assertions, I have argued, lack coherence and empirical evidence. The sociological conception of anomie is a theoretical question to be investigated, not a social condition to be assumed. There is no single correspondence between structural position and individual response, if only because human beings vary so greatly in their perceptions of opportunities and their definitions of values and goals.

By analyzing some of the implications of Merton's views on social structure and anomie, critics have identified other intervening factors that alter the structure-causes-behavior equation. "Anomie scores" among the lower strata do not invariably indicate alienation.[38] Religion, ethnic solidarity, and cultural definitions, among other conditions, may greatly reduce or eliminate tendencies to deviate. For example, Orthodox Jews, a low-income group, exhibit few symptoms of anxiety, rootlessness, isolation, purposelessness, and despair, which are psychological conditions said to characterize the anomic person.[39]

Furthermore, the presumption that deviant behavior is necessarily related to status problems neglects the extensive vocabulary of motives associated with any deviant act. Drug use, alleged to be a deviant escape from economic failure, may actually serve different purposes, depending on the persons, the setting, and prior drug experiences. A situational analysis suggests that drugs may operate as a form of innovative behavior (e.g., risk taking or "kicks"), as a ritual act (e.g., American Indian use of peyote), as peer conformity among adolescents, as an expression of rebellion for counterculture advocates, or even as a highly esteemed social act (e.g., medical experimentation).

Because Merton and his followers pay so little attention to the social meanings held by participants or the existence of social situations that pattern behavior, they ignore the diversity of social motivation as well as the elements of differential learning and opportunity. Theorists also fail to examine the possibility that some forms of deviance (e.g., addiction) may be a potent cause of failure, rather than the result of failure. Social policies that separate and isolate offenders from conventional society may play a crucial role by precipitating the deviant career, a point stressed by labeling theorists.[40]

Deviant Solutions as Delinquent Subcultures

It may not be a trivial social question to ask why some adolescents break the law, although a more fruitful inquiry might be to ask why so many do not. To turn the former question into a central sociological problem, however, has distorted the issue of deviant motivations. A sociological rationale for assuming a special motivation for deviance has developed. While Hobbes and Durkheim argued that social regulation had to be established to prevent deviance, later sociologists have argued that social regulation has to be disrupted before deviance can occur.[41] The distinction between *established* and *disrupted* social regulation is crucial for theories of juvenile delinquency for it leads to diametrically opposed explanations.

Merton's anomie formulation focuses on disrupted social expectations that result in law violations. This ignores the more crucial issue, which is the organization and distribution of social regulation and its consequences for deprived groups.

The disruption thesis, that informs the greatest bulk of criminological studies, primarily deals with working-class delinquents and their peculiar motives to deviate. This features delinquents as a special social type. It is their low social-economic status plus high aspiration that produces stress, leading to delinquent acts. In the absence of strain, normal regulatory circumstances (the latter left unspecified) operate to keep persons law-abiding.

The search for etiological (or causal) factors in the development of stress turned up other significant variables which were independent correlates of delinquency, such as racially heterogeneous neighborhoods and a low percentage of home ownership.[42] This is nothing new, however. The Chicago School had already discovered these ecological relationships. Studies also found that achievement norms varied between social classes and ethnic groups. Minority persons tended to express lower achievement norms than middle-class whites.[43] This calls for modification of Merton's original statement about homogeneous values. Other research casts doubt on the validity of the class-ethnic origin of the offender as a predictor of delinquency. One study by Reiss and Rhodes found that community structure was the best predictor of delinquency. They show that high crime rates cluster in low SES (Social-Economic-Status) areas, regardless of ethnicity or family.[44]

Other data are contradictory. Whether delinquency is or is not related to anomie remains unclear. One study identified the breakdown of control as instrumental for the movement into deviance.[45] Another held economic deprivation to be the chief source of the problem.[46] The question of high aspiration as a source of law-violating behavior was also debated. Is limited education a better indicator of anomie than low income,[47] or do high educational aspirations (regardless of opportunity) simply indicate identification with conventional values that protect youth from gang influences?[48]

Despite the outpouring of research attempting to test or modify the Mertonian model of delinquency causation, the findings failed to identify which factors accurately predicted delinquency for different samples.[49] Running into blind alleys, the quest for deviance causation took another direction. The study of delinquent subcultures appeared to offer a way out of Merton's atomistic conception of individual role performance.

The subculture focus treats anomie in interactional terms. Strain, conformity, deviance, successes, and failures are viewed as shared behavior learned with others similarly located in the social structure, rather than as isolated properties of individuals.

Cloward's formulation takes issue with Merton's conception of the relationship between a closed legitimate system and the inevitable movement into illegitimate activities.[50] If there are differences in access to legitimate means, Cloward reasoned, there are also differences in access to illegitimate opportunities. Pressures toward deviant behavior are viewed as a function of access to both legitimate and illegitimate opportunity structures. In the lower strata, unsuccessful attempts to innovate in an environment that lacks both legal and illegal means may lead to retreatism, a double failure.

In collaboration with Lloyd Ohlin, Cloward developed a more complete statement of this reformulation to explain the rise of delinquent subcultures.[51] Like Merton, they say that adolescents who form deviant subcultures internalize conventional goals, but are blocked by limited economic and educational options. They differ from Merton by asserting that the availability of illegitimate means is crucial in determining the specific type of subculture, whether criminal, conflict-oriented, or retreatist.

Integrated slum areas, where adult criminals serve as models, tend to produce criminal gangs organized around illegal income and status. Unintegrated areas (characterized by mobility, transiency, and instability) that lack criminal opportunities give rise to conflict gangs which engage in violence and vandalism. The third type, the retreatist subculture, represents the double failure. Slum members who resort to drugs and sensual experiences participate in retreatist gangs, but experience little group solidarity.

Subculture theory had another advocate in Albert Cohen.[52] Cohen conceived of delinquent gang behavior as a collective solution to the status problems, needs, and frustrations of lower-class boys. Drawn together by their common resentment of dominant, middle-class values, Cohen's delinquents display a wholesale negativism, a malice toward things virtuous, a versatility in types of delinquent behavior, a short-term hedonism, nonutilitarian expressions of "fun," and opposition to social control.

In arguing against Merton's means-end conception, Cohen claims that the deviant role may even be a highly coveted one that affirms by gesture and deed that one is a certain kind of person. There is no need to posit delinquency as an adaptation to the insufficiency of other means, a response to disjunction. He points out that

> much deviant behavior cannot readily be formulated in these terms at all [i.e., means-end disjuncture]. Some of it, for example, is directly expressive of the roles. A tough and bellicose posture, the use of obscene language, participation in illicit sexual activity, the immoderate consumption of alcohol, the deliberate flouting of legality and authority, a generalized disrespect for the sacred symbols of the "square" world, a taste for marihuana, even suicide—all of these may have the primary function of affirming . . . that one is a certain kind of person.[53]

The validity of the middle-class reaction hypothesis for analyzing slum boys' behavior is questionable, however. Kobrin suggests that a more plausible explanation should conceptualize the process of becoming deviant, rather than focusing on discrete categories of conformity and deviance. Attention to the role of competence in interpersonal relationships may reveal how status-management efforts by gang boys influence particular behavioral episodes.[54]

Short and Strodbeck present an even stronger argument against the reaction-formation hypothesis. In their study of delinquent gangs, the authors find that disadvantaged youth are not alienated from dominant goals, and express no hostility toward middle-class society. The gang serves as their major reference group, setting standards, providing opportunities, and establishing rewards. Payoffs within this setting are substitutes for out-of-reach rewards. Deviant behavior is an expression of the distinctive life-style and interactive patterns that are played out within the gang arena.[55]

Neither Cloward and Ohlin's reformulation nor Cohen's critique of Merton's limited view of deviant role performances carried delinquent subculture theory very far. Problems inhered in certain assumptions and the dominant research methods. Criticisms focus on the culture-bound orientation, the failure to explore the various meanings of any specific deviant act, the restricted analysis of success-goal aspirations or reactive behavior as sole determinants of deviance, the neglect of extensive violation of norms in all social classes, and the *post hoc* assumptions regarding deviance as a discrete category rather than as a shifting phenomenon.[56]

Uncovering delinquency as an individual adaptation or a collective solution to status deprivation produced little significant data about human behavior or the role that deviance plays in modern life. Even Miller's findings about "normal delinquency," an expression of endogeneous values of slum youth,[57] did little to redirect anomie studies into cultural-diversity and value-conflict issues. Deviance continued to be treated as a special event, participated in by trapped and impotent slum persons.

Social stress, concentrated among surplus populations, is said to create the inexorable conditions that eventuate in large-scale deviancy. However, by emphasizing deviant solutions, rather than structural sources, anomie theorists neglect the impact of social control, which effectively excludes the disadvantaged from political and legal management of their fate.

Deviance Sources: The Culture of Poverty

Sociological institution making was at its zenith in the 1960s, during the antipoverty skirmish. Well-armed with data on correlates of lower-class behavior, research justified social intervention as a necessary corrective for a "culture of poverty." Oscar Lewis, an anthropologist, first introduced the term in his study of slum life in New York, Mexico, and Puerto Rico. Analyzing family relations among the poor, rather than community institutions, Lewis discerned a variety of social pathologies that he claimed were associated with the lower urban stratum. Separated, alienated, ignorant, and uninvolved, the poor are said to be a group apart, disconnected from the larger world. Localism, provincialism, apathy, suspicion, and the absence of class consciousness purportedly characterize those locked into the culture of poverty.[58]

The culture-of-poverty concept is really synonymous with the social disorganization focus on the underclass as a "special" social type. High rates of illegitimacy and parental separation and the absence of defined roles and responsibilities relate to antisocial behavior and failure to absorb into the melting pot. Family structure, not mainstream institutions, create and sustain poverty.[59]

Changing terms to designate the same entity, as Matza points out, is a familiar phenomenon in social life.[60] The historical continuity of disreputable poverty has been obscured by word substitutions which replace negative evaluations with inoffensive labels. "Hard-to-reach," "disadvantaged," "culturally deprived," "multiproblem family," and "anomic man" are the most recent additions to the catalog of names. The stigmatic label, however, inheres in the referent, not in the concept.

By using folk concepts of poverty, social scientists have adopted the rhetoric and concepts of political managers. Subsequent documentation by policy specialists and scientists make it clear that poverty is to be treated as an institutionally and historically bounded issue in public discourse. Descriptive and evaluative definitions give such specifications as living standards, directions of change, human costs of being poor, and determining a "poverty line."[61] The we-they dichotomy strengthens the respectable, middle-class stance of investigators. The "we" alliance consists of scientists, program sponsors, professionals, and a sympathetic public, and "they" are the target populations toward whom programs and efforts are directed.

As a description of poverty, the culture concept falls short in three respects. It neglects crucial structural characteristics of a stratified order, oversimplifies and obfuscates the issues of power and control in industrial societies, and focuses on a single stratum rather than the complex set of transactions between interest groups. Whatever is distinctive about lower-class life may be no more than the situational stresses induced by lack of power, resources, and options.

To policy makers, this theory recommends eradication of the culture of poverty, not the elimination of conditions fostering poverty. The war on poverty, by striking at cultural and environmental obstacles to motivation, attacks symptoms and consequences of deprivation, rather than the generative conditions of poverty located in the political economy.[62]

Despite built-in biases, the opportunity structure formula has generated more concrete proposals for change than any other approach to poverty and its consequences.[63] Conforming youths to the mold of a workaday world requires fitting the unskilled to available jobs. This reduces alienation among the troubled and troublesome, and supports the routine goals of public order.

What are the implications of these various "opportunity programs," optimistically sponsored by sociologists? Morally, they function to uphold negative stereotypes that blame the victim. Their focus is on the presumed special needs and shortcomings of the most severely deprived. Economically, the programs operate to channel the poor into dead-end jobs that retain the underclass as a marginal labor force, to the advantage of employers. Politically, they control social unrest by enforcing rehabilitation, rather than granting political power or money. Correcting people, rather than social institutions, maintains the status quo and prevents basic political and economic reform. By denying serious participation by program beneficiaries, these caretaker policies foster exclusionary tactics that serve to divide strata.

The professional-technical model, presumably producing value-free knowledge to be applied to conditions of social disorganization, is based on false premises. The data-collection process, with its one-sided concern with deviant rates among underclass populations, reinforces theoretical misconceptions about the nature of deviance in modern society. Uncovering deviance by depending largely on official data results in questionable findings that are neither reliable nor valid.

METHOD

Delusive Discoveries: The Rates and Distribution Error

Offical data are social products. Their construction is determined by organizational, legal, and social pressures that involve only a halfhearted attempt to measure criminal or deviant activity accurately. Even under rigorous scientific conditions, ambiguity of meanings makes the data-collecting task a highly uncertain enterprise. When data is collected by special interest or occupational groups for their own accounting purposes, rigor typically yields to subjective interpretations and expediency.

In the administration of justice, for example, built-in constraints mask the "hidden figure" of crime. What the public takes to be "objective" rates are actually outcomes of organizational decisions that are conditioned by contradictory expectations of law enforcement among different agencies, by variable agency responses to public resistance against law enforcement, and by conflicts in interpretations or clashing ideologies of enforcers. It is also apparent that occupational careers and risks of law enforcement activities shape the legal product to conform to agency designs rather than legal imperatives. Reciprocal obligations between bureaucracies further disguise organizational self-serving under the protective guise of a law-and-order mandate.[64] Such conditions introduce a bias into offical criminal records.

Nor is police detection a scientific task. Instead, police rely heavily on simplistic versions of crime causation to resolve work-related problems. Cicourel claims that the police develop

> theories about individuals and groups, morality and immorality, good and bad people, practices and typifications of community settings, and such theories or conceptions are employed in routine ways . . . Police . . . perspectives follow community typifications in organizing the city into areas where they expect to receive the most difficulty from deviant or difficult elements to areas where little trouble is expected and where more care should be taken in dealing with the population because of socio-economic and political influence . . . Thus, the officer's preconstituted typications and stock of knowledge at hand lead him to prejudge much of what he encounters . . .[65]

Moreover, police scrutiny and disposition of juvenile offenders involve a variety of extralegal considerations (e.g., previous record, social class, race, demeanor, and such pragmatic considerations as an overload of court cases). Self-report records further demonstrate that official records exaggerate the differences in delinquency among boys in different status levels. Gold estimates that if records were complete and unselective, the present ratio of five to one, favoring the selection of lower-status offenders, would actually be closer to one and one-half to one.[66] Delinquency is relatively evenly distributed throughout all social ranks, but the infiltration of bias in police dispositions operates to concentrate official violations in the lower strata.

In addition to discriminatory police practices, criminal court proceedings are the most severe on those least able to bear costs. Plea bargaining often depends on social-class position. Securing concessions from the judiciary rests largely in the lawyer's hands, and the well-to-do are most likely to have the best counsel. Bargained justice penalizes the poor most heavily. Chambliss suggests that

> since the guilty plea is obtained by striking a bargain between
> the defendant and the court, the benefit to the defendant
> is going to depend on the strength of his bargaining position . . .
> [which is] reflected in his ability to hire private counsel, his
> knowledge of his legal rights and his sophistication about the law.
> Most middle and upper class persons are as ignorant of the law
> as are most lower class persons, but they can pay for good
> legal counsel to inform them of their bargaining power . . . It
> remains for the poor to receive the brunt of the disadvantageous
> possibilities of bargain justice.[67]

In scrutiny, detection, disposition, and sentencing, the lower strata predominate in official records. The vicious circle goes on as the deviant pool created from former offenders continues to provide an available population for future arrest and prosecution.[68]

Out of such "facts," anomie theorists have constructed explanations accounting for the etiology and epidemiology (or distribution) of deviance. By taking at face value a set of organizational imperatives, sociologists have imposed the doctrines and typifications of those in control on sociological theory.

Researchers who assumed records to be objective statements of events have been profoundly wrong. They have allowed biased and selective agency decisions to be transformed into theories of the social sources of criminal behavior, and are supported by a variety of middle-class and elite publics who continue to finance research that contributes to traditional stereotypes. By adopting this research strategy, sociologists (unwittingly, perhaps) have become part of the state regulatory apparatus. Locating the bulk of offenders among the least powerful, least privileged, and least resourceful sections of the community reinforces discriminatory practices and justifies scientific and official intervention in poor and minority communities.

There are other difficulties in the use of institutional rates for constructing or validating sociological theories. Dunham argues that many of the current epidemiological studies of mental disorder are grounded in methodological and substantive errors.[69] He points out that psychiatric diagnosis lacks objective criteria. Diagnosis tends to vary from one setting to another (e.g., in public versus private hospitals), and even within settings because of the different orientations of individual psychiatrists. It is also shaped by the cultural or class characteristics of patients which affect screening and detection.

Moreover, prevalence rates (the number of cases present in a specific population at any one time) are often confused with incidence rates (frequency of occurrence). If a patient recovers sufficiently to return to family, work, and community, is he or she excluded from the count? This issue is clouded by different reporting systems. Does the category "mentally disordered," include any person who indicates to a clinician that he or she has some difficulty? Psychiatrists may so widen the definition of psychiatric disorder that the greater majority of urban persons would be classified as possessing some form of emotional disorder. In the Mid-Manhattan Study, which was based on a prevalence count, researchers found that 80 percent of their sample exhibited some type of psychiatric problem.[70] Aside from serious definitional ambiguities inherent in such studies, little confidence can be placed in mental disorder rates because the same correlations show large fluctuations from one study to another.[71]

Sociologically speaking, inferences from official statistics about the extent of deviance and its relationship to selected characteristics of social structures are totally misleading. We may be able to infer some generalizations about the attitudes and values of institutional caretakers and their paying publics, but to go beyond this by attempting to construct elaborate theoretical schemes that link structural characteristics to individual behavior is to distort the sociological enterprise. Institutional rate differentials, regardless of the specific population or type of deviance studied, have little validity unless researchers redefine categories sociologically to include the hidden population of noninstitutional offenders.

Conclusion

Proposing a special, middle-range theory of deviance, Merton modified the functionalist conception of consensus to take account of the contradictions and malintegrations in contemporary life. Uncovering deviance through official data, investigators sought to demonstrate how a disjuncture between culture and structure encouraged rule violation and lawbreaking, especially among the economically disadvantaged. However, by accepting official data as objective records of events, investigators tended to confuse official rates with the actual occurrence of deviant behavior. Despite elaborate technical methods and predictive instruments, the social engineering role led researchers down a blind alley. Rates were determined according to scientific criteria, but were gathered by biased officials, whose ideology and practices reinforced stereotypical views of wrongdoers. The accounting and descriptive practices of those in control were not considered relevant sociological data. The consequent distortion of social reality leaves much of the work of the anomie school in a scientific limbo. The extent to which these correlations of deviant behavior with specific types of sociocultural environments are valid cannot be determined.

The anomie theorists never acquired an understanding of social behavior from the perspectives of the actors (both controller and controlled). This requires a situational analysis of time, place, definers, and the consequences of social policy. Social reality appears to be different from this point of view. It is less substantial, more flexible, and even "flimsy."[72] Assumptions about the one-to-one correspondence between structural characteristics and behavior become logically and empirically untenable, if only because social meanings are situational, emerging from interaction and activity.

Later theories reversed Merton's conception of the intact nature of the cultural order. The value-conflict perspective, to be examined next, views law, criminal definitions, and punishment as devices by particular groups to protect their values and interests. In a pluralistic social order, legal obligations are often disconnected from moral ones. Under such circumstances, individuals exercise choices in their behavior which are based on learned definitions and expectations.

NOTES

1. Robert K. Merton, *Social Theory and Social Structure* (New York: The Free Press, 1957), p. 132.

2. Merton discusses this theoretical mode in "On Sociological Theories of the Middle Range," in *On Theoretical Sociology* (New York: The Free Press, 1967), pp. 39-72. Merton's overview of forms of deviant behavior and disorganization is found in *Contemporary Social Problems*, 3rd ed., ed. Robert K. Merton and Robert Nisbet (New York: Harcourt Brace Jovanovich, Inc., 1971).

3. David J. Bordua provides a critical evaluation of delinquency studies in "A Critique of Gang Delinquency," *The Annals of the American Academy of Political and Social Sciences* 338 (November 1961): 120-136.

4. Harold L. Wilensky and Charles N. Lebeaux, *Industrial Society and Social Welfare* (New York: The Free Press, 1965).

5. F. F. Piven and R. A. Cloward, *Regulating the Poor: The Functions of Social Welfare* (New York: Pantheon Books: 1971).

6. Richard M. Titmuss, *The Gift Relationship* (New York: Pantheon Books, 1971), p. 241.

7. Irving L. Horowitz and M. Liebowitz, "Social Deviance and Political Marginality: Toward a Redefinition of the Relation Between Sociology and Politics," *Social Problems* 5 (Winter 1967): 280-296.

8. Daniel P. Moynihan, *Maximum Feasible Misunderstanding* (New York: The Free Press, 1969), p. 31.

9. Morris Janowitz, "Professionalization of Sociology," *American Journal of Sociology* 78 (July 1972): 105-135.

10. Notable exceptions to this lack of significant social research in public commissions includes *The Coleman Report* (edited by James Coleman) commissioned by the United States Office of Education.

11. Janowitz, "Professionalization of Sociology," p. 126.

12. Irving L. Horowitz, "Studies in the Life Cycles of Social Science," in *Professing Sociology* (Chicago: Aldine Publishing Company, 1968), pp. 287-304.

13. Merton, *Social Theory and Social Structure*, p. 569.

14. Robert Friedrichs refers to this doctrine as the "priestly mode" in *A Sociology of Sociology* (New York: The Free Press, 1970), chap. 5.

15. C. Wright Mills, *The Sociological Imagination* (New York: Oxford Press, 1959), p. 96.

16. Merton, *Social Theory and Social Structure*, p. 132.

17. Ibid., p. 146.

18. Merton, *Social Theory and Social Structure*, p. 180.

19. See Merton and Nisbet's discussion in *Contemporary Social Problems*, pp. 1-25, 793-845.

20. A critical overview of anomie theory is found in: Marshall B. Clinard, ed., *Anomie and Deviant Behavior* (New York: The Free Press of Glencoe, 1964). See, also, Ian Taylor, Paul Walton, and Jock Young, *The New Criminology* (London and Boston: Routledge & Kegan Paul, 1973), pp. 91-110 and Jerome H. Skolnick and Elliott Currie, *Crisis in American Institutions* (Boston: Little, Brown and Company, 1973), pp. 6-14.

21. Edwin M. Lemert, "Social Structure, Social Control, and Deviation," in *Anomie and Deviant Behavior*, pp. 57-98.

22. Ralph Turner, "Value-conflict in Social Disorganization," *Sociology and Social Research* 38 (1954): 305.

23. Merton lists a total of eighty-seven theoretical and empirical studies on anomie from 1890-1964 in Clinard, *Anomie and Deviant Behavior*, p. 216. These are also summarized in an appendix of Clinard's study, pp. 243-311, by Stephen Cole and Harriet Zuckerman.

24. T. B. Bottomore and M. Rubel, eds., *Selected Writings in Sociology and Social Philosophy* by Karl Marx (London: Watts, 1956) and Max Weber, *The Theory of Social and Economic Organization*, ed. Talcott Parsons (New York: The Free Press, 1964).

25. Max Weber, *The City*, ed. and trans. Don Martindale and G. Neuwirth (New York: The Free Press, 1958).

26. Merton, *Social Theory and Social Structure*. p. 145.

27. Ibid., p. 145.

28. Daniel Bell, "Crime as an American Way of Life," *The Antioch Review* (Summer 1953): 131-154.

29. This is suggested in Arthur Vidich and Joseph Bensman, *Small Town in Mass Society* (Princeton: Princeton University Press, 1958).

30. Emile Durkheim, *Suicide* trans. J. A. Spaulding and G. Simpson (New York: The Free Press, 1951).

31. This Durkheimian tradition has animated two distinguished studies of suicide. See Andrew F. Henry and James F. Short, Jr., *Suicide and Homicide* (New York: The Free Press, 1954) and Jack P. Gibbs and Walter T. Martin, *Status Integration and Suicide: A Sociological Study* (Eugene, Ore.: University of Oregon Books, 1964).

32. Merton, *Social Theory and Social Structure*, p. 183.

33. Ibid., p. 140.

34. Albert J. Reiss and Albert L. Rhodes, "Are Educational Norms and Goals of Conforming, Truant, and Delinquent Adolescents Influenced by Group Position in American Society?" *Journal of Negro Education* (Summer 1959): 252-267 and Richard L. Simpson and H. Max Miller, "Social Status and Anomie," *Social Problems* 10 (1963): 256-264.

35. See, for example, Michael Crozier, *The Bureaucratic Phenomenon* (Chicago: University of Chicago Press, 1964).

36. Merton, "Social Problems and Sociological Theory," in *Contemporary Social Problems*, p. 844.

37. Merton proposes a model of the social process through which anomie "spreads," in R. K. Merton, "The Social-Cultural Environment and Anomie," in *New Perspectives for Research on Juvenile Delinquency*, ed. H. L. Witmer and R. Kotinsky (Washington, D.C.: U. S. Government Printing Office).

38. See the discussion by Snyder, "Inebriety, Alcoholism and Anomie," in *Anomie and Deviant Behavior*, pp. 189-212.

39. Dorothy L. Meir and Wendell Bell, "Anomia in a Small City," *American Sociological Review* 24 (1959): 189-202.

40. Lemert, "Social Structure, Social Control, and Deviation," pp. 88-96.

41. A critique of Merton's theory of motivation is offered by Steven Box, *Deviance, Reality and Society* (London, New York, and Toronto: Holt, Rinehart and Winston Ltd., 1971), pp. 102-106.

42. Bernard Lander, *Toward an Understanding of Juvenile Delinquency* (New York: Columbia University Press, 1954).

43. Alan C. Kerckhoff, "Anomie and Achievement Motivation: A Study of Personality Development within Cultural Disorganization," *Social Forces* 37 (1959): 196-202.

44. Reiss and Rhodes, "Are Educational Norms and Goals of Conforming, Truant, and Delinquent Adolescents Influenced by Group Position in American Society?"

45. Arthur L. Wood, "Social Organization and Crime in Small Wisconsin Communities," *American Sociological Review* 7 (1942): 40-46.

46. Roland J. Chilton, "Delinquency Area Research: Baltimore, Detroit, and Indianapolis," *American Sociological Review* 29 (1964): 71-83.

47. Arthur Kornhauser, Harold L. Sheppard, and Albert J. Mayer, *When Labor Votes* (New York: University Publishers, 1956).

48. Self-attitudes of delinquents versus nondelinquents are analyzed in W. C. Reckless, S. Dinitz, and E. Murray, "Self Concept as an Insulator Against Delinquency," *American Sociological Review* 21 (December 1956): 744-746 and F. R. Scarpitti, E. Murray, S. Dinitz, and W. C. Reckless, "The 'Good' Boy in a High Delinquency Area: Four Years Later." *American Sociological Review* 25 (August 1960): 555-558.

49. Allen Liska reports from re-analysis of eight critical tests of the "stress model" (high aspiration-low expectation of achievement) that disconfirmation of anomie theory occurs for seven of the eight (87 percent) cases. He concludes that it is not stress (in the sense of a discrepancy between ends and means) that generates deviance, but rather a lack of *both* aspirations and expectations for success (i.e., low commitment to conformity). A. Liska, "Aspirations, Expectations, and Delinquency: Stress and Additive Models," *The Sociological Quarterly* 12 (Winter 1971): 99-107.

50. Richard A. Cloward, "Illegitimate Means, Anomie, and Deviant Behavior," *American Sociological Review* 24 (April 1959): 164-176.

51. Richard A. Cloward and Lloyd E. Ohlin, *Delinquency and Opportunity: A Theory of Delinquent Gangs* (New York: The Free Press of Glencoe, 1960).

52. Albert K. Cohen, *Delinquent Boys: The Culture of the Gang* (New York: The Free Press of Glencoe, 1955).

53. Ibid., p. 7.

54. Solomon Kobrin, "The Conflict of Values in Delinquency Areas," *American Sociological Review* 16 (October 1951): 653-661.

55. James F. Short and Fred L. Strodtbeck, *Group Process and Gang Delinquency* (Chicago: The University of Chicago Press, 1965).

56. A critique of anomie theory is offered by Clinard, ed., *Anomie and Deviant Behavior*, p. 30. Discussion of the situational nature of deviance is stressed by Lindesmith and Gagnon, "Anomie and Drug Addiction," in *Anomie and Deviant Behavior*, pp. 158-188.

57. Walter B. Miller, "Lower Class Culture as a Generating Milieu of Gang Delinquency," *Journal of Social Issues* 14 (Fall 1958): 165-180.

58. Oscar Lewis presents his "culture-of-poverty" argument in an introduction to *The Children of Sanchez* (New York: Random House, 1961), pp. xi-xxxi.

59. Daniel P. Moynihan, *The Negro Family* (Washington: U. S. Department of Labor, 1965).

60. David Matza, "Poverty and Disrepute," in *Social Theory and Social Structure*, pp. 619-669.

61. See Bernard Beck's discussion in "Bedbugs, Stench, Dampness and Immorality: A Review Essay on Recent Literature About Poverty," *Social Problems* 13 (Fall 1967): 101-114 and "Welfare as a Moral Category," *Social Problems* 14 (Winter 1967): 258-277.

62. Moynihan, *Maximum Feasible Misunderstanding*.

63. See D. P. Moynihan, ed., "The Professors and the Poor," in *Perspectives on Poverty I: On Understanding Poverty*

—*Perspectives from the Social Sciences* (New York: Basic Books, 1968), pp. 3-35.

64. A good overview of methodological and substantive problems in the sociological use of official statistics is found in Box, *Deviance, Reality and Society*, chap. 6.

65. Aaron Cicourel, *The Social Organization of Juvenile Justice* (New York: John C. Wiley and Sons, 1968), p. 7.

66. Martin Gold, "Undetected Delinquent Behavior," *The Journal of Research on Crime and Delinquency* 3 (1966): 44.

67. William J. Chambliss, ed., *Crime and the Legal Process* (New York: McGraw-Hill, 1969), p. 294.

68. Vold reports that recidivism (return) rates among prison inmates range from 53 percent to 80 percent. George B. Vold, *Theoretical Criminology* (New York: Oxford University Press, 1958), p. 295). While there are alternative explanations of this high return rate (e.g., lack of opportunity or loss of status because of stigmatization), we strongly suspect that ex-convicts, kept under constant surveillance and control by enforcement officials, offer an available source of suspects for "round-ups" with subsequent high likelihood of resentencing.

69. H. Warren Dunham, "Anomie and Mental Disorder," in *Anomie and Deviant Behavior*, pp. 128-157.

70. L. Srole, T. S. Langner, S. T. Michael, M. K. Opier, and T. Rennie, *Mental Health in the Metropolis*, vol. I. (New York: McGraw-Hill Book Company, 1962).

71. Dunham, "Anomie and Mental Disorder," p. 156.

72. Understanding social behavior from the viewpoint of the actor is the crucial idea of symbolic interactionism. This perspective is reviewed in John W. Petras and Bernard N. Meltzer, "Theoretical and Ideological Variations in Contemporary Interactionism," *Catalyst* 7 (Winter 1973): 1-8.

6

Cultural Diversity and Deviant Motivation

VALUE–CONFLICT CONCEPTION

> Crime is conflict. But it is part of a process of conflict of which
> law and punishment are other parts. This process begins in
> the community before the law is enacted, and continues in the
> community and in the behavior of particular offenders after
> punishment is inflicted . . . The demand for law arises out of the
> conflict in cultures; and because there is a conflict in cultures, the
> law is not effective as a deterrent upon the other groups that
> did not at first demand the law. Thus we have legal obligations
> without the support of generally recognized moral obligations.
> (Edwin H. Sutherland, *The Sutherland Papers*)[1]

If science were a self-correcting enterprise, checking concepts against better data would clarify the position of deviance and criminality in the organization of social life. However, science, as I have attempted to show, is not free of social influences or conflicts in interpretations. Styles of reflection are products of social and intellectual trends that often run in contradictory directions.

By tracing the social and professional sources animating the value-uniformity versus value-conflict polemic, I will focus on social processes internal to sociology as an autonomous domain. Conflict over styles of sociological work, as Merton reminds us, is endemic to the changing contours of the discipline.[2] Distinct theoretical and research traditions in deviance, especially pronounced in the consensus-conflict dispute, provide alternative, if partial, perspectives on deviant phenomena.

Reflecting the continuities and discontinuities within sociology,[3] the value-conflict approach has its intellectual roots in the Chicago ecological tradition, its structural imagery in American pluralism, its theoretical spokespersons in students of social problems and criminology, and its research products in studies of crime and deviance as motivated (i.e., rational) behavior.

Unlike anomie theory, with its clear-cut (if mistaken) assumptions, the value-conflict conception develops only preliminary statements about the sources of deviance in the normative social order. The concepts of differential social organization and association, proposed by the school's leading figure, Sutherland, may be seen as arising out of opposition to notions of deviance as personal pathology and of crime as a product of social disorganization.

The notion of cultural pluralism, inherited from the Chicago School, held that ethnic and neighborhood enclaves support distinct values that clash with the mainstream culture. Sutherland transformed this culture-conflict notion into a structural conception of conflicting interests and organizations. In this scheme, deviance and crime are outcomes of conflicts in values which are expressed in criminal law. Application of this idea, however, stagnated at the social psychological level. For the most part, this focus limited explanations of crime to the learning mechanisms involved in a criminal act. This paradigm is summarized in Figure 6.1.

I.	Social-Professional Conditions	Professional recognition of normative pluralism; continuity of social problems approach; conflict in sociological styles of work generated focus on widespread value dissensus and norm violations; sociological response to wartime and middle-class crime; theoretical attempt to extend integrationist question to include conflict and criminality; specialization of theory in crime studies
II.	Perspective	Normative conflict; differential social organization and association as sources of criminal and deviant behavior; law as a device of one party in conflict with another party; thus crime and punishment perpetuate cultural conflict; deviance as shared cultural tradition learned primarily in face-to-face groups; modalities of interaction stressed: priority, duration, and intensity; social psychological analysis stressed differential identification and deviant vocabularies as crucial elements of deviant act
III.	Metaphor	"Criminal behavior system"—career concept emphasized systematic pattern of deviant motives and acts
IV.	Themes	Criminal behavior types; victimology
V.	Method	Typologies; analytical summary

FIGURE 6.1. *Value-Conflict Paradigm*

SOCIAL AND PROFESSIONAL CONDITIONS

Conflict in Styles of Reflection

The formation of ideas, to reiterate, is a process influenced by many social factors. These may be condensed into five types of influences:

1. Ideas may emerge from existing ideology, philosophy, science, or common sense.
2. Ideas are shaped by existing social structures. The range of theoretical influences includes the position of scientists or intellectuals in the social stratification system of their society, the nature of systems of social stratification established between nations or societies in contact, and the nature of their economic and political relationships.
3. Ideas are shaped in answer to social problems.
4. Scientists and intellectuals, working independently or in cliques, debate with each other and from their dialectic emerge differing views. They also debate the popular conceptions held by nonscientists, and this debate influences their position.
5. New techniques of measurement and new data shift the bases of argument.[4]

Sociological paradigms in deviance have been differently affected by these factors, as shown by the Social Pathology and Chicago School responses to urban problems or the functionalists' ideological convictions about the beneficial role of elites in maintaining social order.

First explicated in Sutherland's first edition of his *Criminology* text in 1924 (and later restated in subsequent editions by Sutherland, and Sutherland and Cressey[5]), the value-conflict perspective represents a dissenter's view of the state of theory and research. Debates and dialectical processes that were internal to the academic enterprise shaped the value-conflict school. Reacting against the multiple-factor approach in criminology, Sutherland and his followers attempted to shift criminological theory away from physical, psychological, and economic determinism toward a sociological explanation of crime rates and behavior. In doing so, they also challenged the poverty-causes-crime proposition.

Professional and ideological differences between schools also influenced this intellectual product. While functionalists chose abstract theories that led to an acceptance of the established order, the value-conflict group took a social problems approach that directed them into pragmatic issues of social turmoil. Middle-class or white-collar crime, previously an almost untouchable subject in sociological research, took on theoretical significance. During the depression and World War II, widespread corporate malingering and black-market crime became highly salient public concerns. A conflict perspective could make sense of these happenings, and alter the direction of criminological research at the same time. Thus, it is not necessarily a change in the social structure that generates dissenting ideas or alternative paradigms. It is change in the way theorists *conceptualize* that structure that alters the content of thought.

Rejecting traditional criminology, value-conflict theorists recognized that law and morality are not one, but reflect unresolvable divisions between interest groups. Law is only a temporary resolution of chronic cultural differences within any social community. Punishment is not a restitutive act commensurate with the crime, but an arbitrary instrument of the criminal justice system for maintaining law and order at the cost of justice and rehabilitation. Crime is a normal expression of differential social organization, rather than reactive behavior to psychological or social defects.

These propositions, and others to be elaborated in the next section, are not radical refutations of the American social system. The value-conflict perspective provides "corrective surgery" for the concept of a monolithic culture. As I shall argue below, the pluralistic doctrine of cultural differences as sources of criminal behavior is too bland and too vague to carry deviance theory very far. The political-conflict issue of inequality created by resource maldistribution is not featured in this early, social problems version of conflict theory.

Any perspective provides a selective rendering of data and problems. The value-conflict orientation eventually became restricted to criminological concerns. Sutherland's biography of his theory of differential association reviews the multiple influences that contributed to this theory's formation, including his University of Chicago colleagues, his efforts to seek sociological generalizations about crime consistent with major findings in criminology, and his own preference for limiting the culture-conflict conception to the area of law and crime. Sutherland never aimed for theoretical closure. He pointed out that the "principle of specificity" in culture conflict required narrowing empirical concerns to a restrictive universe of events. Sutherland's theory itself was to remain an emergent construct, an incomplete, if ever-developing, statement of the genesis of crime. Sutherland says about his own work:

> This is to be a biography of the hypothesis [of differential
> association] and a report of its present status or its rise and
> decline. It is a story of confusion, inconsistencies, delayed recog-
> nition of implicit meanings, and of much borrowing from
> and stimulation by colleagues and students. The hypothesis has
> changed rapidly and frequently, for which I am doubly thankful,
> first because the hypothesis . . . is not dead, and second because
> I have been able to retract many ideas about it before they were
> published.[6]

Given a different intellectual milieu and a different cast of supporting characters, Sutherland might have opted for the "multiple-factor," or eclectic, approach. His decision to concentrate on building a theory of criminality, rather than constructing a sociology of conflict, grew out of his rejection of traditional criminology which was notorious for its catalog of disparate and uncoordinated "causes."

Sutherland failed to recognize the problem of limiting the culture-conflict idea to criminal behavior. A focus on crime rates or criminal careers treats behavior as isolated, nonpolitical events, and the role of the State in creating or perpetuating conflict is not within its purview. Value-conflict theorists, like Sutherland, viewed the State as a disinterested party that negotiates the inevitable conflicts between groups. The role of the State in defining and labeling moral offenders as criminals remained a neglected issue.

Value-Conflict Theory and the Break from Consensus Formulations

Current vocabularies for the explanation of deviance and social problems stem from the two traditions of order theories and conflict formulations. The order vocabulary, reviewed in earlier chapters, views deviance as a problem of social disorganization or system imbalance. At the structural level of explanation, this entails a breakdown in social control, including inadequate institutionalization of goals or inadequate means to achieve institutional goals. At a social psychological level of analysis, the failure of individuals to meet the maintenance needs of the social system is caused by anomie.[7]

The conflict vocabulary draws from two nineteenth-century sources, Simmel and Marx, and involves two distinct interpretations of the role of conflict in social organization.[8] In Simmel's version (adopted by Park and Burgess and other Chicago School theorists), conflict is a universal form of social interaction. Competition initiates conflict which maintains collective action, resulting in the continual struggle of groups to maintain or defend their status positions. The metaphor of "unstable equilibrium" depicts the Simmelian notion of conflict as a basic social process. The criminologist, Vold, articulates this view:

> As social interaction processes grind their way through varying kinds of uneasy adjustment to a more or less stable equilibrium of balanced forces in opposition, the resulting condition of relative stability is what is usually called social order or social organization. But it is the adjustment, one to another, of the many groups of varying strengths and of different interests that is the essence of society as a functioning reality.[9]

The conflict perspective has provided the major source of attacks on functionalism. Coser, in his first major book on conflict, expressed what was to become a typical polemic against functionalism. He held that conflict is not given sufficient attention and that such phenomena as deviance and dissent are too readily described as "pathological."[10] In a vein similar to Georg Simmel, Coser says that conflict provides the maintenance function of preserving the viability and flexibility of institutional patterns. Imbalances, tensions, and conflicts of interest among interrelated parts constitute normal system adaptation. Indeed, Coser insists, conflict functions to strengthen the system's basis of integration.

Dahrendorf, another conflict proponent, borrowed the form and substance of Marx's causal imagery.[11] In his analysis, conflict is an inevitable and inexorable force in social systems, manifested in the bipolar opposition of interests. In the struggle for scarce resources, especially power, conflict is a major source of change in social systems.

Divergences in these two conflict approaches are significant for the analysis of changing paradigms of deviance. While Marx and Dahrendorf assume that intense conflict is a pervasive feature of social systems and change, Simmel, Coser, and other value-conflict proponents assume that conflict is simply one process, varying in its intensity and consequences, within a social whole. The Simmelian version animated most criminological studies, but this approach had shortcomings as a theory of deviance.

Normative conflict is a theoretical halfway house, located somewhere between the integration notion and a political-conflict model of deviance. Because value-conflict theorists take the conventional social order for granted, they significantly underestimate the crucial role that stratification and political opposition play in forming and transforming social institutions. Power and its abuses, the tenuous legitimacy of legal institutions, and the corruption of authority (all crucial aspects of a political-conflict perspective) remained dormant issues. The Hobbesian problem of order had no scientific solution in the work of the value-conflict school. Inspired by the Chicago version of the conflict-adaptation model, value-conflict proponents proposed a tentative and ill-developed statement of crime as conflict. Propositions stating the form, direction, and consequences of conflict were not elaborated.

Despite these theoretical inadequacies, the value-conflict hypothesis began to move the sociology of deviance away from disorganization theory and its implicit correctional bias. Value-conflict theory encouraged recognition of the types of social milieux likely to foster cultural diversity and deviant motives. Sutherland's conception of differential organization and association linked person to situation, providing the most systematic statement of a genetic explanation of criminal behavior yet available.

PERSPECTIVE

Sutherland's Differential Organization and Association Theory

Sutherland's early work on crime and the criminal process grew out of a general notion of culture conflict that was popular in the sociological literature of the Chicago era.[12] In the 1934 edition of *Criminology,* he stated the hypothesis as follows:

> First, any person can be trained to adopt and follow any pattern of behavior which he is able to execute. Second, failure to follow a prescribed pattern of behavior is due to the inconsistencies and lack of harmony in the influences which direct the individual. Third, the conflict of cultures is therefore the fundamental principle in the explanation of crime.[13]

Although the assertion that conflict causes crime was never developed in propositional form, this tentative formulation employs three classes of social phenomena, subculture, social differentiation, and differential social organization, to account for variations in crime rates between groups. Sutherland's theory differs from earlier sociologies of crime in several respects.

In the first place, Sutherland said that subcultures influence crime rates. On the face of it, this assertion moves little beyond the Park-Burgess ecological-causation notion. But Sutherland went further. Subcultures (primarily ethnic groups) vary in their selection of certain values as important and worthy of legal protection. "The law is a device of one party in conflict with another party," Sutherland argued.[14] Reading between the lines, we have the beginnings of a political-conflict statement which takes the following form: value conflict———➤differential power of one group to make laws ———➤law protects social values of group A at cost of criminalizing values of group B———➤punishment for criminal behavior directed against group B by group A regenerates conflict. Thus, "if laws increase and behavior remains the same, crimes necessarily increase."[15] The labeling theorists were later to explicitly emphasize the theoretical importance of viewing crime and law as social definitions that vary with interests and values of powerful groups.[16]

Because Sutherland was primarily concerned with demonstrating how crime rates vary, he neglected the issue of how laws are formulated. His subculture thesis restricts observation to the effects of group membership in promoting deviant definitions and acts.

Second, Sutherland's concept of social differentiation refutes common-sense notions and classic criminological doctrines of punishment. According to earlier beliefs, a decrease in punishment caused an increase in crimes. Increased punishment, of course, decreased crime.[17] This simplistic rendering of social life makes no sense, Sutherland argued, because modern society contains a variety of groups with conflicting interests, ideals, and values. Dissatisfied with one culture, the mobile dissenter moves out and seeks another group who will support his or her unconventional behavior. Thus, punishment may have a reverse effect on the person who has strong in-group support. Punitive policies promote resentment, further isolating the offender from law-abiding norms.

Sutherland held that punishment had little to do with high crime rates in immigrant communities. Ethnic enclaves have few primary contacts with mainstream and other ethnic groups. The immigrant is primarily exposed to America's public culture, including the distorted images of conspicuous consumption, easy money, and luxury standards of life that are presented in politics, business, sports, and the media. Institutional rules about behavior may actually encourage delinquency and crime among ethnics that are cut off from American working-class and Old World cultures.[18]

Sutherland comes close to an opportunity thesis, although this theme has a minor part in his explanation of criminal acts. Sutherland recognized that unlawful behavior is learned in a context of shared definitions, some of which are furnished by the dominant culture. However, neither association nor opportunity are sufficient explanations of the move into criminal behavior. Nearly everyone comes into contact with favorable definitions of theft, and many engage in stealing without additional contacts with thieves (e.g., shoplifting). Breaking the law occurs only when appropriately defined situations arise or can be located. Sutherland explicates the position of opportunity in this situational interpretation of crime:

> It is axiomatic that persons who commit a specific crime must
> have the opportunity to commit that crime. On the other hand,
> opportunity is not a sufficient cause of crime, since some persons
> who have opportunities to embezzle, become intoxicated,
> engage in illicit heterosexual intercourse or commit other crimes
> do not do so. Consequently, opportunity does not differentiate all
> persons who commit a particular crime from all persons who
> do not commit that crime.[19]

A situational analysis emphasizes that neither criminal contacts nor punishment directly affect deviant motivations. Associations and punitive measures must be contextually viewed, a point that almost all earlier sociologies of crime ignored.

Third, Sutherland's differential-social-organization idea rejected theories of lower-class criminality as endemic to a special culture or structural location. Poverty per se does not motivate crime, Sutherland asserted, as some poor persons may be law-abiding citizens while some affluent members of the community may be systematic lawbreakers. Criminalization is a function of the community's conflicting definitions of crime. After analyzing the low rate of conviction for white-collar crimes among corporations or businessmen, Sutherland argued that social reactions to business fraud tend to be tolerant of the businessman offender. Definitions of white-collar crimes as technical violations that involve no moral culpability eliminate the stigma and punishment associated with other law violations.[20]

Differential social organization accounts for crime causation as well as variations in conviction rates among groups. For Sutherland, crime was rooted in social organization as an expression of values and social relations of that organization. Since most communities are organized for both criminal and anticriminal behavior, the crime rate offers a summary statement of the number of persons who commit crimes and the frequency with which crimes are committed.

However, Sutherland never explored the process by which crime rates are constructed. By assuming that high rates reflect basic differences in group values and modes of organization, Sutherland fell into a common sociological error. In most modern communities, crime rates may actually say more about differential power than about differential-social-organization. Sutherland was too close to the Chicago School's view of ethnic variation as the major form of social difference to see the class and caste conflict that characterize urban organization.

Under Sutherland and his followers, criminological theory remained at a social psychological level of explanation. The differential social organization idea, purportedly an explanation of rates and distributions of crime, was little more than a rudimentary, structural framework for the more elaborate learning theory Sutherland termed "differential association." This theory featured deviance as a group product, the result of an excess of "definitions favorable to violations of the law over definitions unfavorable to violation of the law."[21] Repeated editions of Sutherland's *Principles of Criminology* have contained the following nine propositions which summarize this learning theory of crime.[22]

1) *Criminal behavior is learned.* This means that deviant behavior is neither inherited nor invented. Involving skills, codes, and a definition of the situation as appropriate, crime

and deviance are learned in the same way as conventional
behavior.

2) *Criminal behavior is learned in interaction with other persons
in a process of communication.* In the Meadian tradition of
social psychology, communication includes both verbal
and nonverbal gestures. Sutherland explicitly rejected individualistic theories of crime that deny the importance of
shared meanings as an essential element of the act.

3) *The principal part of the learning of criminal behavior occurs
within intimate personal groups.* Rather than presuming
that all social influences were equally significant in the genesis
of deviant behavior, Sutherland emphasized the primary
group as the chief source of social learning. Impersonal
agencies of communication (e.g., films, newspapers, and other
media) play a relatively unimportant part in the specific
process of deviant learning.

4) *When criminal behavior is learned, the learning includes
techniques of committing the crime (which are sometimes
very complicated and sometimes very simple) and the specific
direction of motives, drives, rationalizations, and attitudes.*
Criminal intent precedes the act. Deviant attitudes and
motives prepare the way for the movement into a deviant
career.

5) *The specific direction of motives and drives is learned from
definitions of legal codes as favorable and unfavorable.* Values
in modern society may be contradictory, conflicting, or
ambiguous. Legal codes reflect value splits, and, for some
groups, encourage positive attitudes toward breaking the law.

6) *A person becomes deviant because of an excess of definitions
favorable to violation of law over definitions unfavorable
to violation of law.* This is the principle of differential association. It refers to the "counteracting forces" between
criminal and anticriminal associations. Sutherland believed
that the crucial conditions for entrance into deviance were
contact with criminal persons and codes and exclusion from
conventional patterns.

7) *Differential association may vary in frequency, duration,
priority, and intensity.* While Sutherland admitted that a
formula to quantify these modalities was probably impossible,
he specified indices of these aspects of association. For
example, conditions most likely to confirm a deviant identity
include recruitment into deviance at an early age (priority)
by prestigious intimates (intensity), with extended participation in the deviant role (duration).

8) *The process of learning criminal behavior by association with criminal and anticriminal patterns involves all of the mechanisms that are involved in other learning.* Here Sutherland reiterates the proposition that normal learning processes characterize deviant conduct. Neither compulsive behavior nor imitation operates as modes of induction into deviant careers.

9) *Although criminal behavior is an expression of general needs and values, it is not explained by those general needs and values, since noncriminal behavior is an expression of the same needs and values.* Crime motivated by need had long been a wastebasket category in criminological literature. In Sutherland's formulation, need serves no explanatory role, as it fails to differentiate criminal from noncriminal acts. This position runs counter to the poverty-causes-crime notion, which views criminality as an expression of economic want.[23]

Although Sutherland's theory is probably the leading contender among rival theories of crime, it has its detractors. Various critics have pointed out conceptual and substantive weaknesses, such as its failure to account for influences beyond the immediate environment, overrational conception of behavior, inability to explain the origin of crime, neglect of the role of the victim, and lack of clear definitions of crucial terms such as "systematic" and "excess." It has been criticized as limited in scope (it is neither interdisciplinary nor allied with more general sociological research) and overly comprehensive (it applies to noncriminal acts as well as criminal ones). Other detractors charge that it assumes that all persons have equal access to criminal and anticriminal codes and contacts, it has low practical utility, it is nonpredictive (variables cannot be quantified), and it fails to account for "compulsive criminality."[24]

Matza holds that the theory's presumption that humans are "products" of their environment, rather than choicemakers who negotiate between deviant and respectable worlds, is fallacious.

> Though sensitive to pluralism . . . Sutherland was not always appreciative of the movement of ideas and persons between deviant and conventional realms. Partly obsessed by the idea of ecology, Sutherland nearly made his subject a captive of the milieu. Like a tree or a fox, the subject was a creature of affiliational circumstances except that what Sutherland's milieu provided was meaning and definition of the situation. Sutherland's subject was a creature, but he was half a man. Had Sutherland appreciated the interpenetration of cultural worlds— the symbolic availability of various ways of life everywhere— and more important, had he appreciated that men, but not trees

or foxes, intentionally move in search of meaning . . . if, in other
words he had rejected the notion of radical cultural separation
along with an ecological theory of migration well suited for
insects but not man, his creature would have been wholly
human.[25]

Cressey and others have attempted to answer the critics, but they confront only partially the problems that beset this formulation. Glaser has offered one of the more significant refinements, drawn from role theory, by substituting the notion of "differential identification" for the mechanistic association process specified by Sutherland:

The theory of differential identification, in essence, is that a
person pursues criminal behavior to the extent that he identifies
himself with real or imaginary persons from whose perspective his
criminal behavior seems acceptable. Such a theory focuses
attention on the interaction in which choice models occur including the individual's interaction with himself in rationalizing
his conduct.[26]

The element of choice, omitted in Sutherland's version, is evident in this reconceptualization of deviance as independent of direct social and symbolic support. From this perspective, deviant motives and meanings may follow the act as well as precede it.[27] Matza even questions whether most deviance really involves informed choice before the act. A "drift" into deviance means that individuals may try out the role, and impose meanings on the act only afterward.[28]

In this vein, Sykes and Matza have clarified the concept of motives as "linguistic constructs" circumscribed by the actors' learned vocabulary.[29] Neutralizing rhetorics (accounts for wrongdoing that persons provide to social audiences) form the justifications that protect the deviant from self-blame and blame from others. These verbal techniques are said to render social controls inoperative, freeing the deviant for action without serious damage to his or her self-image. This assumes that deviants internalize standard values and attitudes, but employ appropriate vocabularies to normalize the crime.

Sykes and Matza identify five typical vocabularies. They are denying responsibility (the "billiard ball" conception of self), denying injury (for example, vandalism is called a "prank" or "mischief"), denying the victim (such as rightful retaliation), condemning the condemners (such as accusations against the police), and appealing to higher authority (for example, friendship claims are held to be more valid than general social obligations). Rationalizations that enable the deviant to negotiate between straight and deviant worlds represent strategies of action (not moral imperatives, as in

Sutherland's conception). Sykes and Matza's delinquents make no frontal assault on the dominant normative system:

> In this sense, the delinquent both has his cake and eats it too, for he remains committed to the dominant normative system and yet so qualifies its imperatives that violations are "acceptable" if not "right." Thus the delinquent represents not a radical opposition to law-abiding society but something more like an apologetic failure, often more sinned against than sinning in his own eyes.... It is by learning these techniques that the juvenile becomes delinquent, rather than by learning moral imperatives, values or attitudes standing in direct contradiction to those of the dominant society.[30]

In this revision of Sutherland's "definitions favorable to the violation of the laws," conflict shifts from the environment of organizations to the domain of internalized values. The clash between deviant and conventional codes takes place in a structural void. Ethnicity, class, community, or law enforcement practices do not figure in the calculus of deviant accounts. The entire process has become an internal dialogue in which the offender seeks to mitigate his or her presumed guilt or shame by pulling a ready-made verbal cover for his or her acts out of the cultural hopper. This explains how the individual copes with law violations. It does not address itself to Sutherland's critical proposition that crime is conflict engendered by the normal organization of social life.

Social psychological explanations of deviance (whether cultural transmission, differential association, differential identification, neutralizing techniques, or reinforcement theory[31]) reflect the dominant explanatory mode in American sociology. This theoretical bias is expressed by treating individual motives and acts, rather than organizational conduct. Research features person-role interaction, to the exclusion of superordinate-subordinate relationships, and limits conflict to psychic structures and processes, rather than environmental structures and processes. Despite revisionists' frantic attempts to shore up the faulty architecture of differential association theory, its basic defect, a one-sided view of the deviant process, has not been altered. The focus on criminal learning, to the exclusion of the authority structures within which such learning occurs, contains a now-familiar error in deviance theory. It blames the offender, and ignores the legitimate institutions that generate structured inequality.

Other versions of the crime-as-value-conflict theme have emphasized the implications of this perspective for social problems theory. Fuller and Meyers underscore how lack of cultural cohesion affects community action in defining, solving, and administering a social problem. The law enforcement system itself is merely a microcosm of community conflict.[32] Sellin argues that the criminal justice system discriminates against foreign-born and racial minorities, thereby reinforcing public stereotypes about the higher criminality of the lower class.[33] This situation exacerbates ethnic and racial conflict.

Waller takes the value-conflict theory one idea further. He argues that the conflict of mores not only generates social problems, but also prevents them from being solved. Since resolving social problems necessitates organizational alterations and high social costs, established groups pay lip service to reform and block genuine change.[34]

Two writers have made initial attempts to conceptualize value conflict as power differences between groups. Reacting against the deviance-as-pathology view, Turk outlines the conditions under which the probability of conflict between legal authority and subjects varies and the conditions under which the probability of criminalization of subjects varies once a conflict occurs.[35] For the most part, this orientation has had little impact on criminological research in the Sutherland tradition.

The implications that Vold saw in Sutherland's theory (basic power differentials in the creation, enforcement, and administration of the law) were also not adequately followed up in the research. According to Vold, Sutherland floundered on his own pluralistic ideals. Not content with reforming criminological theory, Sutherland wanted to reform the business-for-profit culture.[36] His value preferences, however, did little to advance the state of the theory. If Sutherland had given more attention to structural sources of conflict and been less concerned with deviant outcomes, he might have provided a long overdue critique of American institutions. Instead, he treated criminal behavior as a discontinuous entity, detached from institutional contexts and basic reforms.

I have stressed some of the deficiencies of Sutherland's conception, especially his restricted view of stratification and political conflict. However, it is only fair to point out, that, when compared with earlier explanations of crime, differential association was a giant step forward, as it broke away from the theoretical potpourri that characterized most criminology. Sutherland's multidimensional view of association helped to eradicate the notion of simple predispositional factors in human behavior, eliminated an individualistic model of crime causation, and ended the, heretofore, almost exclusive attention given to lower-class crime.

THEMES

Criminal Behavior Systems

Sutherland reasoned that if crime is to be studied as a normal social phenomenon, it must first be identified as systematic behavior. In *The*

Professional Thief, written in 1937, Sutherland demonstrated the utility of this behavior-system approach by typifying the criminal role as an occupational type with its own language, laws, history, customs, recruitment patterns, defenses, and reciprocities.[37]

The behavior-system idea considerably extended the scope of criminological concerns. First, studying deviant behavior as an interactional outcome, rather than as a series of aberrational traits, keeps human behavior understandable, whole, and intact,[38] and also avoids the methodological error of grouping factors (e.g., slum dwellings, broken homes, low income, etc.) to explain conduct with an accumulation of facts. Trait analysis and multiple-factor designs, standard data-collecting strategies in criminology, have proved unprofitable. Both are merely shotgun approches to human behavior.

Second, classifying crime as homogeneous social behavior offers a sociological alternative to traditional legal categories. The practice of lumping together different behaviors simply because they are legally classified as similiar confounds any attempt to assess criminality as normal conduct.[39] Furthermore, there is little theoretical significance in using such legal classifications as "felony" and "misdemeanor," as states vary in their assignments of criminal acts to these categories. Arrest records, another legal category, reveal little about the behavioral act. We are not informed about the recruitment process or the original offense itself. The prevalence of plea bargaining (reducing the charge to a lesser offense) means that records are almost useless for indicating what types of acts are actually committed. Legal categories, moreover, omit almost all of the contextual information that is essential for analyzing crime as social behavior. Except for rudimentary information about the person, place, time, and victim, the data is context free and tends to be ordered for administrative purposes.

The behavior-system concept did not depart entirely from legalistic categories. Crime remained that behavior defined as such by recognized political authority. Despite the analytic attention to social context and the reactions of conventional audiences, the research focus clearly centered on the criminal and his or her act. The behavior-system notion did promote a new research direction by classifying criminal types. The typological approach identified common behavioral characteristics in order to specify the set of relationships and meanings that pattern the deviant career.

The Typological Approach to Crime

Treating the deviant as a casualty of a pathological, disorganized, or anomic structure transformed the social act into a mechanistic outcome.

"Bad blood—bad behavior," the primitive physical theory of crime, was replaced by "evil structure—evil acts" in later sociological versions of deviance theory. Behavior-system theorists, in contrast, stressed the developing social act as a series of stages that relate to situational contexts and the changing self-image of participants. Once crime is conceptualized in role-career terms, earlier notions of deviance as a uniform and permanent feature of personal identity can be discarded. Mead's view of social roles as constructed and reconstructed in the course of interaction was applied to criminal acts. In Gibbon's analysis, this meant that deviance may be episodic, as well as involving short-term or long-term commitments to illegal activity. The career line itself entails identifiable changes in different offender types:

> There are some criminal patterns in which role-performance is begun and terminated in a single illegal act, and there are others in which involvement in the deviant role continues over several decades or more, as in the instance of professional criminals. Some delinquent roles lead to adult criminality, whereas other delinquent roles are terminal ones, for they do not normally precede or lead to involvement in adult deviation . . . Then, too, some role-careers involve more changes in the component episodes of the pattern than do others. Semi-professional property offenders are one illustration. This pattern begins at the onset of minor delinquent acts in early adolescence. Such a career line frequently leads to more serious forms of delinquency with advancing age: repeated police contacts, commitment to juvenile institutions, "graduation" into adult forms of illegal activity, and more contacts with law enforcement and correction agencies. Over this lengthy developmental sequence, the social-psychological characteristics of offenders also change.[40]

This view considers social control as a major contributing factor in shaping the deviant identity.

Although not a new strategy in criminology, typologies soon became a favorite device for classifying standard research issues.[41] Whether categorizing offense behavior or offender types, the typological approach attempted to identify homogeneous patterns of deviant conduct. The notion was that, once behavior was sociologically ordered, causal, diagnostic, and treatment propositions could follow. Studies purported to make distinctions between types of crime (e.g., white-collar crimes, property crimes, petty offenses, etc.) or characteristics of offender types (e.g., Negro armed robbers, Negro drug addicts, etc.) in order to demonstrate how social backgrounds and attitudinal variations characterize different behavior systems of offenses or offender types.[42]

Clinard and Quinney's criminal typology, provides one of the most comprehensive, if eclectic, typological schemes, featuring eight types of criminal behavior. Their scheme lists violent personal crime, occasional property crime, occupational crime, political crime, public order crime, conventional crime, organized crime, and professional crime. The social control feature is only one of four elements defining the criminal role. Clinard and Quinney base their construction upon four characteristics: (1) *the criminal career of the offender*—the degree to which criminal behavior has become a part of the life organization, (2) *group support of criminal behavior*—differential association with criminal and noncriminal norms, social roles of the offender, and the integration of the offender into social groups, (3) *correspondence between criminal behavior and legitimate behavior patterns*—the degree to which the criminal behavior corresponds to the goals and means that are regarded as legitimate by dominant groups, and (4) *societal reaction*—the various forms of informal and official sanctions, such as disapproval, censure, prosecution, conviction, and sentencing. These behavior types were linked to legal categories of crime to yield the following typology of criminal behavior systems, as the chart on pages 144-145 shows.

Ordering criminal types enabled investigators to concentrate on problems of limited scope and deal with group properties of identifiable behavior units. However, the assumption that integrated behavior characterized certain types of persons and environments tended to oversimplify and overstandardize the deviant act.[44] Clinard and Quinney's approach attempted to bring together a variety of research findings to explicate the behavioral attributes and social correlates of specific offenses.

Violent Personal Crime

Murder, assault, forcible rape, and child molesting constitute the legal offenses included in the violent personal crime category. The sociological significance of this category is that, despite high public consensus on the seriousness of these crimes, offenders rarely consider themselves to be criminals. Lacking a previous criminal record and a self-announced identity as deviant, the violent offender eschews a criminal rationale for his or her deed, and may blame the victim or the circumstances instead.

Wolfgang and others assert that these violations diverge sharply from middle-class interaction patterns.[45] Suppressing aggression is a dominant norm. However, in lower-class and ethnic cultures, a "subculture of violence" may provide definitions that are favorable to the general use of aggression. As a minority life-style, violence reflects the conflict of values in a malintegrated society.

Some data suggest that acts of violence are not necessarily related to other types of crime. In a St. Louis sample of eighty-eight male offenders, investigators found that persons arrested for crimes of violence are rarely arrested for crimes against property. The reverse also holds true for property offenders.[46]

A London study of violent crime showed that the vast majority (80 percent) of those arrested for this type of offense had committed such crimes for the first time. Nearly half, however, had been convicted of petty offenses (e.g., larceny, malicious damage, drunkenness, and breaking and entering). Previous offense histories were least evident among offenders whose crimes were related to family disputes. The author concludes that "most of the crime is not committed by criminals for criminal purposes, but is rather the outcome of patterns of social behavior among certain strata of society."[47]

This, of course, states the familiar notion that the working class is the criminalistic element in society. It also perpetuates the old error of generalizing from conviction rates. Since middle-class offenders are more likely to be adjudicated through civil proceedings, or, in the case of violent crime, under psychiatric auspices, the typical characteristics or social conditions of non-lower-class offenders cannot be determined. Typologies purport to present a uniform set of attributes for specific offender types. However, most research has focused only on convicted offenders.

The subculture-of-violence hypothesis should not be rejected out of hand, but, we wish to know how never-convicted persons who share with offenders an ideology of violence (which, of course, includes police) assess the situational appropriateness of aggressive acts. Dwelling on the criminal abstracts the offender from the social context that gives the act its meaning and purpose.

Occasional Property Crime

Because the occasional property offender has little identification with law violations, the offender can successfully rationalize stealing a car, shoplifting, check forgery, or vandalism. Noncriminal in orientation, these offenders often regard themselves as adventuresome, fast, reckless, or unattached to traditional ways.[48] Social reaction, which often involves arrests and fines, is a response to violations of the values of private property; no personal injuries are involved.

The subculture thesis has little support from some of the criminal offenses within this type. For example, Cameron's data on pilferers, (noncriminal shoplifters) show them to be predominantly employees or respectable housewives. They are not in contact with deviant subcultures.[49] Their

CLASSIFICATION CHARACTERISTICS	*1* VIOLENT PERSONAL CRIME	*2* OCCASIONAL PROPERTY CRIME	*3* OCCUPATIONAL CRIME	*4* POLITICAL CRIME
Criminal Career of the Offender	LOW Crime not part of offender's career; usually does not conceive of self as criminal	LOW Little or no criminal self-concept; does not identify with crime	LOW No criminal self-concept; occasionally violates the law; part of one's legitimate work; accepts conventional values of society	LOW Usually no criminal self-concept; violates the law out of conscience; attempts to change society or correct perceived injustices; desire for a better society
Group Support of Criminal Behavior	LOW Little or no group support, offenses committed for personal reasons; some support in subcultural norms	LOW Little group support; individual offenses	MEDIUM Some groups may tolerate offenses; offender integrated in groups	HIGH Group support; association with persons of same values; behavior reinforced by group
Correspondence between Criminal Behavior and Legitimate Behavior Patterns	LOW Violation of values on life and personal safety	LOW Violation of value on private property	HIGH Behavior corresponds to pursuit of business activity; "sharp" practices respected; "buyer beware" philosophy; hands-off policy	MEDIUM Some toleration of protest and dissent, short of revolution; dissent periodically regarded as a threat (in times of national unrest)
Societal Reaction	HIGH Capital punishment; long imprisonment	MEDIUM Arrest; jail; short imprisonment, probation	LOW Indifference; monetary penalties, revocation of license to practice, seizure of product or injunction	HIGH Strong disapproval; regarded as threat to society; prison
Legal Categories of Crime	Murder, assault, forcible rape, child molesting	Some auto theft, shoplifting, check forgery, vandalism	Embezzlement, fraudulent sales, false advertising, fee splitting, violation of labor practice laws, antitrust violations, black market activity, prescription violation	Treason, sedition, espionage, sabotage, radicalism, military draft violations, war collaboration, various protests defined as criminal

FIGURE 6.2. *Typology of Criminal Behavior Systems*[43] (From *Criminal Behavior Systems: A Typology* by Marshall B. Clinard and Richard Quinney. Copyright © 1967 by Holt, Rinehart and Winston, Publishers. Reprinted by permission of Holt, Rinehart and Winston, Publishers.)

5	6	7	8
PUBLIC ORDER CRIME	**CONVENTIONAL CRIME**	**ORGANIZED CRIME**	**PROFESSIONAL CRIME**
MEDIUM	MEDIUM	HIGH	HIGH
Confused self-concept; vacillation in identification with crime	Income supplemented through crimes of gain; often a youthful activity; vacillation in self-concept; partial commitment to a criminal subculture	Crime pursued as a livelihood; criminal self-concept; progression in crime; isolation from larger society	Crime pursued as a livelihood; criminal self-concept; status in the world of crime; commitment to world of professional criminals
MEDIUM	HIGH	HIGH	HIGH
Partial support for behavior from some groups; considerable association with other offenders	Behavior supported by group norms; status achieved in groups; principal association with other offenders	Business associations in crime; behavior prescribed by the groups; integration of the person into the group	Associations primarily with other offenders; status gained in criminal offenses; behavior prescribed by group norms
MEDIUM	MEDIUM	MEDIUM	MEDIUM
Some forms required by legitimate society; some are economic activities	Consistent with goals on economic success; inconsistent with sanctity of private property; behavior not consistent with expectations of adolescence and young adulthood	Illegal services received by legitimate society; economic risk values; large-scale control also employed in legitimate society	Engaged in an occupation; skill respected; survival because of cooperation from legitimate society; law-abiding persons often accomplices
MEDIUM	HIGH	MEDIUM	MEDIUM
Arrest; jail; prison; probation	Arrest; jail; probation; institutionalization; parole; rehabilitation	Considerable public toleration; arrest and sentence when detected; often not visible to society; immunity through politicians and law officers	Rarely strong societal reaction, most cases "fixed"
Drunkenness, vagrancy, disorderly conduct, prostitution, homosexuality, gambling, traffic violation, drug addiction	Robbery, larceny, burglary, gang theft	Racketeering, organized prostitution and commercialized vice, control of drug traffic, organized gambling	Confidence games, shoplifting, pickpocketing, forgery, counterfeiting

techniques of crime are unsophisticated. Most demonstrate only vague or hearsay knowledge of criminal activities or criminal vocabularies supporting such behavior. Similarly, naive check forgers do not conceive of themselves as criminals. As Lemert points out, forgery "emerges as behavior which is out of character or 'other than usual' for the persons involved."[50] In the case of vandalism, subculture involvement is the crucial condition that leads to the deviant act. The vandal considers his or her behavior to be spontaneous, rationalizes it as part of the gang's status game, and defines the acts as "pranks."[51]

There are two difficulties that arise in the classification of criminal definitions and motives. First, to what extent does the researcher accept the offender's vocabulary of motives as the basis for deciding that there is a lack of criminal motives? Most persons respond to specific social audiences in terms of the expectations in use. What audience is the pilfering shoplifter responding to? Are vandals talking to one another when asserting their innocence, or to the police? Participant observation could disabuse the researcher of the noncriminalistic definitions associated with occasional property crime. Informal observation of college student shoplifters suggests that this form of deviance is a systematic means for "making it" in a situation of structured scarcity.[52] The gap between expectations and reality may foster the rationale that "everyone's doing it," which normalizes the act for the individual and facilitates a repetition of the criminal behavior.

Second, the notion that occasional property crime can be identified by offender types and specific offenses is probably incorrect. For example, shoplifting is also committed by the professional thief, or "booster," whose life career centers around crime. The same act may have different meanings and purposes. Wanton destruction of property may be a political act, as demonstrated by the actions of radical "weathermen" groups who blew up banks and FBI offices during the late 1960s. The classification of any specific offense in the typology often appears arbitrary. Occasional check forgery, for example, appears to fit under two rubrics, occasional property crime and occupational crime, as offenders appear to have acquired normal attitudes and habits of law observance, and are unacquainted with criminal groups. Which characteristic is defined as the crucial one (e.g., career line, social reaction, group support, or whatever) is left unspecified. If the scheme is only meant to partially organize random, heterogeneous studies, it fulfills its purpose. However, if constructed types are meant to provide a definitive set of basic groupings that inhere in social phenomena, as theorists claim, the scheme is pretentious and nonscientific.

Occupational Crime

White-collar crime (offenses conducted in the course of business or professional life by conventional, law-abiding persons) was a matter of profound concern to Sutherland. His initial work on corporate fraud initiated a sociological tradition of investigating violations by respectable persons and organizations (including embezzlement, fraudulent sales, false advertising, price fixing, fee splitting, black market activities, prescription violations, and antitrust violations).[53] Because it combines low social censure with potentially high rewards, occupational crime frequently pays, and pays well, for those willing to risk possible loss of reputation and moderate penalties.

Certain persons are more likely than others to commit these crimes. Quinney's study of prescription violations by retail pharmacists suggests that the occupational structure itself is the key to understanding which persons are most likely to violate the law.[54] The split between profession and business in the retail pharmacy occupation encourages divergent role expectations. Orientation toward the business role (e.g., by being a good businessman, handling a variety of goods, and maintaining attractive window and counter displays) tends to encourage a profit mentality that reduces identification with a professional role conception (e.g., by reading professional literature and attending professional meetings). Deviant behavior as an outcome of social structure is obvious in this case.

Other data show that, despite exorbitant financial losses to companies and the public, occupational crimes are rarely prosecuted as criminal acts. The low visibility of the offense coupled with the high social position of the offender keeps negative social reactions muted. The "conflict in cultures" which is said to generate lower-class crime and social reaction, is not evident in white-collar crime. There is no conflict in culture (or class ideology) and little or no criminalization.

By examining discriminatory sanctioning practices, Sutherland and company were verging on a political explanation of crime. Political-conflict theorists later expanded their incipient statements into a more fully political analysis of the institutional sources of crime and deviance and the consequences for the social order. In the occupational crime category, the emphasis is still on the type of offense, rather than the type of social control that may promote the deviant act. The Watergate scandals suggest that lack of public accountability and citizen participation in decision making, combined with secrecy in managing public affairs, creates a permissive, "anything goes" orientation. Attention to criminalistic social conditions, rather than to criminals and their offenses, is clearly needed here.

Political Crime

Value-conflict theorists, as we have seen, often moved in the direction of a political-conflict interpretation of crime. Criminal law, in this analysis, is an aspect of politics, one of the results of the process of formulating and administering public policy. Social values receiving the protection of criminal law are those considered important by dominant groups in the society.[55] Vold reasoned that since crime is the by-product of conflicting interpretations of proper conduct by different segments of the population, it is an aspect of political behavior. Minority views become defined and sanctioned as criminal by politically dominant groups.[56]

Most theorists, however, hedged on the notion that crime is a political act. While opting for a political crime category, they failed to push the argument one step further and examine how crime may be defined as minority opposition to the political and economic status quo. Most research failed to distinguish any special social characteristics associated with the nonconformer or ideological criminal. Investigators conceded that political offenders lack a criminal identity. They also noted that law violations tend to be rationalized in terms of achieving certain public goals. Personal and social characteristics also appear to be less crucial than the values of the offender and the value systems to which he or she is actively responding.[57] The research further found that neither SES characteristics as in ethnicity or social class nor personality features predict which persons or groups become involved in radical social movements.

This general lack of specificity in the political crime category suggests that the body of research itself is too limited to establish generalizations. Most of the studies antedate the radical social movements of the late 1960s and early 1970s. Black Power, Red Power, the student counterculture, draft resisters, feminism, gay liberation, ghetto revolts, and other political activities are now recognized as forms of political opposition by excluded social groups. Neither aberrational nor deviant, social movements and collective rebellion are politically meaningful acts in a struggle between power-holding groups and powerless ones.[58] Insipid statements about ideological criminals beg the critical question of how lack of social participation contributes to social conflict and violence among otherwise law-abiding persons. By adopting the conventional rendering of political crime as violations of the law, rather than as a form of political protest, value-conflict theorists missed the essential feature that distinguished political crime from other offenses.

Public Order Crime

Considering that well over 50 percent of all police work involves sur-veillance and control over public order[59] it would seem reasonable to devote research efforts to studying the public and legal definitions in-volved in criminalization. This is precisely what some labeling theorists attempted to do. The criminological tradition, however, has typically limited its scope to the offender and his or her career. This is obvious in studies on prostitution, homosexuals, drunks, narcotic users, gamblers, or disorderly persons.[60] The dominant legal institutions and modes of process-ing moral offenders receive short shrift in most of the literature.

This school has made several discoveries about no-victim offenders. First, the crimes-without-victims category, like the political crime cate-gory, relates to the violation of norms held sacred by dominant groups. Unlike political offenders, though, moral violators develop a counterideology and exhibit behavior learned in a deviant sub-culture. Isolation from conventional society and partial identification with criminalistic norms often typify the no-victim offender. The no-victim criminal takes the existing social order for granted, while rejecting the standard institutional routes to social recognition. Inevitably, this dual-ity in norms creates ambivalence, which is considered to be one factor contributing to the common lack of a clearly defined criminal career for these offenders. Criminalistic skills that facilitate moral passage from a conventional status to a deviant one include secrecy, rhetoric that neutral-izes criminal acts, and a supportive subculture. For example, gamblers, alcoholics, and drug users may also be spouses, parents, taxpayers, and employers. Even for those whose identity is organized mainly around the deviant role (e.g., prostitutes), negotiating with clients and other members of the straight world reduces the likelihood that offenders will maintain exclusive commitment to underworld norms.[61]

However, this no-victim category is not always logically consistent. Ross views traffic law violations as "folk crimes," a type of no-victim of-fense.[62] While there is no victim in the conventional sense, the annual death and injury toll on the highways and the damage to property make this act a highly costly one. Ross was on the right track when he classified certain violations as folk crimes, or customary offenses committed by law-abiding persons. Fornication, adultery, gambling, heavy drinking, middle-class drug use, and traffic violations may be illegal, but they are not typically viewed as crimes. The laissez-faire ethic tends to encourage a variety of departures from conventional norms, and lumping folk crimes with no-victim crimes confuses two distinct behavior types. Rather than clarifying regularities in specific criminal roles, inappropriate classification obscures the identifiable features that distinguish one type of crime from another.

Career Crimes: Conventional, Organized, and Professional Crimes

Crime as a career involves a lifetime organization of roles built around criminal activities, an identification with crime, a conception of the self as criminal, and extensive association with other criminals.[63] Three types of crime qualify for inclusion in the career category. These are conventional, organized, and professional crimes, and all involve the pursuit of crime as a livelihood, although each type displays significant differences in specific offenses, modes of social organization, and social reaction.

Conventional crime, which includes the legal categories of robbery, larceny, burglary, and gang theft, involves at least a part-time commitment to a criminal subculture and identification with success goals. Property violations often involve a progression from early juvenile gang offenses to adult crime. Behavior is said to reflect the way of life and norms of the local slum community. Probably among the least resourceful members of a criminal subculture, the conventional crime offender tends to have few skills, and lacks organized protection. Hence, the risks of apprehension, conviction, and imprisonment are high for this group. Withdrawal from crime careers usually occurs when offenders move into marriage, family responsibilities, and full-time employment. Abandonment of the criminal career, despite definitions favoring law violation, is related to a low degree of success in illegitimate pursuits.

Despite public hysteria about crime waves, perpetuated by "criminalistic elements," few slum boys take up career crime as a full-time occupation. Most juvenile offenders do not become full-time adult criminals because crime as a way of life requires technical and social skills that most lower-class youth do not possess.

Unlike conventional crime, with its high risks, organized crime typically operates with the connivance, if not the protection, of the legal establishment. A major form of invisible crime in American society, organized crime involves economic gain through a variety of illegal activities. As both a feudal system and a highly integrated business monopoly, organized crime has the following set of distinguishing structural features:

1. Hierarchical structure involving a system of specifically defined relationships with mutual obligations and privileges

2. Monopolistic control or establishment of spheres of influence among different organizations and over geographic areas
3. Dependence upon the use of force and violence to maintain internal discipline and restrain competition
4. Maintenance of permanent immunity from interference from law enforcement and other agencies of government
5. Large financial gains secured through specialization in one or more combinations of enterprises.[64]

Whether providing illegal services or controlling legitimate businesses and occupations, organized crime demonstrates how standard cultural motives of maximum returns, efficient organization, and skilled management operate for both legitimate and illegitimate business. Facing little or no public pressure to eradicate organized crime, illegal businesses flourish as long as they satisfy contraband demands that legitimate businesses are legally unable or ethically unwilling to meet. These "bastard institutions," as Hughes calls such illegitimate providers,[65] lack quality control over the product and social regulation of production. A "buyer beware" ethic warns of high risks to unprotected consumers, with costs of the operation (which include protection money, legal fees, fines, etc.) passed on to buyers.

Professional crime may include such conventional violations as robbery and burglary, but, traditionally, this category has been limited to such specialized nonviolent activities as picking pockets, shoplifting, the "booster" confidence game, pool hustling, miscellaneous rackets, and extortion. Isolated from conventional society and other types of criminals, the professional enjoys high status in the criminal world, while reaping the benefits of full-time illegal employment.[66]

In the professional "con game," law-abiding persons serve as naive accomplices, turning over their own or another's money. The victim rarely receives compensation, as the professional's survival depends on highly developed skills, support from legitimate groups, and public indifference. Criminal fraud, or swindling, appears to be a national phenomenon according to Schur, with its own game rules and prescriptions:

> All types of con games fall into a general pattern . . . The swindler
> (or swindlers, for several racketeers often band together to
> form a "con mob") selects a person who appears likely to be a
> good "sucker" (or, in the argot of the con man, "mark"). After
> establishing some degree of rapport with the mark, and once he
> sees that the mark will trust him, the con man tells the mark
> of a dishonest scheme by which they can make some money. The
> mark gives the swindler his money, which he never again sees.
> Because he has placed his confidence in the con man, it never

occurs to the mark (until it is too late) that he is the object rather than the co-perpetrator of the swindle.[67]

If fraud is the most prevalent crime in America, as Sutherland asserts,[68] there must be structural conditions that aid and abet this offense. Rivalry, coalition, and strategy, necessary elements for playing the legitimate social game, are obviously extended into alternative arenas. Focusing solely on the criminal career or interactional set, however, neglects examination of the systematic use of fraud as part of normal operating procedures in legitimate business and government circles.

The crime typology suffers from an inherent weakness. Its contrived categories include patterns that are not analytically distinct and mutually exclusive. For example, occupational and professional crime derive from common structural sources, involve low social stigma, and entail the possibility of high "pay-offs."

Social control might be a better defining characteristic for a typology. The types of regulating organizations (e.g., law enforcement agencies, occupational units, schools, civil courts, etc.) and sanctions (e.g., exclusion, fines, loss of job, jail, etc.) for different violations may indicate how different regulatory settings generate varying risk structures for crime and deviance. Carefully monitored occupations with external surveillance (e.g., elementary and secondary school teaching) may have a lower incidence of violations among members than highly autonomous ones (e.g., the medical profession). Elucidating the extent of deviance within conventional social organizations would enhance our understanding of how social control works and who it serves and who it operates against.

Situational Features in Crime and Delinquency

Some critics resisted what they considered to be the forced classification of certain types of criminal behavior. Impulsive outbursts that ended in criminal acts, crimes of passion, and noncareer violations (e.g., part-time prostitution or drug use) were not readily assimilated into a behavioral typology that viewed the career concept as essential. Sutherland's notion of the counteracting forces of contact with criminal patterns and isolation from anticriminal patterns simply does not apply to many crimes. For example, the naive check forger, unacquainted with criminal techniques and possessing conventional attitudes toward law observance, commits crime virtually as a social isolate.[69]

Cressey reluctantly admits that Sutherland's theory explains only the outcomes of association with criminal patterns, not the organizational sources generating relationships.[70] Why some persons embezzle and others commit illicit sex acts is probably unrelated to prior contacts with criminal codes. Sutherland never used an opportunity-differential risk conception that could link motives to social situations.

This opportunity-risk question invites inquiry about what deters so many persons from involvement in crime. The answer requires a situational analysis of time, place, persons, opportunities, skills, and perception of gains and costs. If deviance is defined, in Lemert's terms, as a behavioral alternative for resolution of a critical situation, the assertion that the environment produces the criminal may be qualified by delineating the types of structures and social situations likely to encourage deviant solutions. Contingencies such as unemployment, business failure, gambling losses, dishonorable discharge or desertion from the armed forces, and marital conflict all figure prominently in the case histories of naive check forgers.[71] These contingencies do not cause forgery, Lemert maintains, as others faced with similar crises do not commit crimes. They merely provide the initial conditions that isolate the person from conventional social controls and offer deviant alternatives as a way out of an untenable situation.

Furthermore, a situational analysis of deviance suggests that Sutherland's differential association hypothesis is not a necessary explanation of sources and rates of deviant behavior. The association concept is too psychologistic and nonpredictive to be very useful. For example, our commercial culture may generate institutionalized pressures to maximize status by engaging in impulse buying, whether the person can afford it or not. Some persons overindulge, then learn to avoid the lure. Others borrow from friends and loan companies until their credit runs out or bankruptcy occurs. Still others contrive to evade failure by cashing bad checks, a simple, relatively unskilled act. Why persons choose one solution over another is not dictated by contact with criminal codes that define the situation in advance. Even though all may face impending financial disaster, it does not follow that all will choose the deviant alternative.

The element of choice, almost totally neglected by Sutherland and the behavior-system advocates, is crucial for understanding both legitimate and illegitimate social acts. The choice concept need not become an over-rational view of behavior which assumes all acts to be motivated and planned, and does not have to include the mechanistic notion of standardized behavioral outcomes learned in social interaction. Choice implies opportunity and the (not necessarily conscious) weighing of alternatives in terms of a specific situation.

Considering that differential association theory has dominated the criminological field, it is amazing that it has remained so conceptually restricted. Despite Cressey's efforts to refine the propositions and extend the scope of the theory, it is limited to explaining how the principle of normative conflict works (lack of value consistency encourages alternative life-styles and behavior). It certainly does elevate the level of explanatory discourse far above Merton's cultural homogeneity thesis, but, as an explanation of crime rates, this theory cannot overcome the same conceptual barrier that besets the anomie formulation. Crime rates are not a function of the incidence or prevalence of criminal activities. They reflect the negotiations and decision-making activities of agencies concerned primarily with their own organizational survival, rather than with precise evaluations of law enforcement work.

Victimology

One interesting, if often conceptually distorted, extension of the criminal behavior-system idea is the recognition of the victim as a necessary element in the total set of criminal relationships. The focus on identifying the criminal (a central concern of Tappan in his rejection of traditional legal definitions[72]) is shifted, and identifying the victim becomes most important, including how he or she figures in, initiates, or facilitates the criminal act.

In victimology, a subdiscipline of criminology, victims are the main targets of study.[73] Understanding victim-offender relationships, investigating the victim's share in responsibility for the crime, using victim-survey reports to assess the total amount of crime committed, and examining the possibilities for compensating victims of violent crimes are typical areas of concern.

Victimization studies demonstrate that police-reported crimes reflect only the tip of the iceberg in criminal statistics. The difference between victim-reported crime and police reporting of these same crimes is often remarkable. Victims indicate that rates of robbery, assault, forcible rape, and burglary are two to five times higher than the numbers turned in by police.[74] The general failure to report crime is a function of citizen reaction to police ineptitude in the face of rising urban crime rates, as well as of the victim's resistance to official harrassment and lack of efficient judicial processing of reported crimes.[75]

Victimology studies often turn the crime causation argument on its head, adopting an ingenious, if somewhat absurd, approach. It is an ironic turnabout that the victim is identified as the culprit in this fine art of blaming the victim.[76] "In a sense, the victim shapes and molds the criminal," one writer says.[77] "In a way, the victim is always the *cause* of the crime," another asserts.[78] Stereotyping the victim as inferior diminishes the seriousness of the deviant act. In extreme cases, fabricating victim-damning stories may neutralize atrocities by justifying the victimization, as the following example indicates:

> After the National Guard killed four students at Kent State,
> several rumors quickly spread: the slain girls were pregnant, so
> their deaths spared their families from shame; the students
> were filthy and had lice on them. These rumors were totally
> untrue, but the townspeople were eager to believe them.[79]

The stereotype of the deserving victim is most obvious in notions about rape.[80] Popular literature and films depict the male success story, from the female's initial struggle to her acquiescence and enjoyment of the act. No distinction is made between seduction and violent rape. The reputed "rape wish" of women "precipitates" sexual attacks, thus legitimating women's victimization.

Scientific studies often reinforce these public stereotypes by reducing the assault scene to the foreplay tussle between a resisting (if unconsciously consenting) woman and a forcibly persuasive man. It is said that the woman who claims rape really suffers from ambivalence about her own motives or from memory falsification:

> Even the woman who is quite sane but who is possessed of strong
> guilt feelings, may convince herself in retrospect that her own
> conduct was really blameless and that she was forced. This
> conviction is the more easily arrived at because it is quite likely
> that her conscious response at the time could not accurately
> be labeled either as consent or non-consent. There may have been
> an ambivalent and confused mixture of desire and fear, neither of
> which was clearly dominant. Most women want their lovers to
> be at least somewhat aggressive and dominating. Some conscious-
> ly or unconsciously want to be forced. Their erotic pleasure is
> stimulated by preliminary love-play involving physical struggle,
> slapping, scratching, pinching, and biting. The struggle also
> saves face for the girl who fears she would be considered "loose"
> if she yielded without due maidenly resistance; it also relieves that
> guilt feeling that might exist if she could not tell herself that
> "he made me do it." Many of the wrestling matches in parked
> cars come within this category.[81]

Courts are reluctant to recognize the woman's claim, in part because of the extremely high penalties associated with rape convictions, but also because of problems in obtaining evidence. For the offender, the use of the rape myth that "every woman really wants it" serves to expiate guilt and escape prosecution. In the rape trial these stereotypes operate against the woman. Evidence against the victim includes her sexual fantasies, her moral character, and her "precipitous" behavior. The burden-of-proof argument is traditionally resolved by requiring the woman to demonstrate her innocence.[82]

Despite the difference in emphasis on criminal and victim, criminology and victimology may converge and demonstrate many commonalities. Both are individual oriented, concerned with attributing cause and moral responsibility to the persons involved in the crime. Both take the perspective of the offender, focusing on factors that affect his or her behavior, thus reducing the offender's culpability. Finally, both are preoccupied with mobilizing public and police forces to fight crime, rather than with the social conditions that foster criminal behavior.

METHOD

Constructing Homogeneous Types

The typological method moved criminological research away from a bits-and-pieces approach toward developing a uniform frame of reference. While not itself a predictive device, the typology parsimoniously orders and describes data from which predictive statements may be generated.

While recognizing its methodological advantages, proponents also acknowledge its limitations. These may be summarized as follows:

(1) Typologies are rarely unidimensional. The choice of characteristics used in constructing types is often arbitrary, depending less on general theory than on decisions about variables and measurements that appear to be associated with crime.

(2) Typologies are never exhaustive. Increasing the number of categories to embrace all types of crimes could make the scheme unwieldy. Because classifications shift with theoretical or popular trends, any attempt to classify must be seen as incomplete.

(3) The assumption of homogeneity of types often contradicts empirical evidence. Apparent similarities and convergences in behavior may be artifacts of the classification scheme.

(4) The theoretical link between offense type and behavior system is often fallacious. Deviant behavior may be a highly variable act within any specific offense category, or the same act may fit a number of different categories.

(6) Typologies are only as useful as the purposes they are designed to serve. Without a theoretical guide to determine

significant characteristics, they are relatively meaningless
exercises. Also, as paradigms change, the set of characteristics deemed theoretically significant changes.[83]

The typological device is clearly no methodological panacea. It is only
as useful as the investigator's selection of theory, concepts, and research
findings, which determines how evidence will be presented and the purpose of the constructed types. The misguided notion that typologies demonstrate cause of specific behavior patterns should be laid to rest. Essentially an ordering and describing tool in Weber's analysis, typologies
utilize theoretical concepts:

> as ideal limiting cases—the various possible combinations of these
> could only be hinted at here; they are pure mental constructs,
> the relationships of which to the empirical reality of the
> immediately given is problematical in every individual case.[84]

While typologies attracted many criminologists who were attempting
to clear away the debris of the discipline, other researchers sought theoretical coherence by using analytic induction. This method attempts to establish causal propositions that must be stated as universals (i.e., the propositions refer to all the cases under consideration), rather than as the
customary probability statements (i.e., the propositions refer to some of
the cases under consideration). Analytic induction involves, first, examining individual cases to formulate generalizations that hold true for all the
instances under investigation, and, second, using each negative case (i.e.,
one that does not fit the pattern) to revise or reject the generalizations.[85]

Lindesmith's research on opiate addiction provides an illustration of
this method.[86] He began his study with the tentative hypothesis that individuals who did not know what drug they were using would not become
addicted and individuals who knew what they were taking would become
addicted if they had taken the drug long enough to experience withdrawal
distress when they stopped using it. This hypothesis had to be rejected
after one physician reported that he had once knowingly received
morphine, but had not become addicted. Lindesmith then revised the
hypothesis to limit his definition of addiction to the self-conscious recognition of withdrawal distress, with drugs used primarily to alleviate this
distress.

Other research has challenged this generalization. The use of drugs
primarily for their euphoric effect appears to be a common pattern among
addicts. Avoidance of the withdrawal symptoms may be linked to regular
use, but a large proportion of street addicts become addicted by seeking

kicks.[87] It is not clear whether research proves or disproves Lindesmith's addiction theory, which is a disadvantage of using the analytic induction method. Data drawn from different samples yield different results. Street addicts may differ from incarcerated ones. The behavior-system analysts realize that motives are situationally defined, but their research often ignores the situational component.

Handling negative cases in this method can be difficult. If they are thrown out, the theory is hardly credible. However, if the theory is revised to include all negative findings, the propositions may become simplistic and commonsensical. There are no methodological guides for determining the point at which the investigator stops collecting counterevidence. Finally, the emphasis on qualitative propositions of a universal nature creates problems when the processes studied are continuous variables (e.g., age, occupation, length of time in the deviant career) that are exhibited only in degree. Age, opportunity, and cost assessments, among other factors, vary widely for different actors in the deviant situation. Reducing the generalizations in order to fit them to all possible cases may eliminate much that is theoretically significant and diagnostically valuable.

Analytic induction reputedly identifies causal factors useful for predicting who would be likely to deviate in a particular situation, who would not, and under what conditions deviation occurs. However, the method, as Lindesmith and others use it, is confined to the behavior of persons who have been socially defined as deviant. This implies that generalizations established by such studies are limited to those persons who have been processed by social control agencies. Until more samples are drawn from never-labeled offenders, we should remain skeptical of these studies's claims to have established causal propositions.

Deviance, like other social conduct, may not be as homogeneous as most theorists assert. The criminologist continues to add a greater variety of methods to his or her research toolbox, but the concepts often remain impoverished and ill equipped for handling deviant phenomena. One of the more major shortcomings of the field is its almost total neglect of the potential and actual applications of its theory and research. For example, drug abuse research produces methadone treatment programs for lower-class addicts, insuring that they will remain addicted and under the direct control of government agencies. Whether taking the side of the police, offender, victim, or outraged public, criminologists rarely examine their ideological positions for the possible effects these may have on the perpetuation of discriminatory legal and social arrangements.

Conclusion

The value-conflict paradigm reflects both continuities and discontinuities in deviance theory. In the Chicago School tradition, the theory focuses on normative conflicts arising out of different ethnic, social, or community traditions. Cultural enclaves transmit diverse values from one generation to another, thus perpetuating cultural differences.

Sutherland's differential association theory was a marked advance over the cultural transmission notion. It emphasizes that, while interaction with deviants and deviant codes may be necessary for the movement into deviance, interaction alone is not a sufficient condition for deviance. The quality of interaction (duration, priority, and intensity of contacts) must also be taken into account. Sutherland also stated that conventional and deviant codes exist side by side in the community. Conflict in norms arises out of the normal social arrangements that characterize a differentiated, competitive society.

However, like earlier paradigms in deviance theory, the value-conflict perspective generated a largely atheoretical research program which was committed primarily to studies of offenders. The behavior-system analysis, using the typological method, sought to identify homogeneous offender types by describing and classifying criminal skills, codes, and career characteristics. Some investigators employed negative cases to transform intensive descriptions of deviant motives into generalizations that supposedly held true across time, place, and persons. The studies failed, however, to identify the necessary and sufficient conditions for deviant choices. Problems of sampling and evidence continued to limit criminological findings to visible offenders, those caught in the social control net.

The search for the ultimate causes and nature of criminal behavior was rejected by the labeling school, my next theoretical concern. Identifying with offenders (whom they viewed as victimized outsiders), labeling proponents expressed a strong ideological and methodological preference for small-scale research on deviant populations. The value-conflict premise that deviance is created by law and social control provided the starting point for the analysis of social reaction and its consequences for a deviant identity.

NOTES

1. Albert Cohen, Alfred Lindesmith, and Karl Schuess, eds., *The Sutherland Papers* (Bloomington: Indiana University Press, 1956), pp. 103, 108.

2. Robert K. Merton, "Social Conflict Over Styles of Sociological Work," in *The Sociology of Sociology,* ed. Larry T. Reynolds and Janice M. Reynolds (New

York: David McKay Company, Inc., 1970), pp. 172-197.

3. Robert Merton points out that sociologists tend to develop their own "systems of sociology" which are typically "laid out as competing systems of thought rather than consolidated into a cumulative product." Robert K. Merton, *On Theoretical Sociology* (New York: The Free Press, 1967), p. 23.

4. Leonard Lieberman has applied the sociology-of-knowledge approach to the study of race in "The Debate over Race: A Study in the Sociology of Knowledge," in *The Sociology of Sociology,* p. 393. Robert K. Merton has formulated an early, and a more complex, paradigm for the sociology of knowledge in *Social Theory and Social Structure* (New York: The Free Press, 1957), pp. 456-488.

5. Edwin H. Sutherland, *Criminology* (Philadelphia: J. B. Lippincott Company, 1924). The book has subsequently been revised as *Principles of Criminology* with Donald R. Cressey, coauthor since the 5th edition (1955). The text is presently in its 9th edition (1974).

6. Ibid., p. 16.

7. John Horton, "Order and Conflict Theories of Social Problems as Competing Ideologies," *American Journal of Sociology* 71 (May 1966): 701-713.

8. Georg Simmel, *Conflict and the Web of Group Affiliation,* trans. Kurt H. Wolff (Glencoe, Ill.: The Free Press, 1956) and T. B. Bottomore and M. Rubel, eds., *Karl Marx, Selected Writings in Sociology and Social Philosophy* (London: Watts, 1956). For an overview of contrasting images of social conflict theory, see Jonathan H. Turner, *The Structure of Sociological Theory* (Homewood, Ill.: The Dorsey Press, 1974), part II.

9. George B. Vold, *Theoretical Criminology* (New York: Oxford University Press, 1958), p. 10.

10. Lewis A. Coser, *The Functions of Social Conflict* (London: Free Press, 1956).

11. Ralf Dahrendorf, "Toward a Theory of Social Conflict," *Journal of Conflict Resolution* 2 (June 1958): 170-183 and idem, *Class and Class Conflict in Industrial Society* (Stanford: Stanford University Press, 1959).

12. Cohen et al. note that Sutherland greatly elaborated the relatively crude culture-conflict idea in his effort to seek a basic principle for crime causation.

13. Ibid., p. 16.

14. Cohen et al., *The Sutherland Papers,* p. 103.

15. Ibid., p. 104.

16. Vold, of all the early value-conflict theorists, provided the most explicit statement of the importance of viewing crime and law as social definitions.

17. Cohen et al., *The Sutherland Papers,* p. 105.

18. Ibid., pp. 117-118.

19. Cohen et al., *The Sutherland Papers,* p. 32.

20. Edwin H. Sutherland, *White Collar Crime* (New York: Dryden Press, 1949).

21. Edwin H. Sutherland and Donald R. Cressey, *Principles of Criminology,* 5th ed. (Philadelphia: Lippincott, 1955), p. 78.

22. Ibid., pp. 77-79.

23. James F. Short, Jr. has tested the differential association theory in: "Differential Association and Delinquency," *Social Problems* 4 (January 1957): 233-239; idem, "Differential Association, Delinquency, and Self-Conception Among a Group of Institutionalized Delinquents," paper delivered at the annual meeting of the American Sociological Society, September 1956; idem. "Differential Association with Delinquent Friends and Delinquent Behavior," *Pacific Sociological Review* 1 (Spring 1958): 20-25; and idem, "Differential Association as a Hypothesis: Problems of Empirical Testing," *Social Problems* 8 (Summer 1960): 14-25. Short concludes that, by and large, research bearing on the differential association hypothesis provides only an extremely limited application of a very broadly conceived principle.

24. By 1960, Cressey had collected a 70-item bibliography on the theory: see E. H. Sutherland and D. R. Cressey, *Principles of Criminology,* 6th edition, p. vi. He has also presented a review of criticisms and attempted reformulations of the theory. Donald R. Cressey, "Epidemiology and Individual Conduct: A Case from Criminology," *Pacific Sociological Review* 3 (Fall 1960): 47-58; idem, "The Theory of Differential Association: An Introduction," *Social Problems* 8 (Summer 1960): 2-5.

25. David Matza, *Becoming Deviant* (Englewood Cliffs, N.J.: Prentice-Hall, 1969), p. 107.

26. Daniel Glaser, "Criminality Theory and Behavioral Images," *American Journal of Sociology* 61 (1956): 433-434.

27. Stephen Box, *Deviance, Reality and Society* (New York: Holt, Rinehart and Winston, 1971), p. 156.

28. David Matza, *Delinquency and Drift* (New York: John C. Wiley and Sons, 1964).

29. G. M. Sykes and D. Matza, "Techniques of Neutralization: A Theory of Delinquency," *American Sociological Review* 22 (December): 664-670.

30. Ibid., p. 666.

31. Robert L. Burgess and Ronald L. Akers attempt to translate the differential association theory into a version of behavior theory adopted from B. F. Skinner in "Differential Association and Modern Behavior Theory," *Social Problems* 14 (Fall 1966): 128-147. This behavioristic revision has been attacked for its "fundamental theoretical illiteracy" by Ian Taylor, Paul Walton, and Jock Young, *The New Criminology* (London and Boston: Routledge and Kegan Paul, 1973), p. 131.

32. Richard C. Fuller and Richard C. Myers, "Some Aspects of a Theory of Social Problems," *American Sociological Review* (February 1941): 27-32.

33. See Thorsten Sellin's discussion in "The Negro Criminal," *Annals* 52 (1928): 40 and *Culture Conflict and Crime,* bulletin 41 (New York: Social Science Research Council, 1938).

34. Willard Waller, "Social Problems and the Mores," *American Sociological Review* 1 (December 1936): 924-933.

35. Austin T. Turk, "Conflict and Criminality," *American Sociological Review* 31 (June 1966): 338-352.

36. Vold, *Theoretical Criminology,* p. 261.

37. Edwin H. Sutherland, *The Professional Thief* (Chicago: University of Chicago Press, 1937).

38. Marshall B. Clinard, "Criminological Research," in *Sociology Today,* ed. R. K. Merton, L. Broom, L. S. Cottrell (New York: Harper Torchbooks, 1959), p. 526.

39. An analysis of the criteria of crime from the legal point of view is found in Jerome Hall, "Prolegomena to a Science of Criminal Law," *University of Pennsylvania Law Review* LXXXIX (1941): 549-580.

40. Don C. Gibbons, *Changing the Lawbreaker: The Treatment of Delinquents and Criminals* (Englewood Cliffs, N.J.: Prentice-Hall, Inc., 1965), pp. 51-52.

41. For a discussion of the status of typological assertions and some defects of these arguments, see Don C. Gibbons and Donald L. Garrity, "Some Suggestions for the Development of Etiological and Treatment Theory in Criminology," *Social Forces* 38 (October 1959): 51-58.

42. Representative studies of offender types include, for example, D. C. Gibbons and D. L. Garrity, "Definition and Analysis of Certain Criminal Types," *Journal of Criminal Law, Criminology and Police Science* 53 (March 1962): 27-35 and Julian B. Roebuck and Mervyn L. Cadwallader, "The Negro Armed Robber as a Criminal Type: The Construction and Application of a Typology," *Pacific Sociological Review* 4 (Spring 1961): 21-26.

43. Marshall B. Clinard and Richard Quinney, *Criminal Behavior Systems: A Typology* (New York: Holt, Rinehart and Winston, Inc., 1967), 16-17.

44. Bloch, for instance, claims that a typology of crime and delinquency aims to classify "integrated behavior-forms which characterize certain types of *criminally-prone* individuals," (italics added). Such an assertion betrays an underlying fallacy in types, i.e., reinforcing lay and official stereotypes regarding so-called inherent criminalistic personalities. See Herbert A. Bloch, "Crime Causation: Research and Its Application." *Federal Probation* 21 (1957): 19.

45. Marvin E. Wolfgang, *Patterns in Criminal Homicide* (Philadelphia: University of Pennsylvania Press, 1958).

46. David J. Pittman and William Handy, "Patterns in Criminal Aggravated Assault," *Journal of Criminal Law, Criminology and Police Science* 55 (December 1964): 462-470.

47. F. H. McClintock, *Crimes of Violence* (New York: St. Martin's Press, Inc., 1963), p. 57.

48. Marshall B. Clinard, "Rural Criminal Offenders," *American Journal of Sociology* 50 (July 1944): 38-45.

49. Mary Owen Cameron, *The Booster and the Snitch: Department Store Shoplifting* (New York: The Free Press of Glencoe, 1964).

50. Edwin M. Lemert, "An Isolation and Closure Theory of Naive Check Forgery," *Journal of Criminal Law, Criminology and Police Science* 44 (1953): 296-307.

51. Andrew L. Wade, "Social Processes in the Act of Juvenile Vandalism," in *Criminal Behavior Systems: A Typology*, pp. 94-109.

52. In interviews with undergraduate students of a Social Problems class at Central Michigan University.

53. White-collar crime has been analyzed by: Gilbert Geis, "White Collar Crime: The Heavy Electrical Equipment Antitrust Cases of 1961," in *Criminal Behavior Systems: A Typology*, pp. 139-151; Marshall B. Clinard, *The Black Market* (New York: Holt, Rinehart and Winston, Inc., 1952); and Donald R. Cressey, "The Criminal Violation of Financial Trust," *American Sociological Review* 15 (December 1950): 738-743.

54. Richard Quinney, "Occupational Structure and Criminal Behavior: Prescription Violation by Retail Pharmacists," *Social Problems* 11 (Fall 1963): 179-185.

55. Sellin, *Culture Conflict and Crime*, chap. 2.

56. George B. Vold, "Some Basic Problems of Criminological Research," *Federal Probation* 17 (March 1953): 40.

57. A summary and review of the literature on political crime is found in *Criminal Behavior Systems: A Typology*, pp. 177-189.

58. The politics of violence is discussed in Joe R. Feagin and Harlan Hahn, *Ghetto Revolts* (New York: Macmillan Publishing Co., Inc., 1973).

59. Jonathan H. Turner, *American Society: Problems of Structure* (New York: Harper & Row, 1972), p. 145.

60. For an alternative approach, see Edwin M. Schur, *Crimes Without Victims* (Englewood Cliffs, N.J.: Prentice-Hall, 1965).

61. See, for example, James H. Bryan, "Apprenticeships in Prostitution," *Social Problems* 12 (Winter 1965): 287-297.

62. H. Lawrence Ross, "Traffic Law Violation: A Folk Crime," *Social Problems* 8 (Winter 1960-61): 231-241.

63. Marshall B. Clinard, *Sociology of Deviant Behavior*, rev. ed. (New York: Holt, Rinehart and Winston, Inc., 1963), p. 210.

64. Clinard and Quinney, *Criminal Behavior Systems: A Typology*, p. 383; see, also, Edwin M. Schur in *The Crime Establishment: Organized Crime and American Society*, ed. John E. Conklin (Englewood Cliffs, N.J.: Prentice-Hall, 1973).

65. Everett C. Hughes, *The Sociological Eye: Selected Papers* (Chicago: Aldine-Atherton, 1972), chaps. 1, 2, and 10.

66. Professional crime is reviewed in Clinard and Quinney, *Criminal Behavior Systems: A Typology*, pp. 428-437.

67. Edwin M. Schur, "Sociological Analysis of Confidence Swindling," *Journal of Criminal Law, Criminology, and Police Science* 48 (September-October 1957): 296-304.

68. Sutherland and Cressey, 5th ed. *Principles of Criminology*, p. 42.

69. Lemert, "An Isolation and Closure Theory of Naive Check Forgery."

70. Sutherland and Cressey, *Principles of Criminology*, 7th ed. (Philadelphia: Lippincott, 1966), pp. 82-83.

71. Lemert, "An Isolation and Closure Theory of Naive Check Forgery."

72. Paul W. Tappan, "Who is the Criminal?", *American Sociological Review* 12 (February 1947): 96-102.

73. A historical analysis of the field of victimology is offered by B. Mendelsohn, "The Origin of the Doctrine of Victimology," *Excerpta Criminologica*: 239-244. The idea of the victim as *initiating* the crime has been applied to homicide by Marvin E. Wolfgang, "Victim-Precipitated Criminal Homicide," *Journal of Criminal Law, Criminology and Police Science* 48 (May-June 1957): 1-11.

74. *The New York Times* (April 15, 1974) recently compared crime victimization rates in 13 selected cities (1972 data). The report concluded that the ratio of unreported crime to reported crimes varies from a low of 1.5 to 1 (St. Louis) to 5.1 to 1 (Philadelphia).

75. This is discussed in Phillip H. Ennis, "Estimates of Crime from Victim

Survey Research," in *Criminal Behavior and Social Systems,* ed. Anthony L. Guenther (Chicago: Rand McNally and Company, 1970), pp. 123-148.

76. Stephen Schafer, *The Victim and His Criminal: A Study in Functional Responsibility* (New York: Random House, 1968).

77. Hans von Hentig, *The Criminal and His Victim: Studies in the Sociobiology of Crime* (New Haven: Yale University Press, 1948), p. 384.

78. Menachem Amir, *Patterns in Forcible Rape* (Chicago: The University of Chicago Press, 1971), p. 258. Amir's victim-causation argument is borrowed from Wolfgang whose study of homicide clearly demonstrates how victims often precipitate their own death by aggressive threats or acts, provoking a violent counterresponse.

79. Elliot Aronson, "The Rationalizing Animal," *Psychology Today* (May 1973): 493.

80. Kurt Weis and Sandra S. Borges, "Victimology and Rape: The Case of the Legitimate Victim," *Issues in Criminology* 8 (Fall 1973): 71-115. See, also, Curtis who refutes the guilty rape victim notion on grounds that inferences drawn from police reports are not valid; no reliable evidence exists that shows victims of rape lie more than victims of robbery or other violent crimes; and recent data that reports low percentages of precipitation for all-black contexts (where the majority of rapes are reported) from national surveys and participant observation studies. Lynn A. Curtis, "Victim Precipitation and Violent Crime," *Social Problems* 21 (April 1974): 594-605.

81. Henry Weihofen, "Victims of Criminal Violence," *Journal of Public Law* 8 (1959): 210.

82. The Michigan House Judiciary Committee is considering a proposal to change the rape offense to sexual assault. Proponents believe this revision would greatly enhance enforceability. Thus far, however, legislators have held out for *inclusion* of the woman's sexual history as evidence in court, a blatant victim-blaming strategy (June 1974).

83. Clinard and Quinney, *Criminal Behavior Systems: A Typology,* p. 13 reviews certain problems connected with underlying principles in the construction of criminal typologies.

84. Max Weber, "Ideal Types and Theory Construction," in *Readings in the Philosophy of the Social Sciences,* ed. May Brodbeck (Toronto, Ontario: The Macmillan Company, 1968), p. 507.

85. Norman K. Denzin, *The Research Act: A Theoretical Introduction to Sociological Methods* (Chicago: Aldine Publishing Company, 1970), pp. 195-199.

86. Alfred R. Lindesmith, *Opiate Addiction* (Bloomington, Ind.: Principia Press, 1947).

87. William E. McAuliffe and Robert Gordon, "A Test of Lindesmith's Theory of Addiction: The Frequency of Euphoria Among Long Term Addicts," *American Journal of Sociology* 74, no. 4 (January, 1974): 798-840.

7

Sociological Outsiders' View of
Insiders' Deviant Identities

LABELING THEORY

> In the course of our work and for who knows what private
> reasons, we fall into deep sympathy with the people we are study-
> ing, so that while the rest of the society views them as unfit in
> one or another respect for the deference ordinarily accorded a
> fellow citizen, we believe that they are at least as good as anyone
> else, more sinned against than sinning. Because of this we do not
> give a balanced picture. We focus too much on questions
> whose answers show that the supposed deviant is morally in the
> right and the ordinary citizen morally in the wrong. We neglect to
> ask those questions whose answers would show that the deviant,
> after all, has done something pretty rotten and, indeed, pretty
> much deserves what he gets. In consequence, our overall assess-
> ment of the problem being studied is one-sided. What we
> produce is a whitewash of the deviant and a condemnation, if
> only by implication, of those respectable citizens, who, we think,
> have made the deviant what he is. (Howard S. Becker, "Whose
> Side Are We On?"[1])

Accusations of bias in social science research occur when conflicts
over styles of work become conflicts over political commitments. Whose
perspective is taken into account (the official morality or the deviant
viewpoint) becomes a political concern, arousing anxiety for the profession and challenging conventional judgments of citizens and official caretakers. Becker uses the notion of a "hierarchy of credibility" to understand
this phenomenon.[2]

In a system of ranked groups, superordinate parties are assumed to
have the right to define reality. Because those at the top supposedly have
access to a more complete picture of events (information flows are said
to move down the scale from top-to-bottom rankers), their account of the
organization's workings is usually regarded as the most credible one. Un-

derdogs, however, may be studied, their complaints may be listed, and their grievances may be reviewed, but they lack the right to challenge statements of responsible officials. Credibility and the right to be heard, Becker observes, are differentially distributed throughout the ranks of the system.

As long as sociologists took the prevailing social order for granted, the issue of "sides" was neither relevant nor essential. Academia and politics were believed to be separate and distinct entities. Sociologists were expected to debate the merits of theoretical propositions or methodological approaches without fear of professional reprisals or accusations of bias. The intellectual orthodoxies of democracy, rationality, pluralism, reform, and the blessings of an educated populace dominated the field. An occasional voice from the wilderness might question: knowledge for what?[3] But few heeded the message. Like naive explorers traveling in a new terrain, sociologists remained overwhelmed at how far they had come, and disregarded how little they really understood where they had been.

Once a perspective is reversed, however, with statements of reality taken from persons discredited by conventional morality, and used against the claims and interests of superordinates, in-house charges of bias and treason against objectivity split the field into opposing political camps. Other recriminations follow, with both sides charging the other of professional and moral culpability. Sociology becomes ideology; research becomes special pleading; academics become politicos; professors become hard-line careerists. As for those newly converted it is perhaps in the nature of conversions that former truths appear to be egregious errors, and the new reality, screened through different philosophical and political lenses, takes on a unity and validity that denies the old one.

Labeling analysts reversed the commonsense conception of crime and deviant behavior, designating deviants as more deserving (or at least as credible) as those who condemned them as outcasts. Turning away from the sociological preoccupation with the problem of maintaining social order, labeling theorists studied the problems deviants have with this order. Rejecting formalistic sociology (exemplified by functional theory), and throwing aside the positivistic doctrines and bureaucratic apparatuses that supported traditional treatment of deviants, theorists identified with underdogs as the new truthsayers.

Concern with how society, through its social control agents, negatively reacts to and victimizes moral offenders, lower classes, and minorities provoked a different set of research issues and methods. Predominantly focusing on micro-sociological happenings and interactions, labeling theorists developed mastery of small-scale research on outsider populations.

Getting where the action is required intensive observation, often direct participation, in the underworld life. By taking the outsiders' role, deviance researchers charted the contradictions in the conventional rules that granted controllers the power to reject and punish the troublesome and denied the controlled any effective opportunity to determine their moral careers. In an indirect fashion, labelers indicted conventional society as the evils of the system became known and accounted for by their attention to the inhumane and arbitrary treatment accorded deviants.

Attention to victims, rather than victimizers, however, tended to decontextualize deviant events. Abstracted out of a historical or structural framework, deviance was reduced to a simplistic formula: social control produces deviant careers. The strength of the labeling formulation is apparent in its revised version of social order as itself problematic. Its weakness is its failure to specify conditions under which official labeling works. Its underdog ideology closes off all questions, but one: how does social control escalate the devalued identity into a deviant career? A brief outline of the labeling perspective follows in Figure 7.1.

I.	Social-Professional Conditions	Liberal reaction to bureaucratic state; counter-intellectual tradition; humanistic orientation; identification with underdog as victim; debunking of establishment institutions and sociologies; rejection of formalistic, structural sociology; alternative professional ideologies.
II.	Perspective	Secondary deviation; social control leads to a deviant identity; i.e., deviance a product of negative reaction by social audiences (usually formal control agents); moral entrepreneurs create rules against the interests of underdogs; rule breaking common; social change inevitable.
III.	Metaphor	"Stigma"—defining, isolating, and punishing the rule breaker creates and perpetuates the deviant identity.
IV.	Themes	Collective rule making; social reactors; deviant careers.
V.	Method	Ethnography, participant observation; *Verstehen* or understanding.

FIGURE 7.1.   *Labeling Paradigm*

SOCIAL AND PROFESSIONAL CONDITIONS

Sociological Populism and the Debunking Tradition

In the larger intellectual tradition of sociology, exemplified by European classicism and the Chicago School, social criticism provided an integral tool for examining public values and institutions. Frequently opposing social trends, early social scientists pointed out the flaws and slippages in the structure that generated social dislocations and personal breakdowns. When the drive toward professionalism and social accommodation began, however, this polemic was all but silenced. Value neutrality and technical expertise replaced the older ethos. Sociology, as a science, supposedly thrived on an intellectual diet restricted to traditional morality, status quo social arrangements, and methodological critiques.

Beneath the apparently placid surface of the uncommitted professional stance, an underground culture of sociology, the forerunner of labeling theory, flourished. The emergence of what Gouldner calls "Young Turk Movements"[4] occurred initially in response to the depression and later to the social crises of the 1960s (e.g., poverty, race problems, cold-war normalcy and the civil rights struggle). These movements found scholarly outlets in such new associations as the Society for the Psychological Study of Social Issues (SPSSI) and the Society for the Study of Social Problems (SSSP). By reviving a humanistic tradition and promoting value-related issues, this underground movement opened up the possibility of a committed sociology that could generate an ethical sensitivity to injustice, repudiate inequalities, and propose radical public policies for a brave new world.

These dissenters were caught between the conflicting roles of detached scientist and committed citizen, and became politically strangled by their disenchantment with the status quo and their inability to accept the utopian myths that nurture revolution. They finally resolved this ethical and political conflict by a type of proletariat "cool," remaining occupationally secure in the academic world, while staying detached from its middle-class images and moralistic compulsions.

Early labeling proponents adopted a counterintellectual tradition; a critical, antitechnical posture animated much of their work, serving as a means of escaping what some asserted was the bureaucratic oppression of the age and opening up what others considered to be musty intellectual closets filled with theoretical and research debris. Like some intellectuals in the 1930s who identified with the oppressed working class, labelers took on the deviant's plight as their own.

The debunking strategy romanticizes social rejects and attacks cultural stereotypes. By adopting an "unconventional sentimentality," to use Becker's term,[5] these sociological rebels turn conventional wisdom on its head. Like the followers of the Jacksonian Populist movement in American politics,[6] they scorned bureaucratic expertise, repudiated elites' definitions of social order, and castigated the control apparatus as degrading and dehumanizing. Unfortunately, the evidence for these charges was often sketchy and poorly conceived.

Theirs is not a dogmatic egalitarianism, however. On the contrary, the urban-liberal experience and reformer impulses that influenced labeling thinkers are based on a keen awareness of the complex realities of organized life. They recognize that organizational routines befuddle purposeful collective action for elites as well as underdogs. Their plea is for working out social meanings and symbols that link disparate ranks and are more than public relations devices. Becker and other labeling analysts express a liberal sentiment in their concern with the gap between myth and practice in social life, contending that this situation undermines institutions and increases conflict and alienation. The social-problems-reformer spirit is evident, despite their counterintellectual protests. Becker shifts allegiances and becomes the partisan for professional elites, as when he advises that:

> Professional education tends to build curricula and programs in
> ways suggested by the symbol and so fails to prepare its
> students for the world they will have to work in. Educators might
> perform a great service by working out a symbol more closely
> related to the realities of work life practitioners confront, a
> symbol which could provide an intelligible and workable moral
> guide in problematic situations.[7]

Perhaps debunkers, as younger, untenured, usually unpublished academics, express the frustrations of a marginal class. Once established, they allow moral concerns to take precedence over muckraking efforts. At every stage of their personal careers, however, these Chicago-trained labeling advocates incorporate a dual tradition. One is the adherence to what Horowitz calls the "occupationalist" orientation, characterized by an irreverence for authority and established tradition, a pragmatic view of academic roles, a basically unstructured image of reality, and an emphasis on criticism.[8] The other tradition is the naturalistic attraction to the underlife of modern society, which Gouldner refers to as the "hip" style:

> This group of Chicagoans finds itself at home in the world of hip,
> Norman Mailer, drug addicts, jazz musicians, cab drivers,

prostitutes, night people, drifters, grifters, and skidders, the cool
cats and their kicks. To be fully appreciated this stream of work
cannot be seen solely in terms of the categories conventionally
employed in sociological analysis. It has also to be seen from the
viewpoint of the literary critic as a style or genre and in
particular as a species of naturalist romanticism . . . That is, it
prefers the offbeat to the familiar, the vivid ethnographic detail
to the dull taxonomy, the sensuously expressive to dry analysis,
naturalistic observation to formal questionnaires, the standpoint
of the hip outsider to the square insider.[9]

Humanistic criticism expressed by this dual perspective takes on a
mock-serious quality. The disavowal of middle-class proprieties and hy-
pocrisies illuminates the mystifications that cover up such democratic
failures as the persecution of minorities and homosexuals and the degradation of mental patients and drug users. But modeling society in the image
of a carnival,[10] a con game[11] or a theatrical performance[12] entails certain
hazards for genuine humanism. The extreme relativism implied in this
approach releases the sociologist from moral commitment and reduces
social life to an absurdity.[13] Also, the cooly scientific commentator may be
tempted to view the act of understanding the precariousness of all social
constructions as his or her only relationship to phenomena. Disengagement
from political responsibility may become the most logical act for the morally uninvolved.

In fact, labeling proponents never seriously examined the nature of
stratified social systems and the economic and political relationships that
perpetuate these ranking orders. Nor have they shown systematic concern
for altering, through planned intervention, the institutional coercions they
so brilliantly describe. Evidently, they have been content with creating
an alternative professional ideology which challenges the dominant sociological reality. By introducing human biases and assumptions into the
research task as essential elements, they have engendered what Kai Erikson terms an "epistemological crisis," a breakdown of the normal assumptions of the discipline:

During the decade [1960s], many sociologists began to take a
hard new look at the shape of the sociological enterprise itself,
partly in response to challenges raised by a younger and
more radical generation of students and partly in response to
doubts felt by an older and more established generation of scholars. Together, these re-evaluators have resulted in a widespread
suspicion that the field is experiencing a number of related crises
at the political, moral, and even metaphysical levels. Among
these crises is one that might be called the "epistemological

crisis "—it takes the form of a recognition that the conceptual
underpinnings of sociology may be a good deal more slack than
most of us have been accustomed to thinking, that our professional
house may rest on very soft methodological ground.[14]

Paradigm shifts begin with doubts about the nature of existing knowledge. In time, the paradigm may congeal into orthodoxies that claim to be
unitary truths or present a limited conception of the phenomena it seeks
to explain. Reacting against earlier versions of deviance, labeling theory
initiated a new tradition of sociological research that incorporated sub-
conscious impulses, cultural values, class biases, and political positions.
These elements enter into thinking in ways that cannot be satisfactorily
understood or controlled. Awareness of these constraints, however, is the
first requirement of a reflexive sociology which examines the basic premise of sociological reality and its implications for the human condition.
As I shall argue in the sections that follow, it is unlikely that the labeling
perspective can do more than provide a catalyzing role in energizing a
critical structural sociology. One critic of labeling theory, Peter Manning,
contends that it is presently undergoing a state of exhaustion and conceptual decay.[15] Like other deviance sociologies, the labeling perspective
expresses the professional interest and values of its proponents. Allegations
of conceptual erosion imply that it is time to seek an alternative mode of
explanation which fits different social conditions, professional inquiries,
and contemporary problems. In the concluding chapter, I will suggest
such a direction.

PERSPECTIVE

The Neo-Chicago or Labeling School: New Wine in Old Bottles[16]

Claiming direct descent from G. H. Mead and Herbert Blumer, labeling practitioners have identified with the symbolic interactionist perspective.[17] They emphasize the social psychological process viewing it as the
determining element in social life. The Mead-Blumer brand of Chicago
sociology takes exception to the use of biological, psychological, and structural causation as explanations of human conduct. An interactional perspective focuses on the open-ended, situational construction of reality, in
which meanings (or symbols) arise and are defined and altered by participants in the course of action. The self, as a social object, is an ever-
emerging product, and not, as other psychologies claim, a set of traits.

Society is seen as a residual category, rather than as an entity capable
of acting or relating. Thus, interactional processes tend to be explained
in reductionist terms. Individuals engage in joint conduct in small face-to-

face groups. Institutions are not "self-operating entities," to use Blumer's phrase, that follow their own dynamics.[18] Institutions, as formative transactions, exist because people link their individual lines of action through shared meanings. Because diverse sets of participants belong to different associations and occupy different positions, they approach each other with different meanings. Such collectivities as a family, a juvenile gang, an industrial corporation, or a political party can only be comprehended by examining their settings in the processes of social interaction.

Human nature is essentially social, as collective forms precede individual persons. Through socialization, which involves taking the viewpoint of significant others, the person is linked into the ongoing community of norms and rules. Society and self are reciprocal processes, two sides of a single coin. The human organism is not merely responsive to stimuli or malleable to environmental influences. Blumer emphasizes that the ability to engage in a process of self-indication (i.e., taking note of objects, giving them meaning, and using meanings as the basis for directing action) differentiates humans from all other living forms. Symbolic interactionism stresses that designating, defining, and interpreting behavior gives a fluidity to social existence that precludes theoretical isolation of the structure or the individual as units of analysis. Its philosophical preference, however, has been to emphasize the self as a social object, an entity which is formed, sustained, weakened, and transformed in its interaction with others. Blumer says of this perspective:

> Symbolic interactionism provides the premises for a profound
> philosophy with a strong humanistic cast. In elevating the "self"
> to a position of paramount importance and in recognizing that its
> formulation and realization occur through taking the roles of
> others with whom one is implicated in the joint activities of group
> life, symbolic interactionism provides the essentials for a pro-
> vocative philosophical scheme that is peculiarly attuned to social
> existence.[19]

Interactionists were on less secure ground in viewing self and society as dual aspects of a common behavioral process. In his attempt to reconcile the objective and the subjective, Mead tended to conceive of collective norms as unitary entities, outcomes of a homogeneous collective conscience.[20]

What are the implications of applying this scheme to the labeling analysis of deviant behavior? Societal-reaction theory, as the labeling perspective is also called, stresses the primacy of official constructions of reality over personal ones, neglects structural elements of the deviant act, and features local groups, rather than networks of differentially ranked participants. This perspective also exaggerates the extent to which the self is altered by negative social reactions, ignores the plethora of rules which officials and deviants must choose from when determining alternative lines of action, and bypasses the complex interplay of many groups, out of which materializes new categories of moral and legal control.[21]

Pouring new wine into old bottles may yield only an outmoded residue. The model of interaction generated by the psychologically oriented thought of Mead and the work of the value-conflict theorists[22] provides an inadequate conception of modern social control. Further elucidation of labeling theory will clarify this point.

Fundamentals of Labeling and Societal-Reaction Theory

The neo-Chicago School asserts, as a major tenet, that deviance is an outcome of societal reaction, or labeling by official control bodies.[23] In this scheme, definitions cause deviant careers by generating the symbolic processes that define actors negatively. When stamped as inferior or morally unfit, these actors undergo a transformation of status. The notion of "unconventional sentimentality" posits a culprit-victim relationship with society as the offender. This view of social name-calling, or labeling, reverses the conventional conception of the deviant as evil, maintaining that "the underdog is always right, and those in authority always wrong."[24] The moral burden of control is shifted from the victim (the labeled) to the victimizers (control agents).

Working within a normative approach, this school typically follows the rule breaker as he or she is separated out, processed through the social control agencies, confronted with the formal degradation ceremonies, institutionalized or imprisoned, and subsequently stigmatized with a deviant identity.

The effect of such legal processing is a durable, if not permanent, loss of status.[25] The outsider is created by the forces of law or tradition which are reflected in the rules created by specific social groups. Becker has consistently articulated a relativistic, political-conflict model of deviance within a normative context.

> All social groups make rules and attempt, at some times and
> under some circumstances, to enforce them. Social rules define
> situations and the kinds of behavior appropriate to them,
> specifying some actions as "right" and forbidding others as
> "wrong." When a rule is enforced the person who is supposed
> to have broken it may be seen as a special kind of person, one
> who cannot be trusted to live by the rules agreed on by the group.
> He is regarded as an *outsider*.[26]

Deviance, in this approach, is situational and contingent. It is an outcome of official decisions in a particular social context. The differential definition and application of rules is influenced by the class, ethnic, occupational, sex, and age statuses of persons in complex societies who operate in opposition to social control groups.

While Becker focused his theoretical attention on the societal-reaction aspect, it was Lemert who provided the most sophisticated statement of the labeling view.[27] Lemert distinguishes "primary deviation," which is polygenetic, arising from a variety of social, cultural, psychological, and physiological factors, from "secondary deviation." The latter term refers to the socially defined responses the actor makes to the facts of his or her deviance. These definitions alone have direct implications for status and psychic structure.[28] Labeling, then, is the social process that transforms one conception of self (normal) into another (deviant). Thus, female promiscuity, a primary deviation, is not defined by the actor as immoral until deviant motives are imputed by others (formal or informal control agents), requiring a reconstitution of her self-concept.[29]

The secondary-deviation thesis generated large outpourings of research, in spite of Lemert's warning that such processes did not cause deviance, but were only one of the mechanisms that acted to stabilize the deviant identity.[30] The core propositions of Lemert's social control model included the structural emphasis on social differentiation, power exchanges, and conflict. Lemert's followers, however, by choosing the reaction of the labeled rather than the policies and decisions of the labelers for the starting point of research, have bypassed social control. The examination of classic sociological problems of power differences and ideological struggles is abandoned for an almost exclusively social psychological orientation which is centered on the deviant actor or group. The deviant becomes defined in primarily cultural and behavioral terms in the research, entirely separated from social organization.[31]

The interactional process, theoretically articulated as the relationship between the deviant actor and the conventional audience, has frequently become unbalanced in deviance research, with the consequence that a one-sided, actor-dominated brand of sociology threatens to emerge.[32] While the work of this school is often highly insightful and imaginative, the theory has been largely astructural, ahistorical, and noncomparative, promoting a sociology of the segmental, the exotic, and the bizarre.[33] This becomes apparent when this school's dominant metaphor is examined. The conception of stigma as the crucial process in creating and perpetuating deviant careers suggests Leviathan qualities of social control. Typifying deviants as passive receptors in an all-powerful social mechanism, labeling theory views actors as more acted upon than acting.

METAPHOR

Stigma

Because social control remains, for the most part, a residual feature in most labeling research, the machinations of this apparatus are revealed only indirectly. Rules exist and persons violate them, but the nature of the collective rule-making enterprise is only inadequately specified. Officials appear to isolate and punish deviants. However, the interactive processes by which this stigmatizing activity proceeds is rarely studied. The deviant identity alone becomes real, having a life-force that transcends the individuals possessing it. Labeling advocates prefer to call deviance a master status, a crucial moral career that is both cause and effect of a sequence of personal adjustments.[34] Stigma creates the deviant identity, a transformation evocatively described by Harold Garfinkel:

> The work of the denunciation effects the recasting of the objective character of the perceived other: the other person becomes in the eyes of his condemners literally a different and new person. It is not that the new attributes are added to the old "nucleus." He is not changed, he is reconstituted. The former identity, at best, receives the accent of mere appearance . . . the former identity stands as accidental; the new identity is the "basic reality." What he is now is what, "after all," he was all along.[35]

Stigma is a literary or dramatistic concept which does not readily yield an operational definition of social control and its consequences. Expressed in the impressionistic imagery preferred by labeling practitioners, it conjures up images of blemished selves and discredited bodily or moral attributes that automatically exclude the bearer from the competitive game by assigning labels of inferiority. Goffman translates stigma as a dramaturgical event into life as a theater.[36] It is an action scene set in a courtroom, a mental hospital, a jail, or other institutionalized setting in which degraded actors play prescribed parts in scenarios written and directed by powerful others. Internalized dialogues, out of which the deviant self supposedly emerges, are not expressed. Only the external management of spoiled identities is revealed. Discredited persons control information and develop cumbersome concealments, attempting to pass as normal by using masquerades or deceits.

In a society of "programmed consensus,"[37] in which social misrepresentation is a fine art, the management of stigma symbols is analogous to the manipulation of prestige symbols. In both instances, the individual performs a concealment game in order to reduce the risk of personal exposure.

Stigma is a special case of the split in modern life between the social standards and the discrepant self that the individual must protect with disguises. In the life-as-theater model, the self-other dialogue is an uneasy exchange between antagonists, each of whom seeks to unmask the other as a fraud. Typecasting simplifies the management of tension between hostile participants by assigning roles that require the stigmatized to perform, in almost all life situations, in opposition to normals. Clearly, this has social control functions, as Goffman notes.

> The stigmatization of those with a bad moral record clearly can
> function as a means of formal social control; the stigmatization
> of those in certain racial, religious, and ethnic groups has
> apparently functioned as a means of removing these minorities
> from various avenues of competition; and the devaluation of those
> with bodily disfigurements can perhaps be interpreted as
> contributing to a needed narrowing of courtship decisions.[38]

Scapegoating, victimization, exclusion, and the conferring of invidious properties become the stuff out of which society maintains a semblance of order. By focusing on the modern organization of taboo, dramatizing evil, and emphasizing the differentiating attributes of the morally maimed, labeling theorists critically attack the arbitrary nature of many routine social practices.

Stigma is presented in its objective and subjective phases. Its objective phase is the interlocking of collective rule making and authority structures to define and process the rule breaker. In its subjective phase, stigma isolates the labeled deviant, pushing the outsider into self-protective groups which shield the person from public censure.

THEMES

Collective Rule Making—Creating Deviant Categories

Labeling analysts have never satisfactorily pinned down the nature of collective rule making. The Meadian conception of a single, generalized other, or collective ethic, has obfuscated the complexities, divisions, and dissensus that characterize both conventional and deviant modern groups. While many theorists eschew moral absolutism in norms and values, there is a tendency, inherited from established sociologies, to reify norms as objective entities which are abstracted out of time and space relationships. Norms are viewed as having "consequences," as the normative order defines persons and creates pressures that affect behavior directly. Norms may be in a state of breakdown, conflict, discontinuity, impotence, evasiveness, or stress, which creates the conditions that result in large-scale deviance.[39]

Other observers are more cautious, preferring to define norms as the verbal summaries of mass conformities or regularities in human behavior. Lemert refers to norms as "limits in behavior explicitly or implicitly held and recognized in retrospect by members of a group, community, or society."[40] Awareness of norms, according to this definition, occurs only after violating them. Norms may be distributed on a scale, ranging from highly compulsive to permissive, or on a positive or negative continuum, with industrial societies tending to emphasize the negative cluster. Norm violations that provoke a strong societal reaction and subsequent symbolic complication for offenders provide the analytic starting point for separating out approved and disapproved behaviors. Norms, values, and beliefs provide the context out of which societal reaction and labeling emerge. Cultures and contracultures may thus be viewed as conventional or unconventional normative systems.

Labeling proponents argue that norms must be examined in terms of social meanings and actual behavior. Norms may carry heavy sanctions against drug use, homosexuality, abortion, and prostitution, even though such behaviors do no physical harm to members of the society, lacking a victim in the criminal sense.[41] Norms that are deviant from conventional society's standpoint, may actually be normative for particular groups. Incest in some rural communities,[42] heavy drinking among certain ethnics,[43] and delinquency of slum youth[44] reflect cultural diversity and value conflict.

Stereotypes and public attitudes about behavior also shape the collective rule-making process, often in subtle ways. As ready-made categories, stereotypes provide stock interpretative accountings for persons subsumed under their rubrics. While there is a paucity of research about the stereotyping of deviants, preliminary work suggests that they are one of the basic mechanisms at work in the social construction of deviance.[45]

The labeling implications of stereotypes may be crucial in defining the parameters of belief within which deviance is defined. While there is no one-to-one relationship between definitions and behavior, stereotypes, however misconceived, can shape behavior if they receive almost continual support from the mass media and in ordinary social discourse. For example, stereotypical images of mental disorder (a conception of "crazy people" as "out of control," lacking coherent, cognitive, or behavior skills) may validate professional ideologies that define mental disorder as illness requiring institutional control.[46] When everyday problems that create ambiguities and crises affect deviant individuals, rule violations that are normally tolerated may be interpreted as signs of insanity, thus escalating the labeling process. Scheff describes this secondary-deviation process:

> In a crisis when the deviance of an individual becomes a public
> issue, the traditional stereotype of insanity becomes the guiding
> imagery for action, both for those reacting to the deviant and, at
> times, for the deviant himself. When societal agents and
> persons around the deviant react to him uniformly in terms of the
> traditional stereotypes of insanity, his amorphous and unstruc-
> tured rule-breaking tends to crystallize in conformity to those
> expectations, thus becoming similar to the behavior of other
> deviants classified as mentally ill, and stable over time. The
> process . . . is completed when the traditional imagery becomes a
> part of the deviant's orientation for guiding his own behavior.[47]

In some situations, definitions that are shaped by stereotypical beliefs can have such an overwhelming impact that the individual may find himself or herself unable to sustain any alternative definition of self. Scott reports that misconceptions about the helplessness of the blind are so pervasive that treatment of blind persons may preclude their exercising any independent skills. Blind persons are likely to acquiesce to family or agency assistance, often adopting a facade of compliance out of sheer expediency.[48]

While stereotypes and norms summarize predispositions and retrospective evaluations of conduct, moral crusades generate new collective rules and sanctions. Rule making, from the labeling perspective, has both symbolic and substantive components. Moral entrepreneurs, claiming the superiority of certain values or life-styles, may seek public support for legitimating their norms. Pressure is exerted to reform old organizations, create new ones, or enact legislation that will reflect the crusaders' cherished ideologies. Even unsuccessful moral crusades often whip up symbolic support for threatened groups. The Temperance Movement, analyzed by Joseph Gusfield, demonstrates how new collective rules (Prohibition) grew out of efforts to increase the social prestige of rural, middle-class, Protestant groups.[49]

The moral crusade may also be the product of bureaucratic efforts. According to Dickson, the Federal Narcotics Bureau, rather than outraged citizens, initiated the drug scare and subsequent proscriptive legislation.[50] Rule enforcers can become rule makers, in order to justify their work and their very existence.

One shortcoming of labeling analysis is the view that values are readily converted into rules, or that norms automatically translate into laws. Schur takes exception to these assertions of value-action consistency by emphasizing the complex features involved in rule making:

> Rules arise from (and can be fully understood only in) terms of the complex sociocultural setting. At least three aspects of this setting usually warrant examination: the general social forces that permit (or "create") categorization of a particular kind of behavior as "deviant," the sequence of events culminating in specific efforts at rule-making and rule-enforcement, and the rule-making processes themselves, for example, legislative debates, hearings, and commission reports . . . there must [also] be public consciousness of a particular "category" of behavior (conscious classification singling out of specific acts as troublesome and requiring special attention) if rules are to be made. Such categories must, then, be in a sense "created"; they have not always existed "all along." Indeed, in the strictest sense there was no such thing as "juvenile delinquency" before the development of the juvenile court, and "mental illness" as a technical classification is partly a product of the mental-health movement.[51]

Most labeling advocates err by assuming that norms, rules, and laws constitute equivalent processes with similar consequences. To understand the deviance-making process, it may be analytically useful to distinguish these concepts. Since norms are made visible or reconstituted during or after the social act itself, a breach of norms may go unsanctioned because participants were not aware that behavioral boundaries were being violated. Rules, however, are the often unexpressed, deep structures that underlie cognitive categories. More general and ambiguous than norms, rules involve the perceptions, preconceptions, implicit understandings, and commonsense meanings that enable us to modify and organize reality. Commonsense meanings (or, what every competent group member knows) provide what Cicourel terms "interpretive procedures," which are programming instructions for processing the behavioral scheme of appearances, objects, gestures, sounds, etc., into inferences that permit action. Rules enable members to assign contextual relevance to events; norms and values, as idealized general policies, are invoked to justify a course of action.[52]

Laws are still another matter, as they involve differential power that is embellished by potent symbolism, formalized behavior, and elaborate ritual. Paul Rock holds that law is an imperialistic code in that it is detached from the mores, excludes the gray areas of everyday thinking, and does not manifest the ambiguities and indecisiveness of most rules. Rock writes:

The transformation of a particular moral code into law thus tends
to reify it, sanctify it and impersonalize it. Those who make
laws are able to change once parochial interests into something
qualitatively different. . . . As a reified entity, law has an authority
and concreteness which is independent of its creators. It typically
constrains the legislator himself.[53]

Because labeling sociologists have largely abdicated the study of law
formulations, they fail to recognize the important contingencies that affect
rule-making outcomes.[54] The micro-settings they study are too restricted
to embrace the interplay of competing groups, out of which codes are
proposed, interpreted, and negotiated and new forms of social and legal
controls are constructed.

Social Reactors—Shaping the Deviant Identity

By delineating the sources of stigma, labeling analysts have focused
on the reciprocal process between the self-other or actor-audience as this
defines and shapes the deviant outcome. Operating within an interactional
and situational framework, practitioners contend that objective data (e.g.,
official records, demographic variables, class attributes, etc.) provide few
cues for demarcating the often narrow boundaries that separate moral
worlds. Processes of social interaction cannot be assumed, but "must be
inspected to ascertain the conditions under which deviance comes into
being, how it is defined, and what consequences flow from that definition."[55] Because deviance is ubiquitous, and much of it is secret, most
forbidden behavior in modern societies goes unobserved and unsanctioned.
Deviance, as subjectively problematic, emerges out of interactional se-
quences between conformists and deviants.

Interactionists also account for the perspective of those who define a
person as being a social deviant. When examining this point of view, their
central concerns are the circumstances under which a person is set apart
and labeled deviant, how the person is cast into the deviant role, the means
of redefining the person, and the values, positive and negative, others
place on the facts of deviance.[56] For example, sociologists have noted that
signs of inappropriate sex-role behavior, such as homosexual behavior,
have been among the most severely punished infractions of our social
codes.[57] The imputation of deviance by others, often in the informal group
setting, shapes many deviants. The relativity of definitions becomes apparent in such instances as the decreased tolerance of deviant members by the
nuclear family or other small social networks, which acts as the primary
facilitator of mental hospital admission.[58] Cultural stereotypes of deviants

create negative categories of undesirables, that facilitate the labeling process.

A central tenet in labeling theory is that deviant acts alone do not make a deviant. Mechanisms of social labeling must also come into play. Social groups, of course, differ in their relative power and opportunities to create deviant categories and apply negative labels. While families, peer groups, and occupational associates may be highly instrumental in shaping deviant outcomes, formal organizations serve as a particularly potent force in activating, propelling, or imposing a deviant self-concept. Both fascinated and repelled by the bureaucratization of deviance, theorists showed how organizational problems of management are central to deviant control, as "deviants come under the regulation of hierarchy, impersonality, specialization, and systematic formal rules."[59] Courts, prisons, welfare agencies, mental hospitals, and residential institutions that process the blind, the mentally incompetent, or the aged are interpreted as deviance-dispensing systems that grind out offenders without benefit of procedural safeguards or standards of equity. Processing organizations are often viewed as monolithic, as they frequently manifest the all-powerful, undifferentiated authority structure of a "total institution."[60] Status transformation within this total institutional context involves highly coercive control, in which identity stripping wipes out the inmate's normal statuses, denies him or her the usual facesaving defenses, and reduces the inmate to a nonperson.

When labeling formulators turn from impressionistic descriptions of total institutions, they typically fasten on the issue of organizational imperatives which dictate the selection of clientele and the mode of processing. Concrete evidence from correctional and welfare agencies supports theoretical allegations about the arbitrary, often dehumanizing, aspects of official control. Studies reveal, for example, that:

(1) *Ad hoc* decision making characterizes police work, with decisions geared more to the special problems of officers than to formal legal categories.[61]

(2) Discretionary practices of judges and other court officials result in systematic circumvention of the law to maintain a smooth working system, with plea bargaining a routinized practice.[62]

(3) Arbitrary enforcement of the law places the most vulnerable populations (e.g., poor, black, young, etc.) in the greatest legal jeopardy (i.e., most likely to be reported, charged with a crime, arrested, sent to trial, sentenced, and jailed).[63]

(4) Preferential selection of clientele in public welfare agencies (e.g., young blind persons, more resourceful poor, etc.)

promotes agency programs and goals rather than client-oriented services.[64]

(5) Absence of consistency and conformity in disposition of cases undermines the law and demoralizes officials and clients alike.[65]

(6) Control groups' use of euphemistic terminology disguises the criminalization of deviance and official intervention.[66]

The organization-as-culprit argument, however, rests on a conception of the organization as a monolithic entity. Evidence of organizational bungling is drawn primarily from correctional or residential institutions. There, middle-echelon or lower-level officials, operating in low-resource settings, attempt to cope with apathetic, rebellious, or even dangerous inmates. Public awareness or support of these activities may be virtually nonexistent. Once locked up, the socially rejected are often deprived of even the most ordinary social needs (e.g., monotonous, ill-tasting institutional food is served and sexual intimacy with spouse or friend is denied). To facilitate the workings of the organization, staff and inmates may strike bargains that corrupt authority and generate widespread resentment.[67]

An exclusive focus on confrontations between the labeling group and the persons it seeks to label overlooks such complex structural features of organizational life as status hierarchies, unofficial norms among labelers, conflicting ideologies of different system agencies, and informal power structures that operate to undermine or alter agency goals.

According to labeling theorists, institutional power implies the application of stigmatizing social labels that push the rule breaker into further deviant behavior, a deviant way of life, and a deviant identity. However, the organization-as-culprit idea seriously biases the investigation.

In the first place, there are no necessary connections between having a deviant experience, moving into a deviant life-style, and having a permanent and exclusive deviant identity. These processes should be considered to be independent. For example, data on self-help groups (e.g., organizations by and for the obese, the compulsive drinker, or the drug addict) suggest that the assignment of permanent deviant labels may be highly effective in changing, or normalizing, deviant behavior, especially if change agents are ex-stigmatized persons.[68]

In the second place, a view of social structure as uniformly oppressive ignores the various paths or careers that contribute to or forestall deviant behavior. One career alternative ignored by societal-reaction theorists is that of benign neglect, the process by which significant others normalize the disability with long-run detrimental effects to the disabled.[69] Lowe and Hodges show that, while whites are as likely as blacks to be alcoholics, alcoholism is more likely to be normalized in the black subculture than in the white.[70] One consequence of this is that blacks may avoid the label of alcoholic; this, however, also means that black alcoholics are much less likely to be linked into the health care system. The results are far from benign, as the higher proportion of blacks who die from their alcohol abuse is an outcome of the absence of official labeling and lack of corrective action that may follow such labeling. The extent to which different rehabilitation models (e.g., total institutional treatment versus out-patient care for the mentally disordered) affect personal functioning and help or hinder reintegration needs to be more adequately explicated by sociologists.

In the actor-audience dialectic, the other side of social reaction is the actor who has been stigmatized as "different." Once typed, the acts are interpreted in accordance with the deviant status to which the person has been assigned. Status reconstitution, which follows the process of social typing, necessitates various accommodations on the deviant's part. Becoming a mental patient, a marijuana user, a lesbian, or a prostitute requires an altered self-conception, behaviors appropriate to the role, intrapersonal adjustments to the facts of stigmatization, and an ideology or vocabulary of motives neutralizing the deviant status.[71]

However, the labelists' preference for dwelling on the inner world of the subject divorces the actor from the audience. In this partial view, the social consequences of reaction have been delineated, while the social sources of reaction and its interactional processes have been merely assumed or ignored.

While this interpersonal-situational approach may be eminently sociological in its conceptualization, the scheme often bogs down into an almost total absorption in the actor or the middle-echelon officials processing him or her. The romantic view of the deviant as victim, dear to the humanist's heart, obstructs a view of the extent of the social problem for the larger society (as in suicide) and the exploration of the possible functions of deviance as a safety valve,[72] a boundary maintainer,[73] an innovative force for social change,[74] or a reflection of clashes and conflicts between rival social systems.[75] The greatest shortcoming in this approach, from a social control perspective, is the neglect of historical, comparative, or structural analysis of patterns of deviant activity and roles.[76] Such a microscopic sociology could contribute to the distorted assumption that only modern urban societies have social problems, a position Merton and Nisbet strongly repudiate.[77]

Deviant Careers—Stabilizing the Deviant Identity

To substantiate their claims about how social reaction stabilizes deviant identities, researchers traced the deviant career sequence from initial deviant acts to full-time commitment to deviance. Inheriting this career concept from the natural history perspective earlier formulated by Shaw in his studies of delinquents,[78] labeling analysts use it to magnify the exploitative and arbitrary features of societal reaction. Like early naturalists, they focus on the isolating effects of the outsider role which divide respectables and deviants into different worlds.

These naturalists express more than a sentimental concern for underworld inhabitants. They recognize the pragmatic problems outsiders wrestle with, such as the homosexual's need to maintain secrecy, the drug addict's circuitous efforts to get a regular supply of drugs, and the institutionalized mental patient's attempts to develop viable accommodations to social control.[79]

Research shows that learning deviant norms is a process common to such diverse forms of deviance as marijuana use, skid-row existence, and prostitution.[80] Studies illustrate how commitment to deviant norms after initial recruitment involves the development of a coherent belief system, an ideology or rhetoric which sustains the behavior, and a system of intra-group cues and slogans which imply deviant action.[81] For example, street prostitutes must learn to walk seductively when hustling clients and prosaically when avoiding police.[82] Cues are thus situationally based symbols.

A common self-defense strategy is movement into the deviant organization or subculture. In this protective milieu, outcasts work out their mutual problems, and, in doing so, help to socialize and maintain the deviant identity.

Viewing subcultures as a major form of adaptation deviant actors make to the fact of their stigmatization, researchers tend to see these groups as permanent, ecologically based underworlds. Outsiders can establish an environment conducive to their common interests and needs, such as the inmate cultures that develop in total institutions.[83] By denying validity to outside contacts, the deviant subculture protects its own from outside intervention, thus assuring the stability of these micro-systems. Members are bound together by their common problems of adjustment, their need to assign status rankings among members (e.g., the pimp-prostitute hierarchy), and their mutual goals of adapting to control.

Labeling analysts were on more tenuous ground, however, in assuming that most deviants take the final step of movement into an organized group or subculture. This stage supposedly crystallizes the deviant identity by confirming the separation of the outsider from conventional society. While occupational deviants (e.g., thieves and prostitutes) may follow this professionalizing pattern, part-time, *demi-monde* residents (e.g., weekend hippies) move back and forth between worlds.

Subculture analysis is linked to the anthropological and ethnographic preference for describing the inside operations of urban exotics. In most research, the subculture as an organized form remains unexamined with little or no attention paid to its origins or to the society-subculture exchange process. Labeling theorists also neglect other types of adaptation to the deviant role, including social movements, individual deviance, suicide, and cycles of abstinence and relapse. Research should demonstrate the conditions under which a subculture may arise, flourish, and decline. A cultist devotion to underworld life-styles is no substitute for evidence.

Perhaps most deviance in modern society is highly situational behavior that constitutes only a small part of the person's life.[84] Abortion clients, prison homosexuals, and nudist camp advocates, for example, do not form a basic identity revolving around the facts of their deviance. A conception of deviant life-styles suggests the situational nature of much rule breaking in modern society. With a life-style conception, it may be useful to study the means used by socially defined deviants to legitimize and manage their roles and the conditions under which deviant organizations emerge and are maintained.

Methodology as Metaphor

Labeling theory, characterized by a symbolic interactionist framework, has suffered from methodological inhibition, a shortcoming often associated with this social psychological approach. Conceptual impoverishment is encouraged by an absorption with general imagery which leaves empirical materials to be presented in an unsystematic, elusive, and suggestive manner, rather than providing definitive tests of the interaction framework.[85]

Blumer's research admonitions about the concepts and propositions of symbolic interactionism addressed the need for "direct examination of the empirical social world."[86] In their studies of the actions of participants in ongoing social interaction in organizations, institutions, and social relations, the Blumerians operate with an open-ended, soft methodology, emphasizing sensitizing concepts and a *Verstehende* approach. The latter stresses understanding the phenomenon, rather than confirming or contradicting theoretical hypotheses. However, the cultlike adherence, in some quarters, to participant observation and the ideology of involvement has promoted a focus on the sociologist "making the scene," "getting where the action is," or obtaining "close-ups" of exotic deviants and their careers.[87] This preoccupation is frequently at the expense of examining exchange systems between the deviant and his or her audience or investigating organizational deviance. Criminals, not the criminal code, are problematic; suicide, not social genocide, becomes featured; hidden deviance, not organizational rule violation, is the main focus of attention.

Analysis of deviant subcultures or behavior is often larded with deviant argot, indicating the researcher's sophistication in "inside dopesterism."[88] This verbal preoccupation with the insider's language not only has limited utility for sophisticated conceptual analysis, but also beclouds the issue in romanticism, rather than elucidating the problem. Intensive interviewing may be the only investigative tool, and, in some research contexts, may provide the entire content of the sociological argument. Collections of personal testimonies by stigmatized minorities, while intriguing, lack scientific or generalizing utility. The prevalent individual or case study analysis, while highly insightful and evocative, often fails to move beyond an impressionistic and narrow concern with specific deviant categories.

A recent ethnomethodological critique of labeling theory offered by Warren and Johnson suggest that the rhetoric of labeling is problematic because it retains the correctional, or traditional, deviant categories.[89] This implicit conventional rhetoric is evident in theorists' concern with deviant acts, rather than explaining them. This rhetoric has obscured the fact that deviance is a relative concept, defined differently by different groups, and is situated in meaning in terms of time, place, and persons. Warren and Johnson also state the nature and uses of power are far more complex than is indicated by labeling analysts. Data from welfare agencies and a community mental health center suggest that a conception of negotiated power is a more useful description of the labeling process than a conception of the monolithic power of control agencies. In many cases, those to be labeled may actively conspire to negotiate deviant labels for themselves by collaborating with officials.[90]

Summary and Conclusion

In this chapter I have argued that the labeling perspective has built-in problems because of its failure to provide empirical support for explanations of social control and social change. Its limitations, as I see them, include overconcern with deviant categories (with subsequent lack of attention to the exchange processes between actors and groups), a culturological and behavioral emphasis which systematically neglects organizational variables, inadequate recognition of the functions of deviance for the actor, small social systems, and the larger society, and a seeming fixation on the actor or subject, to the neglect of the social context. Other weaknesses are an isolated concern with exotic materials (often leading to a distorted view of the deviant and his or her organization *vis-á-vis* the larger social environment), a methodological inhibition that limits the field to ethnographic, descriptive, and overly restrictive sociology, and an inadequate development of concept or hypothesis testing, due to the penchant for insightful, impressionistic observation.

The major proposition of this school asserts that societal reaction in the form of labeling, which stigmatizes deviants, leads to an altered identity and necessitates a reconstitution of the self. This premise has not been adequately demonstrated empirically, as the research focus is on those social persons and categories already known to have been labeled. Little testing of alternatives to this conception of labeling as causing a reconstitution of self has been done, nor is there a systematic search for negative cases in most of the studies.[91]

It is apparent, however, that a variety of possibilities exists for explaining this interaction process. For example, the relationship between official labeling and a deviant identity yields four combinations, which are listed in the figure below. This suggests that official labeling, as the prior or causal variable, is not a crucial mechanism for either the formulation of a deviant identity or the persistence of a wide range of deviant acts.

Official Labeling	Deviant Identity (prostitute, psychiatric patient)
Official Labeling	No Deviant Identity (juvenile delinquent, peers-queers sexual encounters)
No Official Labeling	Deviant Identity (middle-class "secret" homosexual, physician-addict)
No Official Labeling	No Deviant Identity (illegal abortee, poolhall hustler)

FIGURE 7.2.   *Societal Labeling and Imputation of a Deviant Identity*

Even this scheme, however, does not account for still other labeling possibilities. Sociological typing (e.g., Sutherland's white-collar crime), informal labeling by significant others which leads to a deviant identity, the lay person's view of wrongdoing, which may be ignored by both legal agents and informal others (e.g., middle-class adultery), and negative self-labeling because of a series of personal experiences are all instances that contradict the simple link between public control and private definitions.

Labeling theorists who claim that the reactive processes of society constitute the only causal factor in deviance are providing only a partial view of a complex problem. Public labeling may have little or no impact in many areas of life, and many unsanctioned "normals" may engage in illegal or aberrational behavior in regularized fashion. Labeling is neither a necessary nor sufficient condition for a deviant identity or subgroup. Even though some studies show an association between official labeling and a transformed self or emergent organized group, further research that examines negative cases, in order to clarify the conditions under which the labeling premise holds true, is required. Until a more rigorous approach to hypothesis testing is developed, the field will continue to offer little more than a collection of isolated studies which are couched in a romantic imagery and disconnected from the main body of sociological work.

Another problem resides in the conception of labeling. Exactly what is common or essential to all of the varied forms of negative definitions (e.g., official typing, self-labeling, informal censure, etc.) is not specified. What does deviance mean if it involves such a wide range of possible origins and processes? There is an obvious contradiction. Deviance is defined as acts that provoke negative official responses (as in the Becker model), but labeling theorists contradict this definition by giving analytical recognition to secret (or nontyped) deviance. The chief problem is a semantic one; two levels of discourse, one dealing with the process of becoming deviant and the other with specific deviant acts, are merged. A consistent, analytic separation of these two levels would clarify empirical efforts.

A further inconsistency, as Gibbs points out, arises when deviance is defined in relation to prevailing social norms while behavior contrary to a norm is not defined as deviant unless it is discovered and provokes a particular type of reaction.[92] The ideology of extreme relativism and distrust of the arbitrary and often irrational nature of law enforcement in industrial society pushes the labeling practitioner into a theoretical limbo. Cicourel's distinction between natural deviance (the lay notion of deviants as natural social types distributed in some ordered manner) and official deviance (conduct defined and processed by political agencies) may be a definitional route out of this conceptual impasse.[93]

Even with fairly extensive modifications, the conceptual framework of labeling theory is probably inadequate for the task of a sociology of social control. Lemert contends, rightly, that existing theories of deviance are ill suited to account for the complexities of societal reaction in modern society.[94] Rather than attempting a refurbishing job, efforts may be better expended in developing an alternative model, a conception of political economy that links social control to the differentiation of interests and groups. A tentative beginning toward this effort is proposed in the final chapter.

NOTES

1. Howard S. Becker, "Whose Side Are We On?", *Social Problems* 14 (Winter 1967): 240.

2. Ibid., p. 242.

3. Robert S. Lynd, *Knowledge for What?* (Princeton: Princeton University Press, 1939).

4. Alvin W. Gouldner, "Anti-Minotaur: The Myth of A Value-Free Sociology," *Social Problems* (Winter 1962): 199-213. Gouldner takes a more critical view of labeling theory in "The Sociologist as Partisan: Sociology and the Welfare State," *The American Sociologist* (May 1968): 103-116.

5. Howard Becker has been one of the leading proponents of the labeling perspective. His work, which incorporates this view, includes: *Outsiders: Studies in the Sociology of Deviance* (New York: Free Press); *The Other Side: Perspectives on Deviance*, edited. New York: Free Press; *Sociological Work*. (Chicago: Aldine Publishing, 1968); "Labeling Theory Revisited," in *Deviance and Social Control*, ed. Paul Rock and Mary McIntosh (London: Tavistock for the British Sociological Association), 1972.

6. See Richard Hofstadter, *Anti-Intellectualism in American Life* (New York: Vintage Books, 1966): 155-156.

7. Becker, *Sociological Work*, p. 103.

8. Irving L. Horowitz, *Professing Sociology* (Chicago: Aldine Publishing Company, 1968), pp. 208-210.

9. Gouldner, "Anti-Minotaur: The Myth of a Value-Free Society," p. 209.

10. See Peter L. Berger's discussion of the metaphors, hazards, and advantages of the debunking stance in *Invitation to Sociology* (New York: Doubleday and Company, 1963).

11. Erving Goffman, "On Cooling the Mark Out: Some Aspects of Adaptation to Failure," in *Human Behavior and Social Processes*, ed. Arnold M. Rose (Boston: Houghton-Mifflin Company, 1962), pp. 482-505.

12. The dramaturgical model has been an integral part of E. Goffman's work. See, for example, *The Presentation of Self in Everyday Life* (Garden City, N.Y.: Doubleday Anchor, 1959) and idem, *Interaction Ritual* (Chicago: Aldine Publishing Company, 1967).

13. The notion of collective action as little more than negotiated understandings contrived in a world without meaning or which is "absurd" is relativism in starkest form. See Stanford Lyman and Marvin Scott, *A Sociology of the Absurd* (New York: Appleton-Century-Crofts, 1970).

14. Kai T. Erikson, "Sociology: That Awkward Age," *Social Problems* 19 (Spring 1972): 431.

15. Peter K. Manning, "Survey Essay on Deviance," *Contemporary Sociology* 2 (1973): 123-128.

16. A summary version of labeling theory is offered in Nanette J. Davis, "Labeling Theory in Deviance Research: A Critique and Reconsideration," *Sociological Quarterly* 13 (Autumn 1972): 447-474.

17. George H. Mead, *Mind, Self, and Society* (Chicago: University of Chicago Press, 1934); Herbert Blumer, *Symbolic Interactionism* (Englewood Cliffs, N.J.: Prentice-Hall, Inc.). For an excellent overview of theory and research in symbolic interaction, see Jerome G. Manis and Bernard N. Meltzer, eds., *Symbolic Interaction*, 2nd ed. (Boston: Allyn & Bacon, Inc., 1972).

18. Blumer, *Symbolic Interactionism*, p. 19.

19. Ibid., p. 21.

20. B. N. Meltzer provides a critique of Mead in Manis and Meltzer, eds., *Symbolic Interaction*, pp. 4-22.

21. Edwin M. Lemert, one of the early fathers of labeling theory, has recently offered a vigorous critique of this perspective in, "Beyond Mead: The Societal Reaction to Deviance," *Social Problems* 21 (April 1974): 457-468.

22. Labeling theorists have moved little beyond Vold's conception of crime and law as social definitions. See George B. Vold, *Theoretical Criminology* (New York: Oxford University Press, 1958). The concepts of power, conflict, and stratification were never adequately developed by this school.

23. Along with Becker, whose works are cited above, other formative writers who have contributed to this approach are Kai T. Erikson, "Notes on the Sociology of Deviance," *Social Problems* 9 (Spring 1962): 307-314 and John I. Kitsuse, "Societal Reaction to Deviant Behavior: Problems of Theory and Method," *Social Problems* 9 (Winter 1962): 247-257.

24. Becker, *The Other Side*, p. 4.

25. R. D. Schwartz and J. H. Skolnick, "Two Studies of Legal Stigma," *Social Problems* 10 (Fall 1962): 133-138.

26. Becker, *The Other Side*, p. 1.

27. Edwin M. Lemert, *Human Deviance, Social Problems and Social Control* (Englewood Cliffs, N.J.: Prentice-Hall, Inc., 1967). An early statement of labeling activities and their consequences is found in Frank Tannenbaum, *Crime and the Community* (Boston: Ginn and Company, 1938).

28. Lemert, *Human Deviance, Social Problems and Social Control*, p. 40.

29. Nanette J. Davis, "The Prostitute: Developing a Deviant Identity," in *Studies in the Sociology of Sex*, ed. James M. Henslin (New York: Appleton-Century-Crofts, 1971), pp. 297-322.

30. Lemert has reemphasized this in his role as discussant for a section meeting on labeling theory at the 1970 American Sociological Association Meetings in Washington, D.C.

31. Albert J. Reiss, "The Study of Deviant Behavior: Where the Action Is," *Ohio Valley Sociologist* 32 (Autumn 1966): 1-12.

32. John Lofland, *Deviance and Identity* (Englewood Cliffs, N.J.: Prentice-Hall, 1969).

33. This sentiment has been well expressed by Simon and Gagnon, who charge that studies in deviant behavior ". . . frequently have been over-impressed with the 'special' or 'exotic' character of the population or groups studied." There is ". . . a kind of intellectual 'hipsterism' delighting in familiarity with esoteric argot and the ease with which they can display their 'cool'." W. Simon and J. H. Gagnon, "Femininity in the Lesbian Community," *Social Problems* 15 (Fall 1967): 212-221.

34. For elucidation of the concept of "master status," see Everett C. Hughes, "Dilemmas and Contradictions of Status," *American Journal of Sociology* 50 (March 1945): 353-359.

35. Harold Garfinkel, "Conditions of Successful Degradation Ceremonies," *American Journal of Sociology* 61 (March 1956): 421-422.

36. Erving Goffman, *Stigma* (Englewood Cliffs, N.J.: Prentice-Hall, 1963).

37. Lemert, "Beyond Mead: The Societal Reaction to Deviance," p. 459.

38. Goffman, *Stigma*, p. 139.

39. For a sympathetic statement of this position, see Simon Dinitz, Russell R. Dynes, and Alfred C. Clarke, eds. *Deviance: Studies in the Process of Stigmatization and Societal Reaction* (New York: Oxford University Press, 1969), pp. 1-12.

40. Edwin M. Lemert, *Social Pathology* (New York: McGraw-Hill, 1951), p. 31.

41. Edwin M. Schur, *Crimes Without Victims* (Englewood Cliffs, N.J.: Prentice-Hall, Inc., 1965).

42. C. Bagley, "Incest Behavior and Incest Taboo," *Social Problems* 16 (Spring 1969): 505-519.

43. Marshall B. Clinard, *Sociology of Deviant Behavior* (New York: Holt, Rinehart, and Winston, 1968), pp. 435-443.

44. W. B. Miller, "Lower Class Culture as a Generating Milieu of Gang Delinquency," *Journal of Social Issues* 14 (Fall 1958): 5-19.

45. J. L. Simmons analyzes deviant stereotypes and attitudes supporting these negative categories in *Deviants* (Berkeley: Glendessary Press, 1969), pp. 32-33.

46. T. S. Szasz, "The Myth of Mental Illness," *American Psychologist* 15 (February 1960): 113-118.

47. Thomas J. Scheff, *Being Mentally Ill* (Chicago: Aldine, 1966), p. 79.

48. Robert A. Scott, *The Making of Blind Men* (New York: Russell Sage, 1969).

49. Joseph Gusfield, *Symbolic Crusade* (Urbana: University of Illinois Press, 1963).

50. Donald T. Dickson, "Bureaucracy and Morality: An Organizational Perspective on a Moral Crusade," *Social Problems* 16 (Fall 1968): 143-156.

51. Edwin M. Schur, *Labeling Deviant Behavior* (New York: Harper & Row, 1971), p. 105.

52. Aaron V. Cicourel, "The Acquisition of Social Structure: Toward a Developmental Sociology of Language and Meaning," in *Understanding Everyday Life*, ed. Jack D. Douglas (Chicago: Aldine Publishing Company, 1970). Cicourel and other phenomenological interactionists (see Douglas, 1970) working under the banner of ethnomethodology, are allied with symbolic interaction in that both perspectives provide a subjective and social psychological view of social organization. Ethnomethodology departs from the older social psychology in rejecting the Meadian notion of roles, and in emphasizing the routine, taken-for-granted expectations that members of any social order regularly accept. Writers stress the fluidity and provisional nature of the dynamics by which good and evil, and conformity and deviance emerge.

53. Paul Rock, *Deviant Behaviour* (London: Hutchinson University Library, 1973), p. 127.

54. Pamela Roby's detailed analysis of changes in the New York State law on prostitution represents an exception to this general neglect of rule-making processes. See P. A. Roby, "Politics and Criminal Law: Revision of the New York State Penal Law on Prostitution," *Social Problems* 17 (Summer 1969): 83-109.

55. Earl Rubington and Martin Weinberg, eds., *Deviance: The Interactionist Perspective* (New York: The Macmillan Company, 1968), p. 2.

56. Ibid., p. 3.

57. A discussion of sex roles—codes, violations, and sanctions—is found in A. Davis, "American Status Systems and the Socialization of the Child," *American Sociological Review* 6 (June 1941): 350 and J. I. Kitsuse, "Societal Reaction to Deviant Behavior: Problems of Theory and Method."

58. M. Hammer, "Influence of Small Social Networks as Factors in Mental Hospital Admission, *Human Organization* 22 (Winter 1963-1964): 243-251.

59. Schur, *Labeling Deviant Behavior,* p. 96.

60. Erving Goffman examines the social structure of "total institutions" in *Asylums* (Garden City, N.Y.: Doubleday Anchor Books, 1961).

61. Egon Bittner, "The Police on Skid Row: A Study of Peace Keeping," *American Sociological Review* 32 (October 1967): 699-715.

62. Jerome Skolnick, *Justice Without Trial* (New York: Wiley, 1966).

63. See Marvin E. Wolfgang, *Crime and Race: Conceptions and Misconceptions* (New York: Institute of Human Relations Press, 1964). Discretionary practices among police in their dealing with lower-status juvenile offenders are discussed in Irving Piliavin and Scott Briar, "Police Encounters with Juvelines," *American Journal of Sociology* 69 (September 1964): 206-214.

64. Scott, *The Making of Blind Men.*

65. David Matza, *Delinquency and Drift* (New York: John C. Wiley and Sons, 1964).

66. The process by which powerful groups convert terms and manipulate definitions for controlling subjects is analyzed by Anthony M. Platt, *The Child Savers: The Invention of Delinquency* (Chicago: The University of Chicago Press, 1969) and Thomas S. Szasz, *The Manufacture of Madness* (New York: Dell Publishing Co., Inc., 1970).

67. Gresham Sykes, *The Society of Captives* (Princeton: Princeton University Press, 1958).

68. Carol A. B. Warren, "The Use of Stigmatizing Labels in Normalizing Deviant Behavior" (Unpublished paper, University of Southern California, 1973).

69. Walter R. Gove, "Societal Reaction Theory and Disability" (Unpublished paper, Vanderbilt University, October 1973).

70. George Lowe and H. Eugene Hodges, "Race and the Treatment of Al-

coholism in a Southern State," *Social Problems* 20 (Fall 1972): 240-252.

71. These general processes are discussed by David Matza in *Becoming Deviant* (Englewood Cliffs, N.J.: Prentice-Hall, 1969).

72. R. A. Dentler and K. T. Erikson, "The Functions of Deviance in Groups," *Social Problems* 7 (Fall 1959): 98-107.

73. Erikson, "Notes on the Sociology of Deviance"; idem, *Wayward Puritans* (New York: John C. Wiley and Sons, 1966).

74. Lemert, *Human Deviance, Social Problems and Social Control.*

75. Gusfield, *Symbolic Crusade.*

76. Gibb's historical and comparative treatment of suicide is a notable exception to this neglect of societal components in the etiology of deviance. See Jack P. Gibbs, "Suicide," pp. 281-321 in *Contemporary Social Problems,* eds., Robert K. Merton and Robert A. Nisbet (New York: Harcourt, Brace and World, 1966).

77. Merton and Nisbet, *Contemporary Social Problems,* pp. v-viii.

78. Clifford R. Shaw, *The Natural History of a Delinquent Career* (Chicago: University of Chicago Press, 1931).

79. In entering the psychiatric arena, the labeling school has made a significant contribution by its emphasis on the relativity of social definitions and the consequences for the actor and his interpersonal relations. Two representative studies using this framework are: S. P. Spitzer and Norman Denzin, eds., *The Mental Patient: Studies in The Sociology of Deviance* (New York: McGraw-Hill, 1968) and Eliot Friedson, ed., *The Hospital in Modern Society* (New York: The Free Press, 1963).

80. Studies of these specific deviant forms are found in H. S. Becker *Outsiders;* S. E. Wallace, *Skid Row as a Way of Life* (Totowa, N.J.: Bedminster Press, 1965); and J. H. Bryan, "Apprenticeships in Prostitution," *Social Problems* 12 (Winter 1965): 287-297.

81. Matza, *Delinquency and Drift.*

82. From interviews with prostitute informants.

83. Goffman, *Asylums.*

84. A situational interpretation of deviance is emphasized by Jack D. Douglas, ed., in *Observations of Deviance* (New York: Random House, 1970); and *Deviance and Respectability* (edited) (New York: Basic Books).

85. John Lofland, "Interactionist Imagery and Analysis Interruptus," in *Human Nature and Collective Behavior* ed., Tamotsu Shibutani (Englewood Cliffs, N.J.: Prentice-Hall, 1970), pp. 35-45.

86. Blumer, *Symbolic Interactionism,* p. 49.

87. Ned Polsky, *Hustlers, Beats, and Others* (Chicago: Aldine, 1967).

88. A recent example of this "pop" sociology approach in deviance texts is Robert W. Winslow and Virginia Winslow, *Deviant Reality* (Boston: Allyn and Bacon, Inc., 1974).

89. Carol A. B. Warren and John M. Johnson, "A Critique of Labeling Theory from the Phenomenological Perspective," in *Theoretical Perspectives on Deviance,* ed. Jack D. Douglas and Robert Scott (New York: Basic Books, 1973).

90. Jack D. Douglas, *American Social Order* (New York: The Free Press, 1971).

91. Exceptions to this methodology are the work by Alfred Lindesmith, *Opiate Addiction* (Bloomington, Ind.: Principia Press) and H. S. Becker, *Outsiders,* whose analytic induction model uses negative cases to abstract that which is common and essential to all the cases under investigation. (This approach is critiqued in the last chapter.)

92. Jack P. Gibbs, "Conceptions of Deviant Behavior: the Old and the New," *Pacific Sociological Review* 9 (Spring 1966): 9-14.

93. Aaron Cicourel, *The Social Organization of Juvenile Justice* (New York: John C. Wiley and Sons, 1968), pp. 335-336.

94. Lemert, "Beyond Mead: The Societal Reaction to Deviance."

8

Deviance Disavowed

SOCIAL CONTROL PERSPECTIVE

> With Marx, we have been concerned with the social arrangements
> that have obstructed, and the social contradictions that enhance,
> man's chances of achieving full sociality—a state of freedom
> from material necessity, and (therefore) of material incentive, a
> release from the constraints of forced production, an abolition
> of the forced division of labour, and set of social arrangements,
> therefore, in which there would be no politically, economically,
> and socially-induced need to criminalize deviance.
>
> (I. Taylor, P. Walton, and J. Young,
> *The New Criminology*)[1]

Sociological constructions of deviance display blank spots as well as idealized images of American society.[2] A liberal consensus in sociology has nearly blotted out any conception of diversity and dissension. Such terms as power, class, conflict, elites, violence, and repression are rarely used.

In the theories I have reviewed, the liberal-pragmatic tradition has been ubiquitous. While the liberal ideology is not a monolithic doctrine, its political sentiments have infiltrated sociological theory, obscuring the origins and development of legal and institutional control over political minorities.

Two major tenets of this ideology have contributed to the blank spots in social theory and research. The first is the ethos of individualism. Liberal ideology holds that rationality and motives are controlled by the individual. To understand social behavior and its organization, the researcher need only sum up individual attitudes and verbal meanings. Each individual is a unique decision maker who operates to maximize his or her interests and needs, and the social order is preserved by a utilitarian agreement among equal parties not to intrude on the personal liberty of another.

This individualistic, overrational conception of behavior, is refuted by social reality in industrial societies, in which rationality has shifted to large-scale organizations. Organizational doctrines and practices are based on technical considerations and cost-benefit accounting. In the impersonal, bureaucratic settings of work, education, and government, citizen participation in decision making is limited by differential rank, lack of information, and undemocratic methods of organizing resources and personnel. Internal stratification within subordinate groups further militates against the establishment of a community of common interests which could counter the dominance of bureaucratic elites.

Marginal professional groups, such as sociologists, are as caught up in organizational imperatives as are other subordinate groups. Intellectual labor is becoming a marketplace commodity, subject to the fluctuations of student enrollments, administrative discretion, and legislative and agency endowments. There seems to be a "false consciousness" among social theorists. Prevailing methodologies continue to feature studies of decontextualized individuals, who, like the researchers who study them, lack a sense of history, organizational constraints, and the market determinants of conduct.

The second principle of liberalism is its notion that the State acts as a political broker. As an important framework within which contending groups bargain for political prizes, the State works for the benefit of all. This pluralistic conception of politics, in which public interest is served by the competitive balancing of multiple interests, is based on several assumptions, including the beliefs that power is widely diffused, authority is legitimated by consent of the governed, government operates by internal checks and balances, and peaceful mediation invariably serves the common good.

This pluralistic model is denied by a view of society as racked by value antagonisms and chronic strife. The State is not a disinterested party in conflicts, but uses the value-neutral prescription as a powerful legitimating myth to maintain authority and inspire support. In this manner, the State maintains its monopoly over the means of violence and coercion. The State is not, therefore, value neutral; it is a weapon in the hands of those who control it. Chambliss traces this conception of the State to the work of Karl Marx:

> In the Marxist view (as expounded mainly by Engels and Lenin), the State consists of the institutions of coercion: the police, the army, prison officials. These are the principal weapons in the hands of the ruling classes. Law, which rests finally upon the State's self-perpetuating monopoly of violence or instruments of coercion, therefore represents the will of the ruling classes; in

more modern terms, we would say that it embodies the values of
the ruling class. This is a view which conceives of society in
terms of sharp conflict between different classes, each with its
own set of values, and the State as a weapon in the hands of the
class in control of it.[3]

Obviously, the State cannot rule by power alone. Coercion must be
supplemented by legitimated authority which entails acquiescence of the
governed who define self-interests in terms of existing political arrangements. As part of this legitimating apparatus, professional academics have
played a myth-maker role, providing a tacit support source for State control over nonelites. In their preference for examining small-scale social
worlds, their concern for general freedom and security for individuals,
their tolerance of nonpoliticized alternative life-styles, and their opposition to violence from the lower stratum, social theorists betray their liberal
bias. They desire a well-ordered (not necessarily homogeneous) society in
which personal careers and private interests assume priority over collective
inequalities and oppressions.

The liberal ideology has become the common denominator of American
political rhetoric, linking leaders, followers, and academics in a shared
universe of discourse. As a language devoid of conflict and power terms, it
limits the sociological perception of social reality, keeping it within official
boundaries. Within this liberal-pragmatic tradition, sociological constructions of deviance illustrate how relations between the State, social institutions, and the academic community shore up narrow conceptions of moral
order.[4]

Most schools of deviance theory adopt a legal definition of crime,
studying those persons legally defined and prosecuted as criminal or deviant. This focus is parochial, and its legalistic definitions shore up enforcement conceptions of individual violators as abnormal. Criticism of criminal
law or law enforcement agencies is seldom expressed.

Liberalism, for professional sociologists, has been strongly identified
with reformism, a method of humanizing and stabilizing the social control
apparatus under existing economic and political arrangements. No vision
of alternative structures appears in reform work. Lacking a historical or
macrosociological perspective, reform proposals tend to rely on tech-
nocratic solutions to social problems (e.g., improvements of the juvenile
justice system, halfway houses, etc.) that enhance State power over controlled populations.

The pragmatic emphasis has concentrated on making sociology "respectable," while also reaping the career pay-offs, academic practices that

encourage identification with an "enlightened," governing elite, often at the expense of clients' interests. As intellectual mercenaries, social scientists have limited themselves to agency-determined research and problem solving. It is no accident that the observed fads and fashions in deviance studies (e.g., poverty, delinquency, underclass riots, and other high-sell research products) tend to support elites' regulation of potential (or actual) troublemakers. Not only are market-oriented sociologists threatened by loss of autonomy in their choice of significant research problems, but the politicization of research is also an imminent hazard. In the struggle for resources, power, and prestige, academics have succumbed, only too willingly, to inducements offered by government and private granting agencies. Market terms could, eventually, openly state what ideas academics may distribute (rather than tacitly implying such limitations, as is done presently).[5]

Applied to social problems, liberalism offers only short-term ameliorative solutions to social problems which invariably benefit caretakers by producing cynicism and defeatism about human potentiality and significant social change. The debunking tradition, adopted by recent theorists, demystifies authority but fails to provide guidelines for reorganizing repressive social structures. Unmasking the frailty of legitimate authority provides catharsis for debunkers, but when divorced from moral and political commitments, it can contribute to a high degree of moral incoherence, social fragmentation, and political privatism among the disadvantaged.[6]

By operating within mainstream formulas, theorists view deviance as an entity to be described, explained, manipulated, and controlled. In contrast to traditional sociologies, a political-conflict model disavows deviance as a viable sociological phenomenon, and views it as part of an official language of control. This conception of social control rejects behavioristic, astructural, and social engineering models of society. Moving away from microanalysis of deviant categories, a social control perspective raises a different set of questions which focuses on stratification, power and its discontents, organizations as political authority structures, and the requisites of normative theory. While not yet fully articulated, this new conflict approach explores the "blank spots" abandoned by social theorists and attempts to explain deviant acts as outcomes of existing political arrangements.

Rather than attempting to delineate the sprawling domain of recent conflict theory, this chapter takes a more tentative approach. I shall suggest some formal and substantive requirements for developing a fully articulated theory of social control, with discussion focusing primarily on substantive theoretical issues. These include the components of a critical social theory, the concept of structural contradictions, and the themes of the political economy of social control, the social organization of social control, and the responses to control by the controlled. Formal requirements (procedural guides for theory construction) will be included in a chapter note. (Students may wish to consult this section for more complete definitions of terms and statements of preliminary propositions than are offered in the main text.)

The organization of this chapter varies from that of the others. As I am proposing new theoretical directions, the paradigm format has been modified to allow a synthesis of labeling ideas and structural aspects of control theory. Figure 8.1, however, uses an abbreviated paradigm format to present an overview of the control perspective. This theory emphasizes organizations as political authority systems and their consequences for conflict and change.

I. Social-Professional Conditions	Developed industrial state; political economy fosters inequality of power, wealth, and authority; crisis of legitimacy: Vietnam war, student protests, urban riots, government corruption; concern with underdog alienation; disenchantment with "liberal" solutions; counterideological tone; radical sociologists' rejection of status quo.
II. Perspective	Critical theory, political-conflict model of social control; society as struggle between conflicting groups for scarce commodities, organizational analysis; collective activities as outcomes of organizational rivalry and coercion; deviance created by maldistribution of resources inherent in legitimate social order and maintained by exchange within and between controller groups and controlled populations.
III. Metaphor	"Structural contradictions"—opposition and cleavage built into social structure, legitimating processes that foster organization generate counteracting forces.
IV. Themes	Political economy of control; social organization of social control; responses to control by the controlled.
V. Method	Methodological dilemmas and constraints; historical model; generalizations from specific instances of changing events; *Verstehen* or understanding.

FIGURE 8.1.   *Control Perspective*

TOWARD A POLITICAL-CONFLICT PERSPECTIVE
ON SOCIAL CONTROL

Critical Theory

Theories of deviance, long insulated from sociology in general and the classical tradition of social theory, are undergoing metamorphosis. A rising cadre of theorists, drawing on radical images of social order, are demanding a different kind of social theory; one that is historically grounded, structurally sophisticated, value committed, and critical of status quo political arrangements.[7]

The conflict images derive from the following three sources: (1) rejection of the liberal ideology and praxis that reinforces social problems and social inequalities; (2) reexamination of Marxian scholarship, focusing on stratification, power, and class struggle; and (3) personal responses to crises of legitimacy, expressed in widespread opposition to the Vietnam War and in mass alienation (e.g., student protests, urban working-class riots, police brutality, and government corruption).

The intellectual style adopted by recent proponents of normative-conflict theory represents a drastic break with standard sociological styles of thought. The temper is explicitly radical and humanistic, rejecting current models of capitalist development at home and abroad. The praxis (models for social change) is split into two distinct tendencies. The first, based on socialist principles, offers a vision of cooperative, collective efforts which supplant competitive market relationships. The second calls for revolutionary action, aimed at creating a decentralized, debureaucratized, and dehierarchicalized society. Whether committed to reflexive sociology or direct action, the new critics attempt to illuminate how social and political organizations engender coercive social arrangements. As Quinney emphasizes, "only a Marxist critique allows us to break out of the ideology and conditions of the age."[8]

Advocates of this new critical stance assert that social theory has become detached from any tenable explanation of contemporary events. Rather than perpetuating official myths that obscure the deepening crisis of the garrison state in Western societies, theory must be related to alternative, if not utopian, visions of social order.

To cogently address the crucial problems of capitalist society, especially its persistent inequality and widespread alienation, theorists are attempting to eradicate the stereotypes and rhetorics of dominant classes from sociological work. Theorists substitute a conflict vocabulary for the official language of consensus, using such terms as struggle, coercion, opposition, violence, and repression. To counter the myth of egalitarianism, theorists depict the structures of inequality by examining power, privilege, wealth, racism, sexism, and imperialism. By challenging the pluralistic doctrine of stability, they dramatize change and its accompanying dislocation, disequilibrium, discontent, disorientation, and uncertainty.

As interpreted by the new critics, theory is normative, by definition, as it renders a selective picture of the world. The language, images, perspectives, problems, and propositions directing social inquiry all reflect particular world views and social values. It is not enough to objectively know aspects of the social world through the positivistic mode of observing and quantifying events. A critical theory insists on personal knowledge, which involves the participation of the knower in all acts of understanding, and requires a fusion of the subjective and objective. This type of sociological work demands intellectual commitment, as well as technical mastery of subject matter and research procedures. Theory based on personal knowledge cultivates a search for meaning, promotes a critical self-awareness, and redirects political participation.

From the viewpoint of normative theorists, the illusion of objectivism (i.e., reality apart from consciousness) is its assumption that knowledge is one-dimensional. The "facts" are there to be observed. Polanyi notes that the objectivist mode is manifested across scientific disciplines:

> For modern man has set up as the ideal of knowledge the
> conception of natural science as a set of statements which is
> "objective" in the sense that its substance is entirely determined
> by observation, even while its presentation may be shaped by
> convention.[9]

This natural-science conception of sociology has distorted the multiple social realities of modern society into conventional forms. For example, the one-sided versions of social structure provided by functionalists and labeling theorists take for granted the dominant social and economic arrangements. Objectivity implies operating within the conventional wisdom, whether studying top dogs or underdogs. Their unexamined assumptions represent a failure to confront the rapidly changing economic and political contingencies of industrial societies. These theorists tactily reaffirm control structures that perpetuate alienating social arrangements.

The objective mode has additional hazards for the theorist attempting to come to grips with alternative realities. Knowledge known only from the outside, which is gathered from an impersonal, dispassionate, and noncommital position, requires little personal responsibility for false claims of validity or low intellectual standards. Professionals also become easily co-opted and tamed. There is little evidence, for instance, that the penetration of sociologists into government, welfare, or crime-control bureaus has alleviated social problems. Socialized into society as it is, the naive reformer addresses no fundamental questions about the rightness or wrongness of existing social arrangements. As an eclectic problem solver for elites, the objectivist turned reformer fails to confront the basic questions posed by the persistence of crime, deviance, and dissent.

These questions, according to the new critics, can be addressed only within the framework of normative theory. Three leading proponents of such redirection in criminology, Taylor, Walton, and Young, point out that

> it should be clear that a criminology which is not normatively committed to the abolition of inequalities of wealth and power, and in particular in inequalities in property and life chances, is inevitably bound to fall into correctionalism. And all correctionalism is irreducibly bound up with the identification of deviance with pathology. A fully social theory of deviance must, by its nature, break entirely with correctionalism . . . [because] . . . the causes of crime must be intimately bound up with the form assumed by the social arrangements of the time.[10]

Crime and deviance are created and perpetuated by coercive social control. The task of a critical theory of social control is to unmask the contradictory forms and directions that the illegitimate uses of power take in conflict situations.

METAPHOR

Structural Contradictions as Conflict Imagery

From Marx, the conflict imagery of political processes borrows the logic of opposites, the dialectical movement in which built-in social antagonisms lead to structural transformation. Thus, all social systems, whatever their peculiar historical form, undergo continuous processes of development, change, dissolution, and renewal.[11]

This is not a revolutionary idea in sociology. The Chicago School posited a similar unfolding social structure which undergoes continuous organization, disorganization, and reorganization. Their imagery, however, remained locked into obsolete conceptions of social order as a progressive movement which was manifested by the inevitable absorption of backward populations into a unified, middle-class morality and life-style. Limited by these ideological blinders, the concept of social organization remained a stunted one.

When applied to organizational analysis, the idea of structural contradictions compels investigators to examine gaps between managerial theories of participation and organizational practices of exclusion. This directs attention to the organizational processes initiated by elites in order to maintain order and stability, that actually generate dissent, deviance, and rebellion among nonelites. Contrast images constitute an integral element of this explanatory scheme. Unmasking authority structures requires that managerial containment ideologies and coercive bureaucratic practices be identified.

Bureaucracy, from this point of view, is not merely a technical system of administration. It is a system designed primarily for the organization and distribution of power and for the formulation of policy within institutions, between institutions, and within societies. Leaders of large-scale enterprises attempt to extend their own freedom, autonomy, and opportunities for self-interested decision making by repressing the interference, power, and interests of others within their administrative sphere.

Weber provided the foundations for the technical description of large-scale organizations. The key theme in his analysis is the administrator's separation from centers of power similar to the worker's separation from control of production. Vidich and Bensman's updated version of this theme depicts bureaucracy as diametrically opposed to the Jeffersonian and Jacksonian image of viable democracy:

> Bureaucracies are characterized by relatively fixed hierarchies
> and spheres of competence (jurisdictions), and they depend on
> files and legalistic regulations for specifying their operations.
> The entire bureaucracy depends on technical experts who are
> engaged in a lifelong career and who are dependent on their
> jobs as their major means of support. Thus, discipline, obedience,
> loyalty, and impersonal respect for authority tend to become
> psychological characteristics of the bureaucrat.[12]

Large-scale organizations routinize control by making standardized decisions which lump thousands of cases into predescribed categories that are determined by institutional managers' hidden agendas. The rationale for decisions remains clouded in secrecy, thus hiding the purpose and relevance of decisions from lower-echelon, clientele groups and the public. Supporting this control apparatus, an expanding army of experts (e.g., administrators, psychiatrists, social workers, judges, prison wardens, criminologists), who have been assigned the crucial defining and regulating tasks, perpetuate these bureaucratic mystifications in their everyday relations with clients.

Security and secrecy systems, rationalized as organizationally indispensable, actually contribute to the restrictive norms of a closed society. Secrecy, as a standard operating procedure for public and private associations, is a device for controlling politically sensitive information and individuals.[13] Organizational elites use privileged information for their own ends, and rank-and-file administrators, disciplined to carry out orders, may avoid or ignore questions about this information's fundamental value. According to Lowry, secrecy systems, when viewed in terms of institutional survival, appear counterproductive.

> . . . secrecy . . . provides a screen behind which shoddy, meaningless, and trivial work (and in extreme cases, charlatanism) can continue with minimum criticism and questioning.[14]

The control of privileged information and the use of democratic rhetoric enable those who run large-scale institutions to maintain order by concealing actual sources of power and authority. A conflict perspective uncovers ideological obfuscations to reveal the inherent contradictions and inconsistencies of organized life. The following diagram, which compares managerial rhetoric with conflict interpretations of managerial practice, suggests some of the possibilities of this perspective.

Managerial Rhetorics (Democratic Ideology)	Managerial Practices (Conflict Perspective)
Democratic Order:	*Despotic Order:*
Open participation in rule making by all ranks; circulation of elite.	Rule making restricted to elites, centrist tendencies in modern, large-scale organizations effectively exclude bottom rankers from decision making.
Cooperation:	*Coercion:*
Voluntary participation in division of labor; citizen approval and loyalty to existing distributions of power, wealth, and authority. Free choice to enter occupational world based on training, skills, and initiative.	Unwilling involvement in compulsory division of labor; underclass resistance to existing political and economic systems; sanctions and lack of alternatives are organizational tactics to maintain system; dissenters treated as "deviants" —criminals requiring coercive control.

FIGURE 8.2. *Typical Expressions of Managerial Rhetoric and Conflict Interpretations of Practice*

Equality:

Open opportunity and political inclusion of all citizens; "the law is no respecter of ranks"; rich and poor equal access to basic institutions (legal, educational, government, medical, etc.).

Inequality:

Closed opportunity structure for political minorities (women, ethnics, blacks, homosexuals, youth, etc.); differential treatment of minorities in all institutional spheres; lack of access to goods and services for underclass.

Affluence:

Present competitive structure promotes high levels of personal wealth; increasing citizen ownership and control over property; freedom-from-want a reality in advanced democratic state.

Scarcity:

Present system restricts the giant proportion of earning power and profits to elites; permanent inflation in advanced capitalist state creates new and persistent bases of economic inequality and hardship.

Power Diffusion:

Power is situational, mercurial, and lacks a fixed organizational basis (e.g., family or corporation); bargaining among multiple-interest groups in legislative arena negates power build-up for any class or interest.

Power Concentration:

Power, by definition, is a system-based phenomenon; distribution of resources constitutes the power structure of that system. Control over resources (wealth, land, public office, ownership of media, strategic information, etc.) by corporate, government, and military elites determines public policy and private goals; because resources are cumulative (e.g., wealth "buys" influence in politics), power tends to be increasingly concentrated in the capitalist state.[15]

Cultural Diversity:

Pluralistic system encourages multiple values and life-styles; political minorities' views protected by Bill of Rights.

Cultural Hegemony:

Official ideology, expressed in media, policy making and planning, controls tastes and judgements in every institution; commercial values extolled over personal ones; mass education denigrates minority life-styles (e.g., rejection of Black English); monolithic culture ideal undermines working-class solidarity and militance.

Depoliticization of Masses:

Solidarity of interests across ranks and groups; opportunity for mobility and accommodation of ethnics into mainstream

Politicization of Minorities:

Antagonism of interests between top and bottom rankers; politicization (e.g., social movements, protests, riots, revolu-

FIGURE 8.2.   *(Continued)*

Depoliticization of Masses:

society mitigates against political uprising.

Politicization of Minorities:

tion) seen as only recourse for excluded (e.g., blacks, migrant workers, radical feminists, etc.); ruthless suppression of some minority actions (e.g., Kent State, Black Panthers) demonstrates threatened power structure.

Legitimacy:

Authority maintained by consent of governed; citizen participation assured by voting and local party activities; competence of officials and legality of procedures guarantees that the public interest is served.

Illegitimacy:

Authority maintained by tactics of exclusion and repression of diversity, and criticized or defied by increasing proportion of citizens; complex registration system eliminates a high proportion of voters; political decisions at local level trivial and irrelevant for directing national policies; officialdom and the law serve private interests.

Law and Order:

Law and enforcement promote order and stability; dissent and militancy deemed un-American; normal political processes suffice for citizen grievance against state.

Law versus Order:

Rule of class law undermines order by selective enforcement; discretionary administration; and police violence against insurgents (e.g., blacks); access to legal and political process effectively closed to political minorities and under-class; order preserved by and for elites by increasingly segregating out in hospitals, prisons, juvenile institutions, welfare settings, and ghetto schools, troublesome populations.

Reform:

Adjustment and amelioration within existing arrangements; institutional policies, aimed to correct structural deficiencies, promote increasing well-being for all ranks.

Change:

Present system unresponsive to political minorities and low rankers; increasing alienation among large segments of working-class and middle-class citizens; need for drastic overhauling of economic and political institutions; redistribution of power, wealth, and authority to restore citizens' rights.

FIGURE 8.2.   *(Continued)*

The inconsistency between democratic theory and exclusionary practices implies a massive degree of slippage in modern life. Sociological portrayals of bureaucracies as monolithic structures underestimate the difficulty elites have in imposing a consistent set of policies for managing and directing the economy. Widespread resistance to elites' control by low-ranking or excluded groups indicates that political institutions are inherently vulnerable. Such structural contradictions as I have described create authority systems that are inherently problematic, subject to repeated crises of legitimacy throughout their institutional orders (e.g., Watergate, violence in ghetto schools, rising divorce rates, industrial sabotage, bargained justice, etc.).

In order to survive, an authority structure must maintain a delicate equilibrium between its demands for conformity and the patterns of resistance that may emerge. How do authorities prevent those who are injured or neglected by political decisions from attempting to change decisions, authority, or the entire political system itself? The management of discontent requires authorities to negotiate with potential partisans, allocating some resources in exchange for compliance. These benefits, however, are limited in order to restrain hostile elements from effectively altering the system. In Gamson's analysis, authorities attempt to control external influence at its source by regulating access to resources (e.g., poor persons cannot afford to run for public office) and denying opportunities to use these resources against decision makers (e.g. co-optation). Authorities also manipulate rewards and punishments in order to keep deviants in line and change the political attitudes of potential partisans, thus neutralizing antiauthority influences (e.g., tactics include organization image making, withholding information, persuasion, behavior modification techniques, and assigning sick or criminal labels).[16]

Control techniques have inherent dangers, Gamson goes on to say. While they forestall an immediate confrontation and increase the temporary maneuverability of authorities, they do not relieve pressure in the long run, and may even intensify it. The subsequent withdrawal of legitimacy by dissenters involves accusations of corruption, erosion of trust, coalition-building, criminal acts, open protest, and various forms of secondary adjustments that undermine institutional goals (e.g., informal factory groups which keep down production rates, teenage gangs, nudist colonies, religious cults, communal families, etc.).

The intimate link between power and conflict in organizational life means that opposition is built into authority structures. The inevitable dissent triggers counteractions by authority in order to maintain the structure. These counteractions are not necessarily punitive. To adapt to threats, organizations may employ a variety of sanctions, including manipulation of the reward structure, toleration of persistent deviance as a necessary evil (e.g., middle-class drug use, black markets), and redistribution of minor resources to partisans. By absorbing new interests and values, authorities forestall confrontation while maintaining existing arrangements. Repression is most likely to be directed at powerless groups who constitute serious threats to dominant life-styles and institutions.

In short, I am arguing for a view of organizations as flexible and adaptive structures which shape control to a variety of internal and external contingencies. To identify sources of stability and change, the scope of a social-control theory should cover several substantive areas. At the macro-social level, the focus is on market and political conditions that sustain and alter institutions. At the organizational and interorganizational level, the theory should explain the various consequences of social control for maintaining and transforming authority relations. Finally, at the personal level, the theory must account for the consciousness of deviant actors, whose deviations give rise to new forms of control and to institution building. These themes will be expanded in the following section.

Political Economy of Social Control

At the macro-social level, the theory should explain how contingencies (i.e., the chain of action and reaction) of control in market and political structures affect institutional maintenance and change. Social control must be viewed as directly related to the legitimate institutional order. Master institutions, serving as distributive systems, define what constitutes proper demand and determine the types and extent of legitimate resources available to different groups. As a characteristic set of supply-demand exchanges, institutional allocations operate through socially defined rules, roles, and sanctions.

This means that, in an unequal society divided by class, ethnicity, sex, and political and economic differences, politically powerful groups make and enforce rules that are detrimental to the interests and needs of powerless groups. At the initial stage of institutionalization, defining, labeling, and categorizing provide the commonsense reality within which social control proceeds. Becker summarizes how defining activities by dominant groups channel behavior of subordinates by imposing certain statuses:

> Elites, ruling classes, bosses, adults, men, Caucasians—super-
> ordinate groups generally—maintain their power as much by
> controlling how people define the world, its components
> and possibilities as by the use of more primitive forms of control.

> They may use more primitive modes of control to establish a
> hegemony and moral legitimacy based on control of definitions
> and labels, but the latter works more smoothly and costs less . . .
> When we study how moral enterpreneurs get rules made and
> how enforcers apply those rules in particular cases, we study the
> way superordinates of every description maintain their
> position. Put another way we study some of the forms of
> oppresssion and the means by which oppression achieves the
> status of being "normal," "everyday," and legitimate.[17]

The market and political imperatives of dominant groups, incorporated into law, administrative rulings, and enforcement procedures, constitute the next link in the social control chain. Legal processes exclude politically subordinate groups from participation in rule making and allocation decisions. Subsequent control practices protect and perpetuate entrenched interests by maintaining the resource deprivation of powerless groups.

The control chain is still incomplete, however. We need to pursue how institutions, by denying opportunities in legitimate sectors to deprived groups, contain the seeds of their own destruction or modification.

The rise of bastard institutions as illegitimate channels for distributing goods and services is one outcome of a division of labor based on structured inequality.[18] These institutions are what Merton calls innovative responses to normative scarcity.[19] Such alternative institutions may arise out of collective protest, or may reflect chronic, long-term deviations. They may operate without benefit of law, although often with the connivance of the legal establishment. Although they arise from different sources, bastard institutions develop social processes similar to those of legitimate institutions. They may be illegitimate distributors of goods and services or satisfy wants not considered legitimate, and are organized around gambling, prostitution, rackets, and black markets (e.g., adoption, abortion, "quack" medical practitioners, professional crime, and bootlegging). They often assume standard organizational forms, not unlike legitimate institutions. Bastard institutions are directed against the law or the declared moral values of society. While equivalent, in many ways, to institutional forms, they have the following distinguishing characteristics:

1. They are corrections of faults in institutional definitions and
   distributions.
2. They entail high risks for participants.
3. They are very likely to be unstable, often changing
   organizational forms and personnel to adapt to new conditions
   and demands.
4. They usually serve politically subordinate groups (e.g., the
   poor, blacks, youth, women, and so on).

5. Unsupported by collective protest, they are unlikely to influence legitimate distribution because they lie outside the realm of respectability.

6. Because of the lack of legal control and their efforts to maximize profits, they are likely to have inferior products and lower standards of production and to involve marginal producers.

7. Operating under dual constraints (i.e., the pressure to provide *sub rosa* distributive channels on the one hand, and the need to avoid sanctions from legitimate producers on the other), they are likely to undergo sharp breaks in routine. To cope with crisis situations, ideology and practice are modified drastically.[20]

Bastard institutions endure as long as they give expression to the values and wants of a deprived population and can insulate themselves from competition with other institutions. Changes in institutional life probably reflect a cyclical pattern which involves deficiencies in institutional distribution, collective protest or chronic deviation, the rise of bastard institutions, further collective protest, and, eventually, the legitimation of former bastard institutions. The crucial feature of institutional survival is that both legitimate and illegitimate institutions adapt through specialization, by orienting themselves to the limited populations they serve. Bastard institutions undergo transformations in form and function that may also include decriminalization. Even with such legal changes, however, the lack of politically disadvantaged groups' participation in policy making tends to perpetuate traditional stereotypes and practices. This fosters a renewed cycle of conflict and reorganization.

Power, in the political-conflict view, is problematic, for, even as it controls, it evokes opposition. Legitimating processes that strengthen organizations also generate countervailing forces that deny legitimacy. Opposition and cleavage are built into the structure, and should not be seen as external to it. As a regenerative force, opposition creates new organizations and stimulates reorganization, as new interests and powers are introduced. Thus, conflict is both the source of social change and the mechanism for modification and adjustment of prevailing social institutions.

This implies that legitimate power is not absolute. The typical order is negotiated, with benefits or values flowing from top to bottom strata in order to mitigate opposition by the deprived. Social control is active control, the adaptive regulation of powerless social groups by powerful collectivities and administrative units in response to the changing conditions or contingencies of control.[21] To control effectively, therefore, groups must continuously assess the values, costs, and consequences of regulation. To categorically deny underdogs certain highly demanded resources would undermine, if not overthrow, control structures. Master institutions prevail because regulation is flexible (even though often corrupt) and because alternative (illegal or quasi-legal) organizations provide desired resources (although these involve high costs for deprived populations). Packer's discussion of the crime tariff, assessed for illegitimate transactions (e.g., prostitution, homosexuality, abortion), suggests that legitimate groups promote the increase of illegitimate resources by making crime costly, rather than eliminating it.[22]

Social Organization of Social Control

At the organizational and interorganizational level of analysis, the theory should explain how organizational adaptations, designed to meet competition, contingencies, and organizational and technological innovations, affect the system of relations between power holders and the controlled. This means that changes in organizational rules and strategic actions enhance the power of some groups and diminish the power of others. We return to the now-familiar thesis that power, whether legitimate or illegitimate, generates opposition, thereby creating new organizations and stimulating reorganization along different lines. The continuous mixture of new interests that arise from reactions to power and the ebb and flow of resources from one sector to another transform and renew the social system.

However, organizations appear to be self-perpetuating units, if examined at only one historical point. Rather than assuming inevitable organizational continuity, a conflict perspective examines the systematic activities of organizations as political authority structures. The focus is upon the conflict process, during which organizations manufacture and manipulate definitions, procedures, bureaucratic priorities, and administrative control instruments. Because of their greater resources, organizations are better able to effect their desired outcomes than are unorganized citizens, and typically operate as self-serving systems.[23] As many of these organizational tendencies toward self-enhancement have been reviewed throughout these chapters, I shall mention only a few in terms of their implications for institutional control and change.

Outcome of value and group conflict. Policies that maintain sectarian values, despite social change and citizen resistance, often create high costs and inevitable weakening of control. For example, the legislation of certain forms of morality (e.g., sex, gambling, and drug laws) has been shown to be totally ineffective in enforcing order or changing behavior.[24] These laws encourage flourishing black markets that remain outside institutional control, and contribute to the withdrawal of legitimacy.

Outcome of differential power. Power arrangements have major effects on the patterning of illegal goods and services (a point I explicated in my analysis of bastard institutions). Regulation contributes to limited supply and product type, resource maldistribution, and higher costs. For example, according to informants, illegal abortions in the late 1960s cost up to ten times more than the present legal ones.

Outcomes of organizational management. Competition for scarce resources by regulatory bodies (e.g., education, welfare, and government units), leads to an efficiency or production conception of client management. Professional skills are subordinated to organizational goals; legal directives are exercised within precise organizational limits; and clientele needs are constrained by organizational quotas and other requirements. Police, social workers, teachers, and others who manage underclass groups frequently manifest this pattern.[25]

Outcomes of exchange between organizational managers and the controlled. Organizational mandates provide broad discretionary powers. This permits a highly structured bargaining system between controllers and clientele groups, relatively free of legal control and supervision. Authority that is maintained by complicity creates a negotiated order that is managed by functionaries to protect their vested interests.

Innovative strategies for client control may be coercive or supportive (e.g., informer systems, "plea bargaining," and advocacy hearings). Their effect is to tie the controlled into the authority network. Exchange, as an outgrowth of intergroup opposition, has the paradoxical effect of inducing innovative practices while it maintains status quo political arrangements. By adapting the legal order to organizational exigencies, control groups exert great influence in political, economic, and professional realms of power.

Outcomes of criminalizing behavior for institutional maintenance. In opposition to the functionalist argument that crime control establishes society's moral boundaries, a Marxist critique emphasizes how the criminalizing processes of dominant groups shore up the existing division of labor. By excluding competition (e.g., draining off surplus labor through welfare, mental institutions, or prisons), maintaining fundamental divisions between classes, and employing a vast retinue of enforcement occupations, institutional beneficiaries use crime to institute order. Writing about this coercive state power to criminalize, Marx held that

> ... crime takes a part of the superfluous population off the labor
> market and thus reduces competition among the laborers—up to a
> certain point preventing wages from falling below minimum—
> the struggle against crime absorbs another part of this population.
> Thus the criminal comes in as one of those natural "counter-
> weights" which bring about a correct balance and open up a
> whole perspective of "useful" occupations . . . the criminal . . .
> produces the whole of the police and of criminal justice,
> constables, judges, hangmen, juries, etc.; and all these different
> lines of business, which form equally many categories of the
> social division of labor. . . .[26]

Thus, crime and its control are part of the normal operating procedures that sustain the advanced capitalist state.

Outcomes of adaptive control. Active social control, I have stressed, is a continuous process by which values are examined, decisions are made about dominant values, and actions are taken to enforce decisions. Resource management by organizations involves a number of control strategies, including *ad-hoc*, practical solutions to police-client problems;[27] the co-optation of occupations and professions, leading to the practice of law as a confidence game;[28] differential selection of offenders;[29] and a variety of other technical and structural devices to facilitate control of offenders.[30] Evidence suggests that many of these practices may eventuate in the corruption of authority and loss of control.[31]

Control also varies with modes of occupational socialization (i.e., the forms of practices, sanctions, and changes). The most problematic features of some occupations are their doubtful and uncertain outcomes and the high probability of failure. An understanding of these contingencies and how they effect workers and clientele groups is crucial for a theory of social control.[32] No occupational group, regardless of status, is immune from the troubles of work. For example, the soaring costs of medical insurance for private physicians (necessary to cover the increasing number of malpractice grievances by patients) may be one factor stimulating reorganization of medical practice (e.g., group practice or hospital-based practice).

Ethnomethodologists, who study organizational classification systems, stress that control is by no means a uniform or automatic process.[33] Regulatory techniques have been shown to be adaptive, coping with a variety of internal and external constraints (e.g., technological and organizational change, struggles between hierarchies within the organization, rivalries between organizations, and resistant clientele and citizen groups). This supports a view of social control as problematic, contingent, and relative to its organizational context and the circumstances of use by participants.

Such structural conditions as innovation, value and group conflicts, power differences, and organizational activities create the basis for the distribution of power and differential enforcement of the law. According to the control perspective, crime itself is political behavior and the criminal is a member of a minority group without sufficient public support or private resources to strongly affect the police power of the State.

Responses to Control by the Controlled. In the interactionist conception of human character that informs labeling theory, the social actor is viewed as creative, open-ended, and existential. Character is dynamic and unfolding; self is a dialectic between conformity and spontaneity; plans of action shift with situational (time and place) definitions of social reality. The merit of this perspective is its uncovering of the deviant as an active participant in the social process who adapts to stigma and exclusion by generating self-protective social worlds.

But, constrained by a social psychology that is not informed by a sense of history or social structure, the labeling school takes as problematic the deviant outcomes, rather that the social sources that generate conflict.

We are exposed to deviants' hostile reactions to control, but lack a conception of the conscious alternatives that permit persons to plan, act purposefully, and rationally control the course of their social lives and history. Deviants are seen as persons who drift into deviance by "specific actions rather than by informed choices of social roles and statuses."[34] Locked into conventional social categories, the deviant plays out ideological struggles by efforts to normalize the stigmatized self.[35] The thesis that "authority acts, deviants react" reduces the conflict process to a product of an all-powerful officialdom.

This view shares with traditional sociologies of crime and deviance a static conception of pathological or passive deviants caught in the grip of an all-embracing, abstract System. It denies that actors are conscious choice makers,[36] and ignores the recent evidence of increased political organization among minorities. While these exploratory efforts toward self-determination have usually been quashed by symbolic reassurances, co-optation, or outright violence, self-help programs (e.g., day-care centers, free meals, liberation schools, medical care centers, legal defense) demonstrate that militant partisans are quite capable of consciously confronting their human condition. For example, while formulating Black Panther doctrines, Huey Newton once stated that "we see major contradictions between capitalism in this country, and our interests."[37] Even in the nonradicalized context of middle-class women's movements, we can observe the transformation of civil rights issues into political and economic ones, related to the distribution of power and material rewards. Marx has observed that the politically disaffected, especially militants, are more likely to be cognitively correct about the forces that shape their behavior or impede their ability to realize personal goals.[38]

In short, I am arguing for a drastic revision of current models, academic and lay, which regard deviants as passive, irrational, and quiescent. By studying criminals and providing rulers with knowledge, academics provide a scholarly support for political authorities which solidifies their power over the disadvantaged. Because of this absorption with the infractions of the powerless, the criminogenic character of the society remains undisclosed. Studying "slaves," rather than the institution of slavery, reaffirms existing arrangements, as Thomas Szasz notes:

> Suppose that a person wished to study slavery. How would he
> go about doing so? First, he might study slaves. He would then
> find that such persons are generally brutish, poor, and
> uneducated, and he might conclude that slavery is their "natural"
> or appropriate social status.[39]

Szasz emphasizes that the path out of this image of social reality is a relational, institutional view:

> Another student, "biased" by contempt for the institution of
> slavery, might proceed differently. He would maintain that there
> can be no slave without a master holding him in bondage; and he
> would accordingly consider slavery a type of human *relationship*
> and more generally, a *social institution*, supported by custom,
> law, religion, and force. From this point of view, the study of
> masters is at least as relevant to the study of slavery as is
> the study of slaves.[40]

C. Wright Mills once said that human beings "everywhere seek to know where they stand, where they may be going, and what, if anything, they can do about the present as history and future as responsibility."[41] Like Mills, I am seeking a historically grounded social science that is willing to confront the consciousness of actors who struggle with inequality and alienating organizations, threatened by declining individualism and expanding state power. To study historical structures is to understand the ways in which they are and can be controlled. To formulate choices within the broad limits of human possibilities is to suggest directions away from the present political incoherence, fragmentation, and drift and begin moving toward personal freedom and responsibility. To do otherwise is to perpetuate a science of control used by and for the powerful against the needs and aspirations of the powerless.

Summary and Conclusion

A conception of social control as legitimate institutional order was used to demonstrate how inequalities, created and perpetuated by dominant groups, generate opposition and alternative organizations. By positing the inherent maldistribution of resources in standard institutional arrangements, we observed the emergence of a legal order and political economy that shores up a restrictive segment of the moral order of society. Subordinate populations are excluded from rule making and the determination of crucial allocations.

By employing a dialectical model of control, I showed how structured scarcity has implications for social change by generating new organizations and stimulating reorganization of existing structures. For example, bastard institutions represent alternative structures that meet consumer needs, although they involve high costs for market participants. Power and conflict, stability and change are interrelated processes built into authority systems.

The reemergence of a conflict perspective in the study of deviance and social control is a promising development. Among other things, it holds out the prospect of theory that is informed by a sense of history. Studies of law, crime, and deviance may be characterized by a conception of complex interactions between developing institutions and social structures and of the consciousness of persons living within such structures, rather than by a static conception of immobilized deviants, irrationally compelled to play out the outsider's scenario. It implies an approach to deviance in which officially labeled deviance is not simply a product of powerful interests, but is, also, the product of collective action taken to resolve inequalities of power and interests. Law and professional occupations are viewed as flexible, adaptive instruments of control which modify strategies in order to accommodate themselves to situational contingencies. This approach avoids the determinism implicit in the labeling conception of a monolithic control apparatus which grinds out uniform deviant identities.

I have attempted to open debate by pointing to certain substantive requirements of a sociology of social control. A critical social theory should be able to explain the forms assumed by social control and deviance within developed societies. The theory is characterized, I have argued, by market and political imperatives, a division of labor that involves armies of experts who sustain and legitimate social inequalities, and the increasing use of repressive laws to criminalize proletariat dissent.

At one level, the theory should explain the wider origins of social control in the context of the political economy. At another level, it should explain the different ways in which structural constraints are instituted, reacted against, and used by persons at different points in the social structure. This implies that actors may consciously choose the deviant path as one solution to the problems posed by existence in a contradictory society. Deviance is a normal social fact, as Durkheim said.[42] Because the deviant rejects traditional stereotypes and asserts the right to human diversity, he or she may be seen as a political dissenter. As a temporary solution to structured inequality, deviance may be the necessary first step toward social reorganization and resource redistribution.

Shifting to a sociology-of-knowledge perspective, we could also speculate that deviance essentially becomes what the sociologist says it is. Isn't this sociological category making simply another way of stating moral evaluations about society and how to perceive, order, maintain, change, and correct it?

A conception of deviance is not simply an analytic description. It contains within it a variety of moral, political, and practical implications. The "facts" of deviance, drawn from lay and official stereotypes, are reinforced by some of the generic features of this concept. To deviate means to alter course, depart from, go astray, revolutionize, or step aside.[43] The lay person's rendering of these words is likely to imply that the deviant is immature, inadquate, irresponsible, unsocialized, destructive, degenerate, and so on. These terms are the traditional ones of sin and immorality on to which newer concepts (drawn from functional, psychiatric, or social disorganization notions) have been grafted, and an increase in social prestige and credibility has been given to these social science definitions. Such categorical treatment of deviants as a special social type often justifies authoritarian techniques of social control under the guise of a benevolent science.

The sentimental version of deviation offered by the labeling school does not provide a way out of the definitional bind. The humanistic tradition that animates much of the labeling school reflects a rejection of both the status quo and formalistic sociology. By assuming the relativity of normality and abnormality, identifying the observer with the observed, and celebrating the diverse and the socially rejected, labeling theory has constructed the framework for a critique of the routine moral order and a sociology that is an apologia for such an order. The human proportions of the thief, the prostitute, and the mental patient are delineated from these outsiders' perspectives by describing their social systems, definitions, and efforts to cope with stigmatization. Transformed from victimizers to victims, such groups become more credible and significant than the standard institutional world that has forced them into being. From this perspective, conventional institutions no longer appear to be given, unalterable, and self-evident, but only to be as legitimate or illegitimate as the condemned.

However, fixation on the controlled, to the neglect of the controllers, blocks the development of a critical sociology that attempts to account for institutional life and its various manifestations. What is needed is not a sociology of deviance, but a sociology of social control, which aims at accounting for social order as a tentative and problematic process, itself an outcome of organizational conflict and exchange. The classical sociological concerns of societal analysis, articulated by Durkheim, Weber, and Marx, and later restated by Lemert and recent conflict theorists, posit a social order that contains built-in opposition and cleavage. The major sociological task in this era of chronic and often drastic change is the development of a theory that accounts for institutions as an outgrowth of power struggles and ideological conflicts. By recognizing the power and conflict inherent in organized life, the sociologist may seek explanations of crime and deviance in the institutions that define and regulate behavior and in the social relations created by these structures. This distribution of power, organization of production, legal definitions, and controlling activities are central concerns which provide analytic starting points for the delineation of the structural conditions that generate rule breakers. Labeling, in a sense, is a consequence and symbol of power. Exactly how such power is appropriated and maintained by organizational exchange and a legitimating apparatus remains a persistent question in sociological theory and research.

CHAPTER NOTE

Formal Requirements of a Social Control Model

Formal requirements for theory are the procedural rules that guide the construction of theories, including their causal structure and scope. The causal or logical structure involves identifying that class of phenomena (e.g., events, relations, ideas, etc.) that causes (i.e., determines, influences, affects) or has consequences for the events or relations in question. Concepts describe classes of phenomena by stipulating what events or relations are to be covered, and how they are to be defined, operationalized (i.e., translated into variables), and measured. In addition, propositional statements must be falsifiable (i.e., capable of being proved wrong), and connected into a logical structure that explains the phenomenon at different levels of generality.[44]

Taking the bare-bones outline of procedural tactics, let me indicate in a very preliminary way, how we might proceed to construct propositions for a political-conflict model of control, and what kind of facts might be derived from these suggestive propositions.

At the highest level of generality, we wish to posit some general ideas about causality, about what can be accepted as a fact. In our analysis, this is:

ASSUMPTION 1.1   *Power exists, and causes all observed deviance.*

It is obvious that this statement says very little about the empirical world. It is too general, as it catches too many phenomena within its scope. We will need to move to a lower level of generality in order to specify more adequately the relationships between power and deviance. These relations can be summarized as:

PROPOSITION 1.1   *A higher degree of illegitimate power in any political system causes a higher rate of deviance.*

While this statement contains the basic concepts of the theory (power, political structure, deviance) and shows the expected connections between them, it remains in a definitional limbo. Therefore, key terms will be defined in order to clarify theoretical meanings and provide guides for observation.

DEFINITION 1.1   *Power is the capacity to affect outcomes in any system, where "system" refers to any specified set of relations.*

1.2   *Power is operationalized as the resources that persons or groups may use to effect system outcomes.*

1.3   *A resource is any attribute, circumstance, or possession that increases the ability of its holder to influence a person or group (e.g., wealth, land, public office, reputation for power, high social status, access to influential persons, social memberships, strategic information, etc.).*

1.4   *The value of any specific resource is determined by the system. (The investigator, therefore, must make judgments based on existing knowledge, social practices, and the actors' definition of the situation about what constitutes a resource for any specific system.)*

The next set of definitions deals with the political structure as an exchange system, in which the rules that govern high-resource classes determine allocations for low-resource classes.

DEFINITION 2.1   *A political system is a set of relations in which resources are distributed and exchanged.*

2.2   *Rulers are in the relatively high-resource class which allocates resources in the system. The ruled are the relatively low-resource class which receives resources.*

2.3   *Rulers set the values, rules, and terms for distribution and exchange in any political system of relations.*

Power is further differentiated into legitimate and illegitimate rule.

DEFINITION 3.1   *Legitimate power is the control of resources in accordance with legally established rules, principles, or standards (also termed authority).*

3.2   *Illegitimate power is the control of resources that violate legally established rules.*

4.1   *Deviance is any behavior of the ruled class that is defined by rulers as violation of established rules and standards.*

4.2   *Deviance is any form of opposition to the rules and standards of rulers that is displayed by the ruled class.*

4.3   *Since any opposition to rulers creates conflict, deviance is a form of conflict.*

Proposition 1.1, translated according to these definitions, means that, as the accumulation of resources within the ruler class begins to violate the legal codes or standards established by rulers, the incidence of conflict (i.e., deviance) will increase. As resources accumulate for rulers, they decrease for the ruled. The following proposition summarizes this relationship:

PROPOSITION 2.1   *A decrease in resources among the ruled leads to a higher rate of conflict.*

This implies that any change in resource distribution that favors one class (i.e., a particular group, class of persons, or sector) over another is likely to generate opposition. For example, in 1974, the United States "oil crisis," created by a monopolistic industry and supported by government controls, resulted in the scarcity and sharply increased costs of gas, fuel, and oil-related products. Consequent rebellion by truckers, whose livelihood depends on cheap, readily available gas supplies, led to strikes, boycotts, barricading of major highways, and open violence.

This case suggests that the resources of subordinate groups need not appreciably decline for opposition to occur. Any group that loses a favored position or fails to influence decision making is likely to respond negatively. This argument may also be stated in propositional form:

PROPOSITION 3.1   *A decreased ability of any party to effect system outcomes will lead to increased conflict in any political system of relations.*

The obverse, that increased power for the ruled will decrease conflict, should hold as well. Thus, institutional managers may prevent or reduce conflict by providing additional benefits (including some power) for potential troublemakers, but only up to the point where partisans could seriously affect the system and change it in their favor.

Still another consideration related to the "power-causes-conflict" assumption is the contradiction that appears when rulers set the terms for exchange, then violate them with their practices. This is illegitimate power (e.g., democratic ideology expressed by despotic rulers) which entails the denial of opportunities to relatively low-resource groups, preventing them from affecting system outcomes. I shall refine and extend Proposition 3.1 as:

COROLLARY 3.1   *A perception by any party in a system of power relations that their existing resources will not affect system outcomes leads to conflict.*

This corollary implies that actors' definitions of the situation must be taken into account. What are the political expectations promoted by ruling groups? To what extent do organizational elites manipulate symbols of inclusion while effectively excluding lower orders from participation? What are the conditions under which lack of participation generates conflict? These questions can be answered only by understanding concrete systems of relations.

For example, why are some populations docile and others rebellious? One answer is that authority relations have different historical sources and existing structures. Another consideration is that behavior may be an outcome of changed expectations. To use a specific case, protests among the black underclass of Northern cities may reflect a change in expectations as a result of increased participation in the political system. Because they have more contact with mainstream persons (e.g., work, shopping, media watching), urban blacks may come to recognize the systematic forms of exclusion that operate against them as a class. As a consequence of perceived deprivation (relative to what others in the system receive), rebellion may occur, taking the forms of crime, deviance, and dissent.

Obviously, if any system of relations generates an excessive amount of opposition and rebellion, it cannot survive. Underdogs may withdraw completely (e.g., suicide); they may seek alternative relationships or organizations (e.g., black markets rather than legitimate ones); they may keep situations stirred up by open dissent; or they may establish coalitions with other deprived groups or with defected elites in an attempt to drastically alter the system. By carefully manipulating the reward system, managers may be able to forestall rebellion and enhance their social position. To further discuss the maintenance of political structures, an additional definition is needed:

DEFINITION 5.1 *Sanctions are the systems of rewards and penalties manipulated by rulers against the ruled in order to maintain any existing political system.*

An understanding of the relationship between power, conflict, and control requires that we locate various deviant forms in an organizational context (e.g., neighborhood, school, family, work place, etc.) by identifying what constitutes deviance for that specific social system, who defines it, who sanctions it, and against whom the sanctions are directed. I suspect that the most severely sanctioned acts are those that constitute the greatest threat to the authority system in question. Thus, if our "power causes deviance" hypothesis is correct, we would expect to find the following derived statement about the relationship between power, deviance, and control to hold true:

PROPOSITION 4.1 *The severity of the sanction is related to the relative amount of resources held by the conflicting party, and to elites' perception of the degree to which the behavior constitutes a threat to the authority system.*

Immediate consequences of this differential sanction system can be further spelled out, as these corollaries to proposition 4.1 indicate:

COROLLARY 4.1 *Token (or no) penalties will be associated with deviance committed by high-resource persons, as part of highly regarded occupational activities (e.g., white-collar crime, corporate and government fraud) that sustain the existing political system.*

COROLLARY 4.2 *Moderate penalties (e.g., loss of reputation, social exclusion, loss of job, fines) will be associated with deviance, committed by moderate-resource persons in groups which do not constitute a serious threat to the political system.*

COROLLORY 4.3 *The most severe penalties (e.g., prison, police harassment, or brutality) will be associated with violations committed by low-resource persons, that constitute the greatest threat to the political system.*

Depending on their structural location, actors commit different forms of deviance, but the extent of deviance is probably the same for most social classes and groups. How these deviant acts are defined and penalized, the type of offense, and the degree to which it is perceived as threatening to the system varies with the group committing the offense (e.g., riots by poor blacks are punished, while police brutality is ignored). Crimes against property and persons and other infractions by lower working-class groups that constitute serious threats to the life-style and authority systems of dominant classes are the most severely sanctioned.

Sanctioning, as an expression of power, has varying consequences for actors in the system. Deviance is normalized for high-resource violators, tolerated for moderate-resource violators, and severely punished for low-resource persons and groups. Those who make and enforce rules establish the boundaries of normality, determine who falls within or outside these boundaries, and affix penalties to violations in terms of the degree to which they perceive them to undermine or destroy the authority system.

To falsify the "power-causes-deviance" hypothesis, it is necessary to observe cases that run counter to the expected direction. For example, social movements that result in citizen-sponsored legislation and decriminalization (e.g., new gambling and abortion laws) reflect successful efforts to effect structural outcomes in line with alternative interests and values. This means that my hypothesis requires refinement in order to include those conditions under which authorities are likely to respond to contingencies by modifying control tactics. These are stated as conditions for maintaining political authority:

CONDITION 1.1   *Under conditions of low threat (as defined by rulers), rulers will tolerate various alternative (quasi-legal, illegal) forms of behavior.*

CONDITION 1.2   *Under conditions of moderate threat (as defined by rulers), rulers will incorporate new interests, leading to redistribution of resources.*

CONDITION 1.3   *Under conditions of severe threat (as defined by rulers), rulers will repress dissent.*

Thus, control involves manipulation of the reward system, tolerance of various forms of illegality and deviance, incorporation of new interests, or outright repression of conflict. Manipulation of the control system may be most often practiced but, if that fails or is not completely effective, a "live and let live" attitude may become a typical response. Under relatively intense and persistent citizen pressure, organizations may also adapt to threat by absorbing new interests and values, in order to obviate the possibility of any basic alterations in existing arrangements. Repression is a final tactic of control that invariably carries inherent dangers. Since open repression (e.g., police shoot-outs) can mobilize sympathetic outsiders, necessitating the extension of repression into formerly "friendly" territory, it is used cautiously and, preferably, invisibly. It is likely to be mythologized for public consumption as something else (e.g., the law-and-order myth).

At this preliminary level of theory construction, I have suggested some directions that a political-conflict theory of control could take in spelling out the relationships between power and conflict and between organizational adaptation and change. Key concepts (including power, authority, political system, conflict, control, sanction) have been defined in a propositional form that states the expected relationships between them. A more complete theoretical construction requires that propositions be ordered from the most general level of causation to derived statements of relationships between variables (how variables covary). The latter serves as hypotheses, requiring observations that support or refute these postulated relationships. This task, it is hoped, will be a major concern of theorists who attempt to explain the role of power and its varied consequences for social order and change.

NOTES

1. Ian Taylor, Paul Walton, and Jock Young, *The New Criminology* (London and Boston: Routledge & Kegan Paul, 1973), p. 270.

2. Ralf Dahrendorf, "European Sociology and the American Self-Image," *European Journal of Sociology* 2 (1961): 324-366.

3. William J. Chambliss and Robert B. Seidman, *Law, Order, and Power* (Reading, Mass.: Addison-Wesley Publishing Company, 1971), p. 53.

4. Anthony Platt reviews the implications of the prevailing ideology which underlies most research and theory in criminology in "The Triumph of Benevolence: The Origins of the Juvenile Justice System in the United States," in *Criminal Justice in America*, ed. Richard Quinney (Boston: Little, Brown and Company, 1974), pp. 356-389. Reynolds and Henslin also critique the liberal ideology in terms of its emasculating impact on social organization theory in Larry T. Reynolds and James M. Henslin, eds., *American Society: A Critical Analysis* (New York: David McKay Company, Inc., 1973), pp. 1-21.

5. Gans argues that the "politics of culture" (struggle for resources and ascendancy in the marketplace) involves the same market and political manipulation of ideas as other mass merchandizing of products or politicians. Constraints from patrons, distributors, or constituents thus limit the production of ideas to "safe," popular, and marketable commodities. Herbert J. Gans, "The Politics of Culture in America," in *Social Problems and Public Policy: Inequality and Justice*, ed. Lee Rainwater (Chicago: Aldine Publishing Company, 1974), pp. 353-360.

6. Richard Flacks has an excellent discussion of authority in *Conformity, Resistance, and Self-Determination: The Individual and Authority* (Boston: Little, Brown and Company, 1973), pp. 4-18.

7. For other representative works employing a social control-political conflict perspective, see K. Marx in *Karl Marx, Selected Writings in Sociology and Social*

Philosophy, ed. T. B. Bottomore and M. Rubel (London: Watts, 1956); R. Dahrendorf, "Toward a Theory of Social Conflict," *Journal of Conflict Resolution* 11, 1958; E. M. Lemert, *Human Deviance, Social Problems and Social Control* (Englewood Cliffs, N.J.: Prentice-Hall Inc., 1964); Richard Quinney, *Crime and Justice in Society* (Boston: Little, Brown & Co., 1970); idem. *Criminal Justice in America,* (Boston: Little, Brown & Co., 1974); A. Turk, *Criminality and the Legal Order* (Chicago: Rand McNally & Co., 1969); Taylor, Walton, Young, *New Criminology.* Conflict theory is not necessarily critical (or normative) theory. Importantly, both functional and conflict explanations, until recently, either take an explicitly pro system point of view (e.g., Lewis A. Coser, *The Functions of Social Conflict* (London: Free Press, 1956) or consider how existing authority relations generate conflict and criminality (e.g., Dahrendorf, Turk, and Lemert). Critical-conflict theory, therefore, represents a sharp break away from existing value-neutral paradigms. In line with this, I use a radical critique to construct an alternative theory of social control that joins Weber's conception of multiple-interest groups and their struggles, to Marx's dialectical theory of power and its opposition in transforming structures.

8. Richard Quinney, "Crime Control in Capitalist Societies: A Critical Philosophy of Legal Order," *Issues in Criminology* 8 (Spring, 1973): 75-99. This article is also summarized in *Critique of Legal Order,* Chapter 1. Quinney, among American criminologists, is the leading advocate for a critical theory of conflict. In England, Taylor, Walton and Young have forcefully argued for this position. See, also, John Rex, "Sociological Theory and Deviancy Theory," Unpublished paper delivered to the 1971 Annual Conference of the British Sociological Association; and J. Rex and R. Moore, *Race, Community and Conflict: A Study in Sparkbrook* (London: Institute of Race Relations: Oxford University Press). Two British writers have compiled a collection of papers taken from the proceedings of the National Deviancy Conference that examine empirical cases of social control as political action. See Ian Taylor and

Laurie Taylor, *Politics and Deviance* (Baltimore, Md.: Penguin Books, 1973).

9. Michael Polanyi presents his own highly complex version of critical philosophy in *Personal Knowledge* (New York: Harper Torchbooks, 1964), p. 16.

10. Taylor, Walton, and Young, *New Criminology,* p. 281.

11. The naive view that Marx saw only two classes, the bourgeoisie and the proleteriat, in capitalist societies engaging in struggle that eventuates in social transformation is, of course, fallacious. The significance of the analytic division into opposing classes provides a handle for sorting out fundamental antagonisms between those who rule, and those who are ruled. See the excellent discussion and review of conflict theory in William J. Chambliss, "Functional and Conflict Theories of Crime," New York: MSS Modular Publication, Module 17, 1973: 1-23.

12. Arthur Vidich and Joseph Bensman, *The New American Society* (Chicago: Quadrangle Books, 1971), pp. 21-22.

13. The sociological character of secrecy has been most fully developed by Georg Simmel. See *The Sociology of Georg Simmel,* Kurt H. Wolff, ed. and trans. (New York: The Free Press of Glencoe, 1950), pp. 307-376. Ritchie P. Lowry also offers a discussion of organizational implications of information manipulation in "Towards a Sociology of Secrecy and Security Systems," *Social Problems* 19 (Spring 1972): 437-450.

14. Lowry, *Social Problems,* p. 44.

15. A recent analysis of power emphasizes its *systemic* properties. See Mary F. Rogers, "Instrumental and Infra-Resources: The Bases of Power," *American Journal of Sociology* 79 (May 1974): 1418-1433.

16. William A. Gamson combines two perspectives on power and discontent, the influence perspective and social-control perspective, to present a model of the potential-partisan authority relationship. *Power and Discontent* (Homewood, Ill.: Irwin-Dorsey, Limited, 1968), ch. 6.

17. Howard S. Becker, "Labelling Theory Reconsidered," in *Deviance and Social Control,* ed. Paul Rock and Mary McIntosh (London: Tavistock, 1973).

18. How institutions come into being and survive or fail to survive is a central question guiding Hughes' study of occupations and the moral division of labor. See *The Growth of an Institution: The Chicago Real Estate Board* (Chicago: Society for Social Research, University of Chicago) series 2, monograph 1, 1931; and idem, *The Sociological Eye: Selected Papers* (Chicago: Aldine-Atherton, 1972) chaps. 1, 2, 10. The "bastard institutions" conception of alternative institutions is drawn from the latter work.

19. Robert Merton, *Social Theory and Social Structure* (New York: The Free Press, 1957), pp. 141-149.

20. I discuss bastard institutions with specific reference to the transforming abortion market in N. Davis, "Bastard Institutions as Alternative Distributive Systems: Toward a Sociology of Social Control" (Paper presented to the annual meeting of the Society for the Study of Social Problems, Montreal, Canada, August 24, 1974).

21. Lemert, in *Human Deviance, Social Problems and Social Control*, rejects the view of the organization as Leviathan. I draw on his discussion of social control as "adaptive control."

22. Herbert L. Packer, *The Limits of the Criminal Sanction* (Stanford: Stanford University Press, 1968).

23. See E. Hughes, *The Growth of an Institution: The Chicago Real Estate Board;* and idem, *The Sociological Eye: Selected Papers;* also *Man, Work and Society: A Reader in the Sociology of Occupations*, ed., Sigmund Nosow and William H. Form (New York: Basic Books, 1962).

24. See, for example, Lemert's preliminary formulation of alcohol use and control costs in *Human Deviance, Social Problems and Social Control*. Edwin Schur also discusses outcomes of value conflict in legislating morality in *Crimes Without Victims* (Englewood Cliffs, N.J.: Prentice-Hall, 1965) and *Our Criminal Society* (Englewood Cliffs, N.J.: Prentice-Hall, 1969).

25. Lee Rainwater, "The Revolt of the Dirty-Workers," *Transaction* 5 (November 1967): 12.

26. Chambliss, *Law, Order, and Power*, p. 7.

27. Egon Bittner, "The Police on Skid Row: A Study of Peace Keeping," *American Sociological Review* 32 (October 1967): 699-715.

28. A. S. Blumberg, "The Practice of Law as Confidence Game: Organizational Cooptation of a Profession," *Law and Society Review* 1 (June 1967): 15-39.

29. William Chambliss draws on his participant observation in two urban mileux (Seattle, Washington and Ibadan, Nigeria in Africa) to emphasize the ubiquity of crime and deviance across social classes in "Functional and Conflict Theories of Crime," module 17 (New York: MSS Modular Publications, Inc., 1973), 16-20. For a recent analysis of differential application of criminal labels, see T. G. Chiricos, P. D. Jackson, and G. P. Waldo, "Inequality in the Imposition of a Criminal Label," *Social Problems* 19 (Spring 1972): 553-572.

30. J. H. Skolnick and J. R. Woodworth, "Bureaucracy, Information and Social Control: A Study of a Morals Detail," in *The Police: Six Sociological Essays*, ed. David Bordua (New York: John C. Wiley and Sons, 1967).

31. See William J. Chambliss's discussion in *Crime and the Legal Process* (New York: McGraw-Hill, 1968).

32. See, for example, H. S. Becker, B. Geer, D. Riesman, and R. S. Weise, eds., *Institutions and the Person* (Chicago: Aldine Publishing, 1968).

33. Relevant studies include, for example, David Sudnow, "Normal Crimes: Sociological Features of the Penal Code in a Public Defender Office," *Social Problems* 12 (Winter 1965): 255-276 and Aaron Cicourel, *The Social Organization of Juvenile Justice* (New York: John C. Wiley and Sons, 1968).

34. Lemert's discussion of secondary deviation as "drift," may be only one alternative for moving into the deviant role. See *Human Deviance, Social Problems and Social Control*, p. 51. We prefer to emphasize the *consciousness* of actors as choice makers. Undoubtedly both of these processes (drift and conscious choice) are involved, although, perhaps, for different actors in different control situations.

35. The issue of neutralizing techniques, as coping mechanisms that devi-

224   SOCIAL CONTROL PERSPECTIVE

ants typically employ, approaches the status of a doctrine, among labeling theorists. This places opposition within conventional moral frameworks, a thesis we reject. See G. M. Sykes and D. Matza, "Techniques of Neutralization: A Theory of Delinquency," *American Sociological Review* 22 (December 1957): 664-670.

36. The concept of choice as an integral element of actors' transactions has been developed by social anthropologists (as well as symbolic interactionists). For representative works, see Victor W. Turner, *Schism and Continuity in an African Society* (Manchester: Manchester University Press for the Rhodes-Livingston Institute, 1957); Fredrick Barth, "The Role of the Entrepreneur in Social Change in Northern Norway," (Acta Universitas: Bergensis Series Humaniorium Litterarum No. 3. Bergen: 1963); and "Models of Social Organization," Royal Anthropological Institute, Occasional Papers, 1966; and J. Clyde Mitchell, ed., *Social Networks in Urban Situations* (New York: Humanities Press, Inc., Distributors, 1969).

37. Charles H. Anderson, *The Political Economy of Social Class* (Englewood Cliffs, N.J.: Prentice-Hall, Inc., 1974) p. 300.

38. This interpretation of Marx is offered by Stanley Aronowitz in "Law, the Breakdown of Order, and Revolution,"

in *Criminal Justice in America,* ed. R. Quinney, pp. 394-414.

39. Thomas S. Szasz, "Involuntary Mental Hospitalization: A Crime Against Humanity," in *Ideology and Insanity,* ed. T. S. Szasz (Garden City, N.Y.: Doubleday Anchor, 1970), p. 123.

40. Ibid., p. 124.

41. C. Wright Mills, *The Sociological Imagination* (New York: Grove Press, Inc., 1959), p. 165.

42. What Durkheim meant by this idea is often misinterpreted as the inevitable acceptance of widespread illegality as a "normal" event in society. What we mean is that *under conditions of inequality and resource deprivation,* characteristic of advanced capitalist states, deviance and crime are "normal" reactions to powerlessness, or conversely, are standard operating procedures among power holders. See E. Durkheim's discussion in *The Rules of Sociological Method,* S. A. Solovay and J. H. Mueller, trans. (New York: The Free Press, 1938).

43. Stanley Cohen provides a highly lucid discussion of the implications of these linguistic constructs in his introduction to *Images of Deviance* (Baltimore, Md.: Penguin Books, Ltd., 1971), p. 10.

44. Arthur L. Stinchcombe provides one of the more readable analyses of theory construction in *Constructing Social Theories* (New York: Harcourt, Brace & World, Inc., 1968).

GLOSSARY

Active control Term used by E. Lemert, referring to bureaucratic mode of adapting regulation of powerless groups by continuous managerial assessment of costs and consequences of control.

Analytic induction Method of abstracting generalizations by examining negative cases; propositions are to be universal generalizations that hold for all cases investigated; e.g., Lindesmith's drug addition study.

Anomie Applies to social characteristics of society, as in breakdown of regulatory norms (Durkheim); or faulty arrangement of status and roles (Merton); in characterizing persons, it refers to anxiety, normlessness, and purposelessness induced by social disorganization.

Anomie theory Robert Merton's theory of deviance in which cultural goals and institutional means to goals are out of joint, producing stress and deviant behavior especially among disadvantaged groups.

Amelioration Correctional mode of addressing social problems; emphasized adjusting individual to industrial sector through clinical, public health, or manipulating public opinion models of rehabilitation.

Authority Legitimate power in accordance with legally established rules, principles, or standards.

Bastard institutions Scarcity of legitimate allocations lead to alternative social organizations; any form of relatively persistent and organized opposition which effects supply and distribution of resources.

Boundary maintenance Autonomy of a social system that preserves the existing structure of relations. Functionalists view deviance as defining the outer limits of the moral order, thereby strengthening in-group bonds.

Bureaucracy (or bureaucratic state) Large-scale organizations stressing technical goals (e.g., profits or numbers of persons processed) and cost accounting methods. Features include hierarchy, strict division of labor, technical skills, value neutrality, centrism, and secrecy.

Career crime A generic term for roles built around criminal activities; includes crime as a livelihood, criminal identity, and extensive association with criminals and criminal life-styles.

225

Chicago School   Ecology and interaction focus to social organization; cultural transmission notion of learned behavior; theory emphasized direct observation of local urban milieux, appreciation and often identification with the deviant enterprise, taking the actor's perspective, and the ethnographic style. Predecessor of the value-conflict approach and, especially, the labeling perspective.

Choice behavior   Assumption that persons plan and weigh alternatives in terms of specific situational constraints and opportunities; presumes actors to be conscious agents.

Coercion   In conflict theory, legitimate social organization is the compulsory division of labor exerted by dominant groups.

Collective determinism   An assumption that society is greater than the individuals composing it; society as *sui generis,* or acting unit, determines individual actions.

Conformity   Compliance and institutional loyalty in accord with dominant rules and practices.

Consensus   Value agreement or moral cohesion among members of a social group or society. Functionalist theory holds that social order is based on social arrangements that foster moral unity.

Conventional crime   Generic term for offenses committed by lower-class groups, including violent crime, property crime, or street crimes (public disorder, etc.).

Crime tariff   Costs of transaction (as in increased costs, fines, loss of reputation, etc.) for negotiating in illegitimate markets; token penalties assigned to make crime costly without eliminating it.

Crime without victims   Criminalizing moral offenses; business or sex crimes that lack a victim in the conventional sense; e.g., prostitution, abortion, homosexuality; victimless and public order crime constitutes over 50 percent of law enforcement work.

Criminal behavior system   Study of crime as an occupational role, involving its own traditions, recruitment patterns, and exchanges. Differs from personality trait analysis and multiple-factor designs in stressing social aspects of crime.

Critical theory   Normative or value-oriented explanations of social reality; the new critical-conflict theory rejects liberal (or status quo) solutions to social problems, and takes a radical (i.e., Marxian) perspective toward institutions and change.

Cultural hegemony   Literally, the oneness of culture; an official ideology extolling commercial values and monolithic culture ideal; rhetorical device of dominant groups to control opposition.

Cultural pluralism   Ethnic and community divisions generate distinct values that clash with mainstream culture; idea underlies value-conflict school.

Culture of poverty   The assumption that restricted lower working-class culture causes or reinforces poverty. Circular effect occurs: pathological culture causes poverty; poverty reinforces pathological culture.

Deviance   Any form of opposition to established rules, standards, or practices of elites; deviance may be a political label, a popular stereotype, or a form of sanctioned behavior. In conflict theory, deviance is political opposition to coercive control.

Deviant career   Organization of roles around the deviant activity involving a belief system, a rhetoric of action, and strategies of group defense; the term is usually associated with subculture.

Dialectic   Mode of investigating social organizations as a chain of actions and reactions; a cognitive style emphasizing social contradictions and lack of fit between cultural and structural elements leading to change.

Differential association   Social psychological theory of deviance by E. Sutherland emphasizing the mechanisms of learning crime within intimate groups. Variation in frequency, direction, priority, and intensity of associations accounts for selective definitions of law as favorable or unfavorable.

Differential identification   Theory of criminal learning, offered by Glaser, stressing the actor's choice behavior in identifying the real or imaginary role models in learning criminal conduct. This conception implies that deviance is learned independently of direct social and symbolic supports.

Differential-opportunity structure   Assumption that structured discrimination causes deviance among working class; also a metaphor in anomie theory describing deviance as a normal response by lower-class offenders to closed systems.

Differential organization   A conception of social organization as divided by values, occupations, social classes, ethnicity, and life-styles. As proposed by Sutherland, differences in the power to define crime account for variations in conviction rates, e.g., high rates among lower working-class violators and low rates among middle-class offenders; and variations in distribution, e.g., concentration of crime in inner cities.

Dramaturgical model   Impressionistic method of depicting social life as theater popularized by Goffman and the labeling school; tends to portray actors as game players and manipulative agents for self-interested ends.

Eclecticism   A theory that lacks a consistent set of orienting ideas; also varied observations that are unconnected to theoretical principles.

Epidemiology   Rates and distribution patterns of behavior among a specific population; e.g., data showing frequency and location of delinquent acts or mental illness; term drawn from medical studies.

Equilibrium   Continuity and stability of a social system over time. Functionalists stress that social control is a major stabilizing mechanism.

Ethnography   Fieldwork method where investigators participate in the social scene by taking the perspective of the actors; also a descriptive writing style.

Ethnomethodology   A mode of investigating "everyday" meanings and classification systems of persons or organizations; emphasizes the naturalistic study of meanings and conduct apart from abstract and artificial sociological categories.

Etiology   Cause or origin of a particular behavior type, e.g., poverty causes crime; term drawn from medical usage.

Falsification   The notion that theoretical propositions must be capable of being proved wrong; statements that refer to unobservable events (e.g., God is dead) do not qualify for propositional status.

Function   Any values, social practices, or institutions that contribute to maintaining social order; may be manifest (i.e., known by participants) or latent (i.e., unrecognized by participants).

Functional theory   Also Structural-Functional Theory; a major theoretical framework developed by Talcott Parsons, focusing on the interdependence, interrelationship, and equilibrium features of institutions or relationships; stresses stability, order, and persistence of social systems.

Illegitimacy   Decision making that violates established rules and procedures, sometimes called power.

Innovation   A deviant adaptation (Merton) that involves acceptance of monetary goals, but rejection of legitimate means, e.g., professional crime among working class.

Integration   Mutually complementary role exchange, with actors performing in terms of norms grounded in common values; key concept of functionalist school.

Labeling theory   Also called social-reaction theory; theory that considers the source of deviance in control practices; negative labels affixed to powerless dissenters creates stigmatizing and isolating effects.

Laissez-Faire   Literally, hands-off; doctrine of elites supporting nonintervention in social problems; this idea was widely adopted by early American sociologists (e.g., Sumner) who rejected planned social change as a violation of natural social processes.

Latent function   Unrecognized or unconscious social pattern that contributes to societal stability, e.g., Merton's analysis of boss rule.

Law Formalized codes often detached from mores, that reflect a society's differential power, i.e., powerful interests make and enforce rules against powerless groups.

Legitimacy Power to make decisions in accordance with legally established rules and procedures; also authority.

Liberalism An eighteenth-century doctrine that stresses individualism and personal freedom; also contemporary ideology fostering status quo political institutions in the interests of dominant classes; set of beliefs about the State as an important bargaining agent for all interest groups.

Macro-social Applies to institutional level of analysis especially market and political arrangements.

Means-end disjuncture Key tenet of anomie theory, developed by R. Merton, that holds deviance to be a product of the gap between cultural goals of success and lack of institutional means to monetary goals. Thus, deviance is caused by economic deprivation.

Metaphor A term (or set of terms) that depicts the typical cognitive and symbolic style of a perspective.

Micro-social Applies to interpersonal level of analysis; e.g., small group, subculture, or deviant life-style.

Middle-range theory Theory encompassing restricted fields of experience (e.g., delinquency, race relations, social problems). Merton developed the idea as a reaction to Parsons's master conceptual scheme.

Neutralizing techniques Rhetorics or linguistic constructs justifying deviant acts; assumes that conventional norms are internalized by offenders who reduce guilt by denials of wrongdoing.

Norms A social standard that sets limits to behavior explicitly or implicitly held and recognized in retrospect by members of a group, community, or society; norms justify actions.

Official statistics Organizational data or records depicting typical accounting methods. These are invalid when used to generalize rates and patterns of behavior; but can be useful data to understand organizational constraints and control system.

Order Division of labor based on differential rewards commensurate with occupational rank, level of competence, and social significance of task; major functionalist concept.

Organized crime A type of highly institutionalized career crime that involves economic gain through illegal activities; e.g., drugs, abortion, or sex services; also bastard institution.

Paradigm   An analytical tool for organizing theoretical ideas and research into a comprehensive framework; as used in the philosophy of science, it is a historically based, conceptual framework that guides investigation; paradigm changes occur as a result of accumulations of unsolved theoretical problems.

Perspective   A world view that provides a selective perception of social reality that guides scientific investigation.

Pluralism   A set of political beliefs about the organization of power as widely diffused throughout social ranks; asserts the competitive balancing of multiple-interest groups.

Political crime   Used to describe offenses directed against state authority; in control theory, all crime is political opposition by minorities.

Political system   A set of authority relations; system of resource distribution and exchange.

Politicization   Political organization by disadvantaged groups; efforts to redistribute resources by underclass groups by exerting pressure on legitimate systems (e.g., legal reform) or creating alternative structures (e.g., day-care programs for the working poor).

Power concentration   As a part of conflict theory, power is defined as a system-based phenomenon and operationalized as resources persons or groups bring to bear in effecting favorable decisions. The concentration of resources in capitalist societies implies that power is heavily concentrated among the few.

Power diffusion   As part of democratic ideology, this emphasizes the situational nature of power; also wide circulation of power throughout social ranks.

Professional crime   Specialized, nonviolent crime, as in confidence games, rackets, or "booster" shoplifting.

Rebellion   A deviant adaptation (Merton) that involves rejection of institutional goals and means, and substitution of alternative ones; e.g., radical social movements.

Resource   Any attribute, circumstance, or possession that increases the ability of its holder to influence political decisions. Because resources differ for different social systems (e.g., beauty is a high resource in courtship, but has less value in public office), actor's definitions as to what constitutes political valuables must be taken into account.

Retreatism   A deviant adaptation (Merton) that involves rejection of institutional goals and practices; e.g., drug addiction, psychosis, or other withdrawal behaviors.

Ritualism   A deviant adaptation (Merton) to structured frustration, as in avoidance of competition or restricting aspirations, e.g., lower-echelon bureaucratic roles.

Rule   A perception, implicit understanding, or commonsense meaning that codifies and organizes reality; e.g., Cicourel's analysis of rules as interpretive procedures; may also refer to social norms, standards, and directives.

Ruled   Relatively low resource persons or groups who are excluded from political participation and allocation decisions.

Rulers   Relatively high resource persons or groups that determine rules and allocations in an organization or political system; also called elites, managers, leaders, decision makers, patrons, etc.

Sanctions   System of rewards and penalties used by rulers to maintain a political system; varies by class and degree of threat to the political system.

Secondary deviation   A theory of deviance articulated by E. Lemert stressing the crucial role of social reaction (or official labeling) in developing a deviant identity; differs from primary deviation which is rule violation that remains unsanctioned or has little impact on the actor's identity.

Situational behavior   Analysis of social conduct in terms of time, place, persons, and meanings involved in the social act; labeling and control perspectives stress this approach.

Social control   Legitimate institutional power; in conflict theory, it is a form of coercive management practices by elites against powerless groups that generate deviance and dissent.

Social Darwinism   A doctrine stressing social selection as demanding adjustment of population to industrial sector; although borrowed from Charles Darwin's evolutionary concept of biological change, the theory became associated with strategies for controlling underclass groups; early doctrine held by elites and rising academic and professional reformers regarding inevitable biological process of the selection of the fittest, elimination of unfit, and deviance as maladjustment requiring correction.

Social disorganization   Generic term for social change as imbalances in social order (e.g., breakdown of regular norms, faulty arrangement of status and role assignments); also used to describe lower working-class life-styles; conveys images of modern society as undergoing acute decline and breakdown, dissolution of social bonds; absence of social harmony and homogeneity.

Social engineering   Manipulating social reform in the interests of dominant groups, as in social changes to preserve the status quo.

Social pathology An early twentieth-century American framework to study social problems and deviance; stressed conventional morality as "normal" behavior; working-class life-styles as aberrational and "'sick" behavior; deviance as individual maladjustment requiring correction.

Social psychiatry Analysis of mental disorder in interactional terms; also, a critique of psychiatric categories of control.

Social science movement Nineteenth-century American predecessor of sociology; proponents attempted to link academic concerns to social reform to provide secular and scientific world view, replacing theological explanations of society. Ideological sources stem from the radical utopianism of French Enlightment, practical social change in British reform tradition, and organismic, positivistic doctrines of Auguste Comte.

Socialization Social learning of rules and expectations that contains behavior within group limits.

Society as organism: Biological idea borrowed from nineteenth-century positivistic doctrines regarding society as a living organism subject to laws of growth, decay, and change; stressed unity, harmony, order, and progress. Functionalists modified this into a systems conception.

Sociology of knowledge Method of understanding the historical and social influences that inform theories; can be a subdiscipline of sociology or a mode of assessing the social and professional context of a specific theory; also referred to as sociology of sociology.

Status A social rank in a hierarchy, typically based upon power, prestige, or wealth.

Stigma Social typing as deviant that results in devalued status; dominant imagery of labeling school.

Stereotype A conventional category providing an evaluative set of attributes said to characterize a group; e.g., Scott's study of public stereotypes that support policies encouraging dependency among the blind.

Structural contradictions Leading metaphor of political-conflict approach to control emphasizing opposition and cleavage as inherent to social structures; stresses power as creating opposition, thereby altering, renewing, or destroying structures.

Subculture An alternative life-style believed to have an ecological base that characterizes political minorities and deviants; enables outsiders to cope with stigma and discrimination and to reinforce deviant values, e.g., delinquent gangs.

System Dominant metaphor to describe society used by the functional school; the concept is borrowed from Comte's conception of society as organism and recent cybernetic (feedback) models stressing interrelationship of parts.

Total institution Residential institutions that regulate all phases of inmates' conduct by denying the normal identity and forcing compliance to institutional rules, e.g., prisons, mental institutions, hospitals.

Typology A method for organizing research into homogeneous categories; widely used in criminology to identify and define variations in criminal patterns and offenders.

Value neutrality The idea that social theory and research is (or should be) free from personal and professional biases; tends to be associated with conservative interpretations of social order.

Verstehen Method of understanding phenomena from the actor's perspective; also, a mode of subjective explanation in social science that differs from natural science conceptions of objectivity.

Victimology Study of victims in victim-offender relationships by analyzing victim involvement, using victim-survey reports to assess extent of crime, and examining modes of compensation for victim losses. Victim-causation doctrine tends to reinforce popular stereotypes about victims as inferior, e.g., raped woman as "loose" sexually.

Web of life Biological metaphor of Chicago School presenting social organization as competitive adjustment of populations and their environments within a complex system of interdependencies; stressed ecology or physical environment as determining behavior.

White-collar crime Legal offenses committed by middle class or elites in the course of regular occupational activities; e.g., price-fixing and antitrust violations.

INDEX

235